Contents

Illustration: from *The Literary Notes of Thomas Hardy*

Acknowledgements

I wish to thank the editors of the *Hardy Society Review* and of *Notes & Queries*, who printed shortened versions of parts of the book before publication.

My thanks are also due to the Open University and Arnold Kettle for his challenging and stimulating commentary on my work in progress towards a Ph.D.

R. S.

THOMAS HARDY:
Psychological Novelist

Rosemary Sumner

St. Martin's Press   New York

ISBN O-312-80161-0

Library of Congress Cataloging in Publicaton Data

Sumner, Rosemary, 1924-
  Thomas Hardy, psychological novelist.

  Bibliography: p.
  1. Hardy, Thomas, 1840-1928 — Knowledge — Psychology.
2. Psychology in literature. I. Title.
PR4757.P8 1980   823'.8   80-18334
ISBN O-312-80161-0

1 Introduction

"If you mean to make the world listen, you must say now what they will all be thinking and saying five and twenty years hence",[1] wrote Hardy to Mrs Henniker in 1893. It was not till more than 70 years later that Hardy critics began to recognise how much he had to say to the modern world. He is now beginning to be seen less as a traditional Victorian novelist and more as a pioneer in the novel. His affinities with twentieth-century novelists are beginning to be examined; his ideas on man and society are now seen to have much in common with some aspects of twentieth-century thinking, including existentialism, as Roy Morell[2] and Jean Brooks[3] have suggested. Critics are beginning to acknowledge, though in passing rather than in detail, that his psychological insight, subtlety and complexity are much greater, and closer to twentieth-century psychological theories than had previously been recognised. But though critics have paid passing tribute to this aspect of his fiction, sometimes even using the epithet "Freudian", no one has yet examined this in detail. This is rather surprising in view of the central importance of character in novels and of Hardy's own emphasis on this "centrality". In "The Science of Fiction", he says that what a novelist requires above all is "a quick perception of the more ethereal characteristics of humanity", and "a sympathetic appreciation of life in all its manifestations" in order to give "an accurate delineation of human nature".[4] In "Candour in English Fiction",[5] the main theme is the conflict between the necessity for any significant fiction to express honestly what human beings are actually like and the taboo on doing so in contemporary English society. In his best novels, Hardy was continually trying to do just this, in all its complexity, in defiance of the taboo. Even in his earliest novel he is beginning to work in this direction, and by *Jude the Obscure*, if not before, he has achieved a profound and sympathetic understanding of the mind, including some of its more disturbing aspects; he has ventured into those areas of sexuality which many of his contemporaries found so

1

alarming. His analysis is sometimes so minute that Sue Bridehead, for instance, has been said to "move away from being a figure of Tragedy to being a clinical 'case' ".[6] Though some passages might almost seem to have been lifted from a case history, Hardy's imaginative sympathy is so great that she remains to the end a living, suffering, irritating and interesting human being. It is the combination of the "sympathetic appreciation", the sense that Hardy knew what it feels like to be Sue, and what it is like to love her, with the unflinching analysis of her psychological disturbance which makes this character in some ways the culmination of his work.

The nature of Sue's psychological problems made *Jude the Obscure* particularly challenging to contemporary readers. Though he had written about similar problems in many of his novels (in the 1896 Preface to *Desperate Remedies* he said that "certain characteristics which provoked most discussion in my latest story were present in this my first — published in 1871, when there was no French name for them") he had never been quite so explicit before. In "Candour in English Fiction", he said, "Life being a physiological fact, its honest portrayal must be largely concerned with for one thing the relationship of the sexes". Catastrophes must "be based on the sexual relationship as it is. To this English society opposes a well-nigh insuperable bar".[7]

Admittedly, marital problems were a topical subject in the 1890s and Hardy was accused of jumping on the "marriage question" bandwagon with *Jude the Obscure*; but his contemporaries dealt mainly with the social aspects of the problem, unlike Hardy who, in the treatment of human relationships in the novel, is primarily concerned with psychological and sexual difficulties. Grant Allen's *The Woman Who Did*, a popular novel which came out in the same year as *Jude the Obscure*, is about an advanced liberated young woman who dressed in 1890s women's lib style of flowing robes, sandals and hair fillet, rejected marriage and the conventional family set-up and managed to find a man who was prepared to accept her plans for their sexual relationship. They would have children, take equal responsibility, financial and otherwise, for their upbringing, but would not live together, though they would visit one another whenever they wished. Unfortunately, Grant Allen did not have the temerity to let them carry out their plans in the novel; instead, he killed off the father before the child was born and the rest of the novel is concerned with the financial and social problems of the one-parent family. A comparison of *The Woman Who Did* and *Jude the*

Obscure serves mainly to draw attention to Hardy's profound and intense concentration on the psychological complexities of his characters. His understanding of the sexual basis of much psychological disturbance anticipates Freud's thinking on these lines by many years.

As a consequence of dealing honestly and outspokenly with sexual matters, Hardy necessarily included some consideration of the physical aspects of sexual relationships. He even, very cautiously, in *Tess of the d'Urbervilles* suggested that Angel, "with more animalism might have been a nobler man".[8] Tess herself embodies Hardy's vision of a perfect balance between the physical and the spiritual (her anxieties on the subject are seen as superimposed by society's conditioning rather than integral to her nature). In *Jude the Obscure* he writes of "the deadly war between flesh and spirit", but he shows, in Jude's case, flesh winning and implies that the war is an unnecessary one. This is one of the ways in which Hardy can be seen moving towards one of Lawrence's major themes: "Life is only bearable when mind and body are in harmony and there is a natural balance between them, and each has a natural respect for the other".[9]

Many of Hardy's central characters can accurately be described as psychologically disturbed. This is often seen as arising from the fact that they are "modern" men and women. They are frequently intelligent young people who have difficulty in finding harmony of mind and body and who are also attempting to adjust to "the loss of faith in a beneficent deity"[10] and to a sense of rootlessness. Here lies the immense importance of landscape in Hardy's novels. Those characters who retain a sense of oneness with Nature stand a greater chance of survival than those who, like Sue, have completely lost this contact. In *The Return of the Native*, he says, "to know that everything around and underneath had been from prehistoric times as unaltered as the stars overhead, gave ballast to the mind adrift on change and harassed by the irrepressible new".[11] D. H. Lawrence explored the same problems in a much more extreme form in an industrialised society. Here again the two writers share the same concerns, and we can see Hardy embarking on a subject which Lawrence was to deal with more fully.

One of Hardy's greatest strengths as a novelist is his creation of "a sense of felt life", so that his readers can experience what it is like to be Tess or Sue, Clym or Jude. This derives in part from his ability to "let a bucket down into the subconscious" (as Forster describes the process) so that he is imaginatively exploring his characters in the process of creating them. His tendency to tell editors that he is writing a story suitable for their magazines, a story which will, he thinks, be entirely "proper", and then to find that it is going in a quite different direction and proving itself quite unsuitable for serial production, demonstrates his intuitive understanding of human beings, and his honesty in portraying them; in spite of bowdlerisation for magazines, he refused, in most of his final versions, to force events and characters in a preconceived direction. *Jude the Obscure* carried him into "such unexpected fields" that he offered to cancel the contract with the publishers.[12] Instead they published a bowdlerised version in *Harper's New Monthly Magazine* and Hardy's original novel, with a few modifications, was published in book form by another firm. He was prepared to reject his own preconception in favour of ideas that seemed to arise spontaneously in the course of writing; he admitted that he had been unable to make Grace Melbury behave in a way which he himself would have found interesting, "but she was too common-place and straight-laced and I could not make her". This feeling for truth to human nature, forcing him to write in a way opposed to his conscious wish fits in with his statement in the 1912 Preface to *Jude the Obscure* that "no doubt there can be more in a book than the author consciously puts there". As Lawrence said, "Trust the tale, not the teller".

This sympathetic, intuitive insight into human nature, gives the reader such a sense of involvement with the characters that the accompanying conscious understanding and formulation of psychological theory tends to be overlooked or even condemned as being intrusive and spoiling a good story. But Hardy's exploration of the mind and emotions is deepened by his speculations about them; he combined the study of psychological theory with sympathetic observation, analytical comments with creative imagining. This can be seen in all his major novels, and sometimes in a particularly clear way in his minor novels and short stories, where the theory and the imaginative creation have not been fully integrated. The three essays on the novel ("The Science of Fiction", "The Profitable Reading of Fiction", and "Candour in English Fiction") and occasional sentences in the Prefaces and in the *Life of Thomas Hardy*[13] give further evidence that he was well aware that he was probing into relatively unexplored areas of human experience. Further evidence of his interest in psychological theory is now avail-

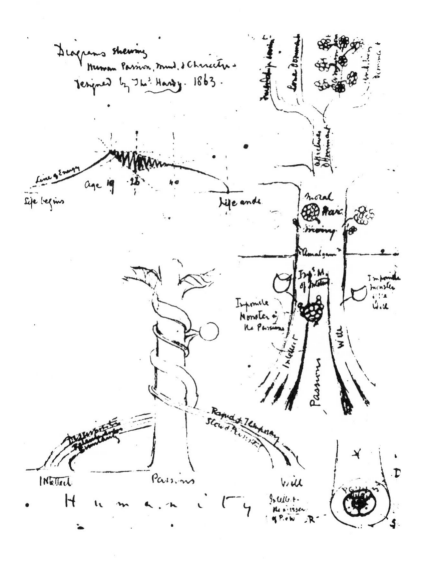

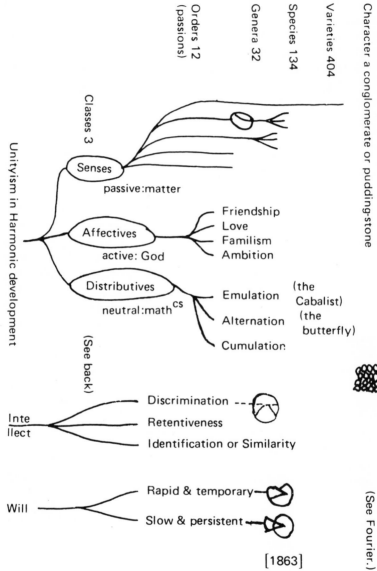

Character a conglomerate or pudding-stone

Varieties 404

Species 134

Genera 32

Orders 12 (passions)

Classes 3

Senses

passive:matter

Affectives

active: God

Friendship
Love
Familism
Ambition

Distributives

neutral:math^{cs}

Emulation   (the Cabalist)

Alternation   (the butterfly)

Cumulation

Unityism in Harmonic development

(See back)

Inte llect

Discrimination

Retentiveness

Identification or Similarity

Will

Rapid & temporary

Slow & persistent

[1863]

(See Fourier.)

able in the *Notebooks*.[14] The first pages consist of "Diagrams showing Human Passions, Mind and Character — Designed by Thos. Hardy 1863". The page is annotated "See Fourier" and is probably based on J. R. Morell's translation of Charles Fourier's *Passions of the Human Soul*, which was the only translation available in 1863 (though Hardy could have read it in French). Since the rest of the *Notebooks* contains material dating from 1876, it can be assumed to be indicative of Hardy's interest in the subject that he preserved these early notes and incorporated them in a later notebook.[15]

Fourier maintained that emotion is the motive power of human activity, and that most of the miseries of mankind stem from suppression of the passions. Though Hardy did not accept such a view wholesale, it is obvious that he felt some sympathy for it (as his treatment of Angel, to give just one example, suggests). There is also in the *Notebooks* a number of passages copied from Comte's *Social Dynamics*, including, among others, such subjects as The Brain, Sensations, Madness, Subjectivity[16] and two long passages on the importance of "studying the laws of mental and social development"; "To the moral world of man with its complicating passions and aspirings must be applied that search for natural laws, for uniformities amid diversities which had already led men to such wonderful results in physics and astronomy."[17] The fact that Hardy copied out these passages supports the other evidence of his interest in theories about psychology.

But it would be wrong to assume that he simply accepted what writers such as Fourier and Comte had to say. Shortly after a group of passages from Comte, Hardy quotes a remark that some French thinkers "fall into the error . . . of supposing in nature a greater simplicity than is to be found there".[18] It is significant that he makes a note of this; the novels illustrate his consciousness of the diversity of human nature and experience, his unwillingness to force his vision into a system, his insistence that "unadjusted impressions have their value".[19] He does not regard himself as a mere pupil of philosophical/psychological writers such as Fourier and Comte (nor indeed of Schopenhauer and Von Hartmann). In his novels he is probing, pushing out the boundaries, going much further in some of the directions in which they had started to advance. It is not altogether surprising that throughout his novels there is much that is closer to Freud and later psychological writers than to their predecessors in the nineteenth century.

A look at Hardy criticism from his own day until now shows how this aspect of his novels has been neglected. Yet many of his contemporaries really understood that Hardy was, at least in *Tess of the d'Urbervilles* and *Jude the Obscure*, challenging emotional atti-tudes to human nature and what it was possible to say about it, and through their shock and disgust they showed their recognition of this (thus giving an excellent illustration of Lawrence's statement that "any really new novel must hurt to some extent"). The Bishop of Wakefield flung *Jude the Obscure* into the fire and wrote to *The Yorkshire Post* to publicise his action.[20] Mrs Oliphant complained that Hardy dealt with matters hitherto "banished from the lips of de-cent people, and as much as possible from their thoughts".[21] Others showed their appreciation of Hardy's power and insight. Gosse called the character of Sue, "a terrible study in pathology, but of the splendid success of it, of the sustained intellectual force implied in the evolution of it, there cannot, I think, be two opinions".[22] Hardy said that Gosse understood his intentions. Havelock Ellis, who was already at work on his vast *Studies in the Psychology of Sex*, made somewhat similar comments and added that *Jude the Obscure* was "the natural outcome of Mr Hardy's development".[23] These com-ments suggest that the points I have been making were already well established by 1896. But, astonishingly, these perceptions then vanished from Hardy criticism for 70 years.

In the mid-twentieth century, Hardy came to be regarded as a very simple traditional novelist, nostalgically recreating a lost rural past, and anything he had written to the contrary tended to be disre-garded in an extraordinarily patronising way. Donald Davidson said, "Hardy professed himself an evolutionary meliorist or almost a convential modern. But this had nothing to do with the stories which started up in his head".[24] The implications of this are that Hardy does not know what his philosophy is and his stories "start up in his head" without conscious thought or volition, and mean the opposite of what he says they mean. This is purely derogatory and is not in-tended to suggest that they derive from profound workings of the unconscious. Later in the same essay, he is "good and innocent," which recalls Henry James's "the good little Thomas Hardy", a phrase which Leavis described as "appropriately sympathetic".[25] Lord David Cecil goes even further and calls him "poor, simple conscientious Hardy".[26] Similar attitudes were taken by writers who concentrate on what they take to be his Fatalism and Pessimism — both of which he repeatedly denied. Cecil is just one among many who maintain that the characters are merely puppets in the hands of all-powerful Fate. This theory leads naturally to the conclusion that characterisation is unimportant in the novels, or, if it is of any interest, it lies in its extreme simplicity. Davidson says, "the event dominates, rather than motive or psychology or comment".[27] Guerard says that in *The Mayor of Casterbridge*, "macabre absurdity, not macabre neurosis spins the plot".[28] Cecil calls the characters puppets, then complains that they are not treated as puppets in *Jude the Obscure* and then has the temerity to maintain that it is Hardy who is muddled.[29]

There are, of course, some exceptions to this trend in mid-century Hardy criticism. Pierre d'Exideuil said that "we should be passing over a point of material importance if we failed to show that the doctrines of the Austrian psychologists are in no respect at variance with anything in the Wessex cycle . . . Hardy was a Freudian before Freud".[30] J. I. M. Stewart, in an essay of 1948, described Sue as "a point of major innovation in prose fiction".[31] But neither of these made any impact on the criticism of their day, nor did Stewart develop his point to any great extent in his book on Hardy published in 1971.

The situation in Hardy criticism has now completely changed. The breakthrough came in 1965 with Morrell's *Thomas Hardy, the Will and the Way*,[32] which proved irrefutably that Hardy was right in asserting that he was not a "Fatalist and pessimist", and suggested that he was looking forward as well as back, and had affinities with the Existentialists. The book was an important turning-point because it rejected the patronised, traditional, nostalgic Hardy and suggested his relevance to the modern world. It has now become commonplace for critics to mention complexity of characterisation, psychology and Freud.

The exploratory nature of Hardy's writing is mainly in this venturing into unfamiliar, even taboo areas of human experience. Nevertheless, his awareness of psychological complexity, of unconscious drives, led him to see that new methods of presenting character in the novel were necessary to convey this. By the time of *Jude the Obscure* he was able to incorporate into the novel the "puzzling" and "unstateable" qualities of Sue Bridehead, but even as early as *The Return of the Native* we can see him struggling to create a technique for expressing this conception. In 1886, he said, "Novel-writing as an art cannot go backward. Having reached the analytical stage it must transcend it by going further in the same direction."[33]

One effect of "going further in the same direction", was that in his next novel, *The Woodlanders* (1888) he expressed his realisation that however far analysis is pushed, there will always be some areas of the personality which will remain unexplored. He calls Grace "a conjectural creature". As he develops the capacity to probe deeper and deeper into the characters he creates, the more he becomes aware of the need to suggest that they extend beyond his understanding. It seems to me possible that if he had continued writing novels, he would have found a means of expressing this perception more fully. Sue certainly embodies it more fully and vividly than Grace. However, it was left to Lawrence to pursue this line of development and to create a style which enabled him to convey that sense of dealing with "unknown modes of being" which we merely glimpse in Hardy.

Hardy's most profound and searching insights seem to me to be into those minds which are "not well-proportioned". He is also interested in those well-proportioned minds whose "usual blessings are happiness and mediocrity", but it is the mind which may "cause its owner to be confined as a madman" or "applauded as a prophet"[34] which leads him to some of his deepest psychological perceptions and to insights into motivation which some of his contemporaries hesitated to accept but which correspond closely to the insights achieved by other means by psychological writers of the twentieth century. In this sense, Hardy was ahead of his time. It is an aspect of his greatness as a writer which has not been fully appreciated; it is only one aspect, but it is an important one. Freud complained of Dostoevsky that "his insight was entirely restricted to the workings of abnormal psychology" and showed how this narrowness warped Dostoevsky's representation of love.[35] Hardy, on the other hand, never presents abnormal psychology in isolation. His novels are nearly always structured on a pattern of contrasts which serves to highlight human variety and multiple ways of reacting to a single occurrence. A neurotic or turbulent character (Sue Bridehead or Michael Henchard) may seem to dominate a novel, but the balanced, or placid or superficial characters are also there to show other modes of being. So though there are major characters who live lives of great emotional intensity and disturbance, they are shown to be a part, not the whole of "the great web of human doings". Hardy's sensitive awareness of the variety of psychological experience is closely bound up with both his aesthetic and his social aims. He was passionately concerned, as "Candour in English Fiction" shows, to make the novel a vehicle for truth about human nature, however disturbing that truth might be, and he hoped by using it in this way to increase people's tolerance and sympathy and so undermine that "inert, crystallised opinion — hard as a rock — which the vast body of men have vested interests in preserving".[36]

A realisation of both the range and the immense depth of Hardy's psychological insights is necessary for a full grasp of his scope and stature as a novelist.

2 Minor works: some psychological explorations and experiments

Hardy's minor works and short stories are relevant to this examination of the psychological insight shown in his major works, since some of them illustrate, sometimes in a rather stark way, his continuing interest, throughout his career as a novelist, in psychological complexities. His frequent focusing on unusual or abnormal states of mind, his awareness that he is probing into areas more usually explored by the medical profession, and his occasional sceptical concern about possible therapeutic experiments all serve to highlight particularly clearly his interest in and awareness of psychological theory. The short stories, especially when they focus on a single psychological oddity, illustrate this interest in a single-minded way, which does not necessarily make a good story but does clarify an element in Hardy's writing which is also centrally and significantly present in the major novels. In the latter the psychological interest is embedded in the multiple and diverse "seemings", in the short stories and minor works it tends to stand out as a separate element because of the starkness and simplicity with which it is treated. The exploratory quality which is important in much of Hardy's major work is also to be found running through his minor fiction. The most outstanding and influential aspect of this is probably his recognition of the importance of sexuality in the psychological make-up of the individual and the bearing of this on human relationships. Here, too, he continues to write with candour in a society which was hostile to such outspokenness; even in these minor works we have glimpses of those qualities which make him a precursor of the twentieth-century psychological writers and novelists.

In his 1896 Preface to his first novel, *Desperate Remedies*, Hardy drew attention to the fact that this particular thread had been running through his writing from the very beginning: "certain characteristics which provoked most discussion in my latest story were present in this my first — published in 1871, when there was no French name for them". Matters both provocative and French are presumably sexual and *Desperate Remedies* is, intermittently, a surprisingly sensual book. The characters are exceptionally aware of one another's physical presence; Cytherea feels, "Edward's warm breath touched and crept round her face like a caress",[1] as he bends near her to adjust the rudder of their boat, and she is conscious of the brush of Manston's fingertips through the palm of her glove even though he is merely handing her money for a charity collection.[2] The connection with *Jude* which Hardy refers to in the Preface lies presumably partly in the situation of Cytherea, torn between two lovers, uncertain whether the passionate, sensual one is more attractive or frightening. But even more striking are the scenes with Miss Aldclyffe. It is these which bring us close to the outspokenness of *Jude* in sexual matters. Critics have remarked that it is surprising to find such Lesbian scenes described in a book published in 1871, and they often make some comment on Hardy's "innocence" in not realising the "Freudian" implications of what he is doing. A close examination of these passages (as well as his comment in the later Preface) make it clear that there is no such innocence here.

Hardy very carefully prepares us for the explicitly sexual scene where Miss Aldclyffe joins Cytherea in bed. At their first meeting at the hotel it is Cytherea's beauty of movement which first attracts Miss Aldclyffe. Hardy ponderously and elaborately stresses that it is a particular way of turning, which captivates men, and which had moved Miss Aldclyffe: "She murmured to herself, 'It is almost worthwhile to be bored with instructing her in order to have a creature who could glide round my luxurious, indolent body in that manner, and look at me in that way — I warrant how light her fingers are upon one's neck and head' ".[3] Hardy could hardly insist more strongly on the physical nature of the attraction. The coachman's account of the rapid succession of lady's maids hurrying away from the house after a single night reinforces his view that "she's an extraordinary picture of womankind".[4] Her violently quarrelsome and bullying manner with Cytherea on her first night at the house seems exaggerated and implausible unless we notice how Hardy gradually builds up the impression of a tormented neurotic being, struggling with conflicting emotions. Her emotional state is partly explained by her tortured, frustrated life, but one of the weaknesses of *Desperate Remedies* is that we do not know about this until the convolutions of the plot are worked out; by this time, the novel has turned into a detective story and the thread of psychological complexity and ambiguity has been lost. Even so, without revealing the factual basis for her neuroses, Hardy displays the violent swings of mood which spring from memories of the past aroused by Cytherea's name and resemblance to her father, from her refusal to be dominated, and from the strong physical attraction which Hardy keeps emphasising: "The idea of my taking a girl without asking her more than three questions . . . all because of her good l _ _ _ _ the shape of her face and body".[5]

Hardy drops these preliminary hints before plunging the reader into the passionate scene which takes place in Cytherea's bed:

> The instant they were in bed Miss Aldclyffe freed herself from the last remnant of restraint. She flung her arms round the young girl and pressed her gently to her heart. "Now kiss me", she said.

She demands kisses and speaks of her love, "as if in the outburst of strong feeling, long checked and yearning for something to love and be loved by in return".[6]

She twice implies that the relationship is a "motherly" one but what Hardy describes is *not* a mother and daughter relationship. As Miss Aldclyffe presses her inquiries about Cytherea's lover, she more and more plays the role of lover herself. She speaks in "jealous and gloomy accents", claims, "I love you more sincerely than any man can", and, when Cytherea defends her right to go on loving him, begins to attack her because she has been "sullied by a man's lips . . . I — an old fool — have been sipping at your mouth as if it were honey, because I fancied no wasting lover knew the spot. But a minute ago, you seemed to me like a fresh spring meadow — now you seem like a dusty highway."[7] Finally, after painting a vivid picture of the lover's imminent unfaithfulness (to be contrasted with her own constancy) she says:

"Put you hair round your mamma's neck and give me one good long kiss . . . ". Cytherea did as she was told . . . flung the twining tresses of her long rich hair over Miss Aldclyffe's shoulders as directed, and the two ceased conversing, making themselves up for sleep. Miss Aldclyffe seemed to give herself over to a luxurious sense of content and quiet.[8]

It is amazing how little comment this scene seems to have provoked at the time. Morley, reporting on the book for Macmillan, comments on "a number of highly extravagant scenes, notably one between Miss Aldclyffe and her new maid in bed", but concludes that the book "shows *power* — at present of a violent and undisciplined kind".[9] There seems to have been very little other direct comment on this scene. *The Spectator* referred to "idle prying into the ways of wickedness"[10] but seems to have been referring to illegitimacy, prostitution and murder; its objection to Miss Aldclyffe is that she is "an unmarried lady" and mother to Aeneas Manston. Presumably Hardy's contemporaries took the same view of the relationship between the two women as the servants in the novel do: "they were woman and woman, not woman and man, the facts were ethereal and refined, and so they could not be worked up into a taking story".[11]

Hardy's claim that the provocative qualities of his last book were already present, though unnoticed, in his first, seems to me fully justified. His interest in the complexities of sexual emotions is clear in *Desperate Remedies*. The treatment of Miss Aldclyffe's Lesbianism stands out partly because of its very nature, being an unusual subject for such detailed examination at that period, partly because it is so very explicit, and because Hardy's method of treatment is very concentrated, most of the material being compressed into two successive chapters. For these reasons, this relationship comes across even more vividly than Manston's powerful sensuality or Cytherea's sensitive awareness of nuances of sensation. Its dramatic, even sensational quality is also emphasised because it is not followed up: as the complications and intrigues of the plot develop, Hardy loses sight of the inner lives of the characters and becomes more concerned with events. Nevertheless, *Desperate Remedies* is important in illustrating, in a limited way, many features which were to be central in the major novels. The interest in complex and neurotic psychological states, the awareness of the importance of sexuality in relation to these states, the determination to deal honestly and explicitly with these subjects are all present in this first novel. We can see now that in his earliest novel Hardy was showing those exploratory and challenging qualities which eventually became dominant in his latest fiction.

Hardy returned to the consideration of specifically homosexual feelings ten years later, in *A Laodicean*, but in a much more tentative way than in *Desperate Remedies*. In Paula Power he created a "modern" young woman torn in a number of different directions by conflicting feelings and interests, most conspicuously between modernity and antiquity (she is "a modern flower in a mediaeval flower pot"[12]) but also uncertain of her sexual drives. She thinks she may be in love with the young architect, but while she encourages him up to a point, she is always poised ready to escape, or to repel him if he is too forthcoming. In these respects she is somewhat similar to Sue Bridehead, but Hardy's intention in *A Laodicean* (before he fell ill and had to cobble the rest of the book together as best he could) seems to have been to explore a slightly different kind of sexual "fastidiousness". Like Sue, Paula is an advanced and independent young woman; she is obviously attracted by Somerset, yet is nervous of being alone with him. Her reaction to his jarring his injured knee when they are together in a lonely part of the castle is to withdraw: "she did not come near him; indeed she withdrew a little . . . a curious coyness seemed to take possession of her".[13] She hurries off and returns with Charlotte as chaperone. After Somerset describes his fall into the tower and says that he thought of her when trying to signal for rescue, "she arose and went across to Miss de Stancy. 'Don't you go falling down and becoming a skeleton,' she said . . . after which she clasped her fingers behind Charlotte's neck and smiled tenderly into her face".[14] Later, Hardy comments, "If Paula allowed demonstrations of love to escape her towards anyone, it was towards Charlotte".[15] Conversation between the two girls makes Somerset feel "superfluous"[16] and on the night of the ball he feels that by refusing to dance Paula is "spoiling his evening for a sentimental devotion to Charlotte".[17] Also there is the famous gymnastic performance when Paula, looking (in pink flannel doublet and hose) like "a lovely young youth and not a girl at all",[18] demonstrates her athletic skill and daring to Charlotte and Mrs Goodman.

It is possible that Hardy was intending to explore her sexual uncertainty more fully; it was probably due to his illness that the novel deteriorates into a travelogue of Europe and Paula changes from her "habit of self-repression"[19] to become the pursuer of Somerset. There are enough hints to suggest that the creation of a bisexual personality attracted him, that he did not conceive of this as having any association with neuroses, and that, without his illness, Paula might have developed as a more complex and complete character. Millgate sums up very interestingly his conclusions about *A Laodicean*:

> If it seems too much to suggest that Hardy saw Paula as a sexual Laodicean, occupying an equivocal mid-way position between male and female, it is none the less evident that here — as in the presentation of Knight in *A Pair of Blue Eyes* and of the Miss Aldclyffe — Cytherea — Manston triangle in *Desperate Remedies* — he is not so much blundering in the pre-Freudian darkness as exploring tentatively and with instinctive sensitivity, some of those areas of sexuality which lay beyond the stereotypes of Victorian fiction. Hardy's explorations reached a remarkable conclusion in the sustained portrayal of Sue Bridehead — whom Paula in her combination of fastidiousness, Hellenism and rather aggressive modernism strikingly anticipates — and it is much to be regretted that in *A Laodicean* they remain only one of many fragmentary elements in a novel which Hardy began so ambitiously but completed in such weary despair.[20]

The bulk of what Millgate says seems to me absolutely accurate and indeed is central to this study, but I cannot altogether accept the implications of some of his phrases; his suggestion that Hardy is "not so much blundering in the pre-Freudian darkness as exploring tentatively and with instinctive sensitivity . . .", while granting Hardy a greater grasp of psychological problems than many critics would allow, still makes concessions to the idea of the naive, unconscious artist, entirely dependent on "instinctive" knowledge of human nature. It would be more true to say that Hardy was exploring both consciously and "with instinctive sensitivity" "the pre-Freudian darkness". This ability is always present, whether in the background or the foreground of his fiction, including some of the short stories, even though because of their brevity he cannot develop the complexities of the characters as fully as in the longer works.

His methods of presenting some of the short stories seem to be especially designed to draw attention to their psychological implications. In *A Group of Noble Dames*, in the interludes of dialogue between the stories, the tellers frequently refer to the "neurological" or "professional" (as with the surgeon's tale) aspects of the stories. The members of the club, after hearing "Squire Petrick's Lady" say that "such subtle and instructive psychological studies (now that psychology is so much in demand) were precisely the tales they desired". Some of the stories themselves illustrate, in a more anecdotal way than the novels, Hardy's fascination with unusual states of mind and strange ways of thinking and feeling. "Squire Petrick's Lady" is described as being about "a curious mental delusion". Though it is called "Squire Petrick's Lady", the story is really concerned with Squire Petrick's changing states of mind. His wife's delusions about the aristocratic parentage of her child is merely the trigger to her husband's curiously shifting mental states; these changing moods and attitudes are what Hardy is interested in, and the story is primarily concerned with examining them. They are not altogether credible because, as in so many of the stories, there is very little personality to embed the mental changes in. Squire Petrick exists merely as a reaction to his wife's deathbed "confession"; he has no other facets. For the sake of compression, a single psychological curiosity is isolated; as a result, we get an account of a psychological oddity but no sense of a complex human being whose experience we are concerned with. This is an instance of Hardy's interest in psychology, especially in its bizarre and unusual aspects, being excessively absorbing to him, so that he presents us with the abnormalities neat, instead of, as he usually does, embedding them in a wide range of life and feeling. Similarly, in "An Imaginative Woman" (*Wessex Tales*), the woman's obsession with the poet she has never met is the whole of her personality. The details of the story, with the poems written on the wall, the expected meetings, the poet's suicide and the birth of the child resembling the loved but never encountered figure provide suspense and surprise so that it is quite a good story at a superficial level. Hardy's interest in the obsession is paramount, but the woman's personality and emotions are not developed enough to create a sense of a complete human being.

There is a similar conflict between the centre of interest of the story and the mode of presenting it in "A Changed Man". As the title implies, the core of the story is a personality change. A dashing cavalry officer, to his glamorous wife's dismay, abandons the army for the church, becomes dowdy and dull, but sacrifices his life working for the poor in a cholera epidemic. The psychological *volte face* is recorded in a factual way but there is no attempt to explore the process of change. As in many of the short stories, the psychological interest suggested by the subject matter and in this case by the title, is not developed and interest is focused more on intricacies of plot. The need for a slight but gripping story for magazine publication and Hardy's interest in psychological complexities have not been integrated.

"The Distracted Preacher" (*Wessex Tales*) is also concerned with the question of the possibility of a complete personality change, in this case in the opposite direction, from a humdrum life to an exciting one. In some respects it is a version, a very slight one, of "the war waged between flesh and spirit" in *Jude the Obscure*, but in this version, the spirit (or perhaps rather the desire for conformity and respectability) is stronger, and the flesh very much weaker. The preacher loves the female smuggler largely because, "her experienced manner and bold indifference stirred his admiration in spite of himself".[21] He thinks longingly, "If only I had stuck to my father's little grocery business instead of going in for the ministry, she would have suited me beautifully".[22] However, after trying in vain to get Lizzie to abandon her exciting life, he sticks to the course he has chosen. This is an appropriate choice; this naive, respectable, emotionally undeveloped young man, whom the Customs men call "an old woman", could not make a major change in his lifestyle (that in his furthest flights of imagination he sees himself as a grocer crystallises this point nicely). He is the opposite of Jude, who, when faced with a similar choice, admits that every fibre of his being is urging him towards Sue, while the pull of the church, which forbids this, becomes meaningless to him. That Mr Stockdale makes the choice he does is completely plausible; that Lizzie eventually joins him is not. Years later, Hardy admitted that he really wanted the heroine to go off with a smuggler instead of settling down with the preacher.[23] This illustrates in miniature Hardy's continuing conflict between his desire to write truly about human feelings and behaviour and the demand for respectability from his public. He argued the point fully in "Candour in English Fiction", and experimented boldly in the major novels. For the magazine public he was prepared to make concessions, and this is why the short stories give us glimpses of psychological insight or seem to promise to explore some psychological idiosyncrasy but fail to fulfil the promise instead of probing deeply into conflicts and motivation.

In the stories, as in much of his writing, Hardy is concerned with how people make choices; he explores the interplay between their psychological states and the events which impinge upon them. In the novels, there is scope for showing how different people respond to a single event (the different reactions to the threatening storm in *Far from the Madding Crowd* for instance). In the short stories he concentrates usually on the reactions of a single character, often in relation to a single decision or a single facet of his personality, as in the changed man's decision to become a preacher or in the distracted preacher's failure to decide to change his way of life. Obviously in the restricted space of a short story he could not achieve the effect of exploring the inner fluctuations of a character in their full complexity which is characteristic of his major work. In spite of their limitations in this respect, these stories do focus attention on the fact that one of Hardy's central interests is the workings of the mind and that he sees times of conflict, indecision and choice-making as particularly revealing.

There is one story in which he presents powerfully the opposite experience — one of those occasions when people become incapable of choice. I am not referring to those times when the characters deliberately decide not to choose, in an attempt to put the blame for whatever may occur on the external world instead of on themselves, as when Troy decides that "Providence was jeering at him" and so all effort on his part is useless, or when Eustacia "would let events fall out as they might sooner than wrestle hard to direct them", or when Tess, after discovering her letter has gone under the mat, displays "that too ready acquiescence in chance so characteristic of the whole Durbeyfield family", but rather to those occasions when, for various reasons, the individual behaves in a way which is involuntary. Tess, her personality eroded by despair, "drifts with the current", in response to the pressures put upon her. When Eustacia and Wildeve dance together it is like "riding the whirlwind" — a mutual experience of trance-like abandonment of conscious control, induced by the music, the movement and sexual attraction.

Cytherea is hypnotised by Manston's powerful sexuality so that he can control her movements as least partly against her will. Here again, music plays an important part in slackening conscious control; Manston's organ music seems to develop "as its libretto the poem of her own life and soul, shifting her deeds and intentions from the hands of her judgment and holding them in its own".[24]

Obviously this area of experience, where reason and conscious thought are dissipated and instinctive responses seem to be at odds with conscious desires, interested Hardy greatly. "The Fiddler of the Reels" (in *Life's Little Ironies*) is a powerful exploration of this loss of normal mental processes and of conscious intentions and desires. Critics have tended to classify it as a "supernatural" story, but in the light of Hardy's ambivalent attitude to the supernatural this seems to me a simplification. His treatment of supernatural themes is rarely unambiguous. The witch in *Under the Greenwood Tree* is something of a behaviourist psychologist who knows how to manipulate people's responses, the weather-prophet in *The Mayor of Casterbridge* probably has shrewd psychological insight rather than magic powers. Susan Nonsuch's witch-like goings-on are described, but they provoke Clym's question, "Do you think I have turned teacher too soon?" Hardy summed up his ambivalent feelings on the subject in 1915: "Half my time — particularly when writing verse — I 'believe' (in the modern sense of the word) not only in the things Bergson believes in, but in spectres, mysterious voices, intuitions, omens, dreams, haunted places, etc, etc. But I do not believe in them in the old sense of the word for all that".[25] It is interesting that most of the things he lists here could be regarded as psychological phenomena. Similarly, in "The Fiddler of the Reels", Mop Ollamor's hypnotic effect on Car'line is not presented simply in terms of bewitchment but examined as a psychological phenomenon. Hardy says that her father is aware of "her hysterical tendencies" and that "it would require a neurologist to fully explain" Mop's influence over her. Thus Hardy announces that he is dealing with recognisable psychological instability, but his method of presenting it is not in the least clinical. His long description (some three-and-a-half pages) of the dance is a powerful evocation of Car'line's emotional and physical state. The prose, though not without some ponderous phrases, creates a sense of continuous flow, of emotional and physical intensity which very effectively draws the reader into the experience. He suggests simultaneously the rhythm and feeling of the music and the sexual implications of what is happening:

> She continued to wend her way through the figure of 8 that was formed by her course, the fiddler introducing into his notes the wild and agonising sweetness of a living voice in one too highly wrought; its pathos running high and running low in an endless variation, projecting through her nerves excruciating spasms, a sort of blissful torture . . . she thus continued to dance alone, defiantly as she thought, but in truth slavishly and abjectly, subject to every wave of the melody, and probed by the gimlet-like gaze of her fascinator's open eye.

"The Fiddler of the Reels" is a powerful evocation of a state of being in which all conscious control and even identity is dissipated. Mop playing the fiddle manipulates and controls every movement and Car'line responds involuntarily but with a kind of willingness which indicates the sexual attraction she feels. The power of this story lies in the vividness of Hardy's evocation of Car'line's experience. By focusing on the music and the dancing and using these as a symbolic expression of sexual domination, he achieves an effect of extreme concentration. It is a rare example of Hardy using the brevity of the short story form to advantage.

The theoretical basis of the story — Hardy's interest in hypnotic states, in the effect of music on a susceptible person, and in the control and manipulation of one person by another — are all completely embodied in the central characters, so that the reader is far more aware of the lived experience of Car'line, of her hypnotised state, her compulsive response to the music and her physical exhaustion than of the possibility of a "neurological explanation" which Hardy suggests would be available if we cared to look for it. This is rare in those short stories which deal with unusual psychological states. In most of them, the *idea* of the psychological oddity is conveyed clearly, but a feeling of what it is like to experience such a state is not usually adequately suggested.

"Barbara of the House of Grebe" (*A Group of Noble Dames*) is also a story about the manipulaton and control of one human being by another. It is far less powerful as a story than "The Fiddler of the Reels" because Hardy does not here manage to create that sense of a lived experience. But it is extremely important as evidence of Hardy's interest in psychological theory. In it, he seems to have foreseen future developments in psychological medicine. This extraordinary story is therefore highly relevant to a discussion of Hardy's psychological insight. It is not only an example of his use of various kinds of neuroses as material for fiction but also shows a shrewd grasp of the mental processes of some types of psychological practitioner long before anybody had begun to practise in the way he described in the story. His wish to be "fifty years ahead of his time" finds a weird fulfilment here.

The story is told by a surgeon, who apologises for his tale being "perhaps a little too professional". It is simultaneously a sensational horror story and an account of an experiment in aversion therapy. Though obviously a potboiler (and rather a lurid one), it also shows in a surprising way Hardy's serious interest in the workings of the mind and in scientific developments in that area. The use of a surgeon as narrator, his introductory remarks about the "professional" aspects of the story, his comment on the nature of the "cure" ("How fright could have effected such a change of idiosyncrasy, learned physicians alone can say; but I believe such cases of reactionary instinct are not unknown") all show that Hardy is deliberately choosing to deal with clinical material.

Barbara is depicted as "a tender-hearted but somewhat shallow lady", and therefore perhaps a particularly suitable case for the conditioning she receives. Lord Uplandtowers who carries out the treatment is "a perverse and cruel man" who "dislikes many people and things". Hardy's lack of sympathy with "behaviour technology" is apparent throughout. He underlines Lord Uplandtowers's coldness, ruthlessness, and lack of interest in Barbara except as something he has decided he wants to possess. One comment in particular highlights Hardy's criticism of his method of manipulating behaviour: "Lord Uplandtowers was a subtle man when once he set himself to strategy; though in the present instance he never thought of the simple stratagem of constant tenderness". Though Uplandtowers claims that his treatment is "done to good purpose and not idly", Hardy depicts him as ruthlessly pushing the technique to its limits and quite aware of the risks he is running; when Barbara faints at her first sight of the mutilated statue, he thinks he may have overdone it and that she may be dead.

There is a good deal of emphasis on how Barbara behaves (rather than on what she feels), though Uplandtowers does not altogether discount feelings as an unverifiable element, as some twentieth-century behaviourists working on such a case might do. But his teasing comments after the first experiment show that he is more interested in what she does than in what she feels: "a baby should not go to closets at midnight to look for the ghost of the dear departed". By threatening to lead her back to the disfigured statue, he tries to elicit a declaration that she no longer loves her first husband. Though he fails in this, her terror convinces him that "another dose or two and she will be cured". And so the therapy continues; he rigs up the horrifying statue in a cupboard at the foot of the bed and forces her to contemplate it each night: "Firm in enforcing his ferocious correctives, he continued the treatment till the nerves of the poor lady were quivering in agony under the virtuous tortures inflicted by her lord to bring her truant heart back to faithfulness". On the third night, when she collapses in an epileptic fit, he is "dismayed by the sense that like many other subtle personages he had been too exacting for his own interests". However, she recovers, and "a considerable change seemed to have taken place in her emotions". She begs him to take the statue away, says she hates the memory of her first husband and says, "It fills me with shame — how could I ever be so depraved! I'll never behave badly again." When he promises that he will not make her see the statue again, " 'Then I'll love you', she said eagerly, as if dreading lest the scourge should be applied anew". The effect of the treatment is permanent: "The strange thing now was that this fictitious love wrung from her by terror took on, through mere habit of enactment, a certain quality of reality . . . the mood of attachment grew and continued when the statue was removed. A permanent revulsion was operant within her." Thus, the aversion therapy has apparently had an entirely satisfactory outcome. Lord Uplandtowers has succeeded in "blocking" the undesirable behaviour (embracing the statue of her dead husband and manifesting love for him) and eliciting "the appropriate behaviour" (expressions of love for her present husband). However, Hardy does not present this as a triumph for "behaviour technology". The "unwanted side-effects" often accompanying aversion therapy begin to emerge: "the cure became so permanent as to be itself a new disease". The "scared and enervated lady" is as annoying to her "strange, hard, brutal" husband because of her clinging jealousy as she was when she was infatuated with the memory and statue of her first husband.

This story is extraordinary in a number of ways. First its date; it was first published in 1890 in the Christmas number of *The Graphic*. Yet it contains a detailed account of an experiment in aversion therapy. But the use of conditioning as a therapeutic process had hardly begun in the 1930s, and it was not really developed until the 1950s. Admittedly, people have always tried to control one another's behaviour through the use of punishment, but I think Hardy's story makes it clear that he is dealing with something more complex than this. As H. R. Beech points out: "it could be argued that behaviour therapy is as ancient as the attempts made by men to shape and control behaviour by rewards and punishments, although this would be rather like crediting the abacus inventor with the same degree of sophistication as the modern computer designer".[26] Lord Uplandtowers's "doses" of terror are certainly contrived with some degree of sophistication, and are conceived as stages of treatment in a "cure", not as simple punishment.

As for the beginning of this kind of treatment, Beech is unwilling to place the origins of behaviour therapy any earlier than the 1920s with Pavlov's experiments with animals and those of J. B. Watson with children. Watson's earliest and most celebrated experiment, in 1920, in which he conditioned a baby of eleven months to be afraid of a white rabbit which he had formerly liked, was not, of course, therapeutic, but was designed to demonstrate Watson's theories about human responses to conditioning. B. F. Skinner is prepared to go back a little earlier in time for the beginnings of behaviourism. He cites H. L. Thorndike's experiments on how cats learn to escape from latched boxes, which took place in 1898.[27] However, this early work was concerned with animals not human beings, with learning theory not therapy (leading to Thorndike's *Psychology of Learning*, published in 1913) and in any case took place some years after Hardy wrote his story. Similarly, C. Lloyd Morgan was mainly concerned with observing how animals learn, though he included some speculations on the relationship of man's and animals' thinking.[28] But though these writers can certainly be identified as the precursors of modern behaviourism, there is nothing in their work which resembles the aversion therapy found in "Barbara of the House of Grebe". It seems rather strange to suggest that Hardy imagined aversion therapy some 50 years before it was first practised; yet I have been unable to trace any written records of similar cases in Hardy's day, nor do specialists in the field of behaviour technology seem to be aware of earlier examples. Skinner

calls Thorndike's experiments of 1898, "One of the first serious attempts to study the changes brought about by the consequences of
behaviour".[29] I can only conclude, then, that Hardy conceived
imaginatively a technique of behaviour modification which was
subsequently developed over a period of 50 years through experiments with rats, pigeons, dogs and so on and through clinical
studies of human beings.

Secondly, the method described in the story is extremely similar to
those adopted in the mid-twentieth century. A brief examination of
behaviour technology supports this view. Blackman sums up the
various methods and terminologies by saying, "behaviour ther-
apies ought to include any behaviourally orientated techniques
used in a recognised therapeutic situation to help patients to
behave in more acceptable and usual ways".[30] This fits Hardy's
story, apart from the "recognised therapeutic situation" which of
course cannot exist without predecessors.

Techniques similar to those described by Hardy have been used in
the twentieth century to change various kinds of "unacceptable" behaviour. Some behaviourists use them for treating "learned" behaviour such as gambling, alcoholism and (very doubtfully in this
category) homosexuality and fetishism. Barbara's case is parallel to
the two latter categories. Her love for a statue is obviously fetishistic.
Her love for her dead husband is deemed to be "inappropriate sexual
behaviour" by Lord Uplandtowers, and this corresponds to similar
assumptions made by some behaviourists about homosexuality.
Beech comments that,

> It is perhaps understandable that the use of aversive conditioning
> has been mainly concerned with the kind of psychological ab-
> normality which produces some gratification for the patient. In
> this way, it is hoped, the behaviour which has afforded grati-
> fication will be effectively blocked, so that the patient is free to
> find some new way of gratifying his needs.[31]

Thus, Lord Uplandtowers was working on accepted modern clinical lines when he chose aversion therapy rather than the "constant
tenderness" suggested by the surgeon who narrates the tale. The
parallel with behaviourist treatment of male homosexuals is very
close. The "patients" are shown pictures of naked men and given
electric shocks or nausea-inducing drugs. One of the difficulties, according to Beech, is that, "the treatment described has been con-

cerned with the symbols of abnormal behaviour rather than the abnormal behaviour itself . . . blocking the response to a symbol may have little impact upon the behaviour outside the treatment laboratory".[32] In Barbara's case, symbol and actuality are one — she loves both the statue and the memory of her husband. Lord Upland-towers's speedy "cure" is explicable in modern behaviourist terms, since in using the symbolic statue as a means of treatment he is making a direct attack on the abnormal behaviour itself. Hardy's description of the results of the violent and terrifying treatment also matches subsequent findings on aversion therapy: "the evidence generally suggests that very intense punishment has the greatest effect in suppressing some piece of behaviour; while this may be true in general, other evidence indicates that intense punishment is more likely to disorganise a response than to suppress it".[33] Here again, the only partially satisfactory outcome (that is from Lord Upland-towers's point of view; from any other it is, of course, totally unsatisfactory) would seem to correspond to later experimental findings. Beech sums up on aversion therapy by asking "can punishment, used in any naive way, ever be enough to produce adaptive, socially acceptable behaviour in cases where clearly the situation is extremely complex?".[34] He then goes on to analyse the more satisfactory "operant conditioning with positive incentive" which has now largely replaced aversion therapy in the treatment of behavioural problems.

Hardy also raises in this story the questions and doubts which have surrounded aversion therapy (and indeed the whole theory of behaviourism) since it first started to be practised. It is quite clear which side Hardy is on in the argument. He depicts Uplandtowers as a hard cruel man to whom it does not occur that "constant tenderness" might be more effective than "subtle stratagems". After the treatment "unwanted side-effects" emerge: Barbara is "broken-spirited", gives birth to large numbers of sickly babies which die immediately, and dies "completely worn out in mind and body". Hardy's attitude is not surprising. It is because he sees human beings as, at least to some extent, autonomous, capable of choice, and having a right to be themselves, that he is strongly critical of Upland-towers's behaviour. (This critical attitude is further evidence, if any were needed, that Hardy does not regard his characters as "puppets"). Though in most ways, "Barbara of the House of Grebe" is an uncharacteristic story, it is typical of Hardy's writing in three ways: in its evident respect for the value of the individual's identity;

in its overt interest in psychological problems and theories; and in its expression of ideas and theories which were not to be of common interest or knowledge till many years later.

It is strange that T. S. Eliot should have chosen this story as the focus for his attack on Hardy.[35] He maintains that "here . . . you get the essential Hardy without the Wessex staging", and goes on to claim that "in 'Barbara of the House of Grebe' we are introduced into a world of pure evil". Eliot does not explain why he thinks this, though he does contrast it with, among other stories, James's *The Turn of the Screw*, which, he says contains Good and Evil. Possibly Eliot was conscious of the element of psychological experimentation in Hardy's story, though he does not mention it; this would account for his antipathy, since he maintained that "psychology is dangerous unless based on sound theology". However, since the story is an exposure, not a condonation of cruelty and manipulation, Goodness is there by implication, as well as being explicit in the voice of the narrator.

This story seems to me far from being "masterly" (in a diabolic way) as Eliot suggests. The events are presented melodramatically, the characters are lacking in complexity, in spite of their bizarre qualities. It is significant only because it shows that even when writing sensationally and superficially, Hardy still has extraordinary insight into how the mind works, and even foresees how men will use such knowledge in the future. It may seem extraordinary to suggest that Hardy's interest in psychology has led him to foresee the development of aversion therapy long before it was practised, but this story, and the introduction to it in *A Group of Noble Dames*, seem to me fully to justify such a claim.

There is one other example in Hardy's fiction of his concern about the medical treatment of mental illness. Though this occurs in a major novel, *The Woodlanders*, I will mention it briefly here since it demonstrates both his sceptical attitude towards unsympathetic experimental treatment and his understanding and acceptance of those who do not behave in "acceptable and usual ways". Fitzpiers is presented as a skilful doctor of physical medicine, but his flippant attitude to human relationships affects his treatment of psychological problems. He shows no understanding of the kind of effect the sale of her head has on Grammer Oliver. His treatment of Mr South's tree-obsession is utterly casual and unconcerned, showing not the slightest attempt to understand his patient's frame of mind. Hardy emphasises his lack of interest in the case:

Mr Fitzpiers entered the sick chamber as a doctor is wont to do on such occasions, and pre-eminently when the room is that of the humble cottager; looking round towards the patient with a pre-occupied gaze which so plainly reveals that he has well-nigh forgotten all about the case and circumstances since he dismissed them from his mind at his last exit from the same apartment.[36]

His comment on the disastrous outcome of his experiment is equally callous: "Damned if my remedy hasn't killed him!".[37] It is an exclamation which might well have been uttered by Lord Upland-towers if his "remedy" had had (as it so nearly did) the same effect.

This attempt at curing mental illness, and the only slightly less calamitous experiment in "Barbara of the House of Grebe", show Hardy's interest in psychological disturbance and also his understanding of the complexity of mental processes and the futility of simple, insensitive approaches to mental illness. They show, too, that Hardy regards abnormal disturbed psychological states as areas of importance for the novelist. His minor fiction is particularly revealing in this respect. The subjects he deals with include mental aberrations such as obsessions, delusions, hysteria; attempts at curing these; Lesbianism and bisexuality; and minds at times of uncertainty, confusion and change. Most of these subjects also occur in the major fiction, where they are embedded in an imagined world that is much richer and more varied and in characters of great complexity; in the short stories, these subjects stand out with clarity and simplicity in their simpler contexts. Sometimes, it is merely as "subjects" that they stand out; we see the interest the subject had for Hardy, but it has not been made an integral part of a fully developed human being. In January 1888, he wrote:

A "sensation-novel" is possible in which the sensationalism is not casualty, but evolution; not physical but psychical . . . The difference between the latter kind of novel and the novel of physical sensationalism — i.e., personal adventure, etc. — is this: that whereas in the physical the adventure itself is the subject of interest, the psychical results being passed over as commonplace, in the psychical the casualty or adventure is held to be of no intrinsic interest, but the effect upon the faculties is the important matter to be depicted.[38]

This is clearly the direction that Hardy's art as a novelist was taking.

"The effect upon the faculties" had always been important in the major novels, and in *Tess* and *Jude* it becomes paramount. In the short stories and some of the minor novels we can see him setting out in that direction, but in these lesser works he rarely completes the journey. The happenings, often grotesque, outlandish, and melodramatic, predominate and "the effect upon the faculties" dwindles into relative insignificance, or partakes of the sensationalism and implausibility of the events.

In spite of this, these minor works are immensely illuminating for anyone who wants to understand Hardy's intentions in his fiction. They demonstrate his interest in (even obsession with) unusual mental and emotional conditions, especially when they are of an extreme or intense kind; they show the enormous range of his understanding and sympathy and his use of fiction as a means of enlarging the sympathies and attacking the prejudices of his readers. In them too, we see how the gifted storyteller, the writer who sets us longing to know what happens next is sometimes handicapped by these very gifts and led to abandon some exciting new perception about human nature for the sake of an intriguing plot. Yet, because the various elements are not fully integrated, these less successful works give us the chance to see particularly clearly almost the raw material of which the major works are made.

APPENDIX TO CHAPTER 2: A NOTE ON "OPERANT CONDITIONING"

B. F. Skinner formulated this phrase and explained its meaning in *Science and Human Behaviour*, p. 65:

> The term (operant) emphasises the fact that the behaviour *operates* upon the environment to generate consequences. The consequences define the properties with respect to which responses are called similar. The term will be used both as an adjective (operant behaviour) and as a noun to designate the behaviour defined by a given consequence.

By a strange coincidence, Hardy uses the unusual word "operant", in a difference sense, in "Barbara of the House of Grebe" — "a permanent revulsion was operant within her".

It is interesting to speculate upon the possibility that Hardy's story gave rise to this technical term of behaviourist psychology. If Skinner had at some time read the story, the word might well be associated with the therapy described there and thus have led him to coin the phrase "operant conditioning".

It would be one of "life's little ironies" if a story which was simultaneously a prophecy and an exposure of behaviour technology was the source of one of its key technical terms.

3 *The Well-Beloved*: an experiment in Jungian theory

The Well-Beloved is without doubt a minor novel. Hardy felt it necessary in his Preface to defend it from "the charge of frivolity". But as part of Hardy's whole work as a novelist it is a significant and in many ways characteristic work — characteristic in that in this, his penultimate novel, he should be experimenting, making innovations, exploring new aspects of psychology, investigating the possibility of exploring man's experience of time in new ways. Even when writing in a "fanciful" vein, Hardy is still expressing a serious concern with psychological theory. His approach is tentative; he is after all experimenting with a new kind of novel, simultaneously theoretical and fantastic. He managed all this, in what was probably a potboiler, while in the midst of his major efforts to push out the boundaries of the novel and attack the "inert mass of crystallised opinion"[1] in *Tess* and *Jude*.

The Well-Beloved is, very largely, a vehicle for theory; Hardy virtually outlines, in a simple form, Jung's concept of the anima, and there are many striking parallels between the novel and Jung's writings. The novel demonstrates Hardy's continuing interest in psychological theory with particular clarity because it presents the central character in a very abstract and theoretical way. Pierston comes across more as an exemplification of a theory than as a plausible, fully developed human being. Hardy subtitled the novel "A Sketch of a Temperament", which indicates his intention to focus on the character of the hero, but he also called it "a fanciful exhibition of the artistic temperament".[2] These remarks support the impression given by the book itself that Hardy intended it to be a light and whimsical treatment of the theme, but he regarded the theme itself as serious and relevant to an understanding of human nature: "There is, of course, underlying the fantasy followed by the visionary artist, the truth that all men are pursuing a shadow, the unattainable, and I venture to hope that this may redeem the tragicomedy from the charge of frivolity".[3]

The theme itself is an ancient one. Hardy says in the Preface that the idea "is by no means new to Platonic philosophers" and he quotes Shelley in an epigraph. The pursuit of ideal beauty is of course one that recurs in all the arts and in philosophy. Yet there is a certain newness and modernity in the way Hardy develops the idea and there are some very close parallels with Jung's theory of the anima. Jung always stressed the antiquity of the concept as expressed in myth and in subsequent literature (he was particularly fascinated by Rider Haggard's *She*, but he does not appear to have encountered *The Well-Beloved*). Jung's aim is to increase our understanding of phenomenon by approaching it from a theoretical and scientific standpoint, while commenting on the inadequacy of science to explore it fully; he therefore attempts to combine the imaginative and the abstract in his analysis. Conversely, Hardy's starting point is imaginative fiction, but this novel contains a large number of abstract statements about the theme, and Pierston's pursuit of the Well-Beloved is frequently presented in theoretical terms, often in summary form rather than dramatically and imaginatively. As a result, the two writers, from their opposite standpoints, tend to converge in their mode of presentation of their common theme.

The theoretical basis of the novel is that Pierston's emotional life is "governed by the migratory elusive idealisation he called Love, who, ever since his boyhood, had flitted from human shell to human shell an indefinite number of times".[4] Hardy presents Pierston as a man with only a limited amount of insight into his own nature. Though Pierston "did not assume that the idol of his fancy was an integral part of the personality in which it had sojourned for a long or short while",[5] he did not see much further than this. Hardy says he recognised "as a fact simply" that "his well-beloved had many embodiments".[6] Thus, although Pierston's fascination with the three Avices forms the central thread of the story, it is repeatedly stressed that the ideal can take on a wide variety of physical shapes. This is presented as particularly advantageous for Pierston as sculptor, providing him with an unlimited source of inspiration, bringing him fame, wealth, popularity, but producing, in Pierston's view, and apparently in Hardy's, a rather low form of art.

If we were restricted to Pierston's view of the Platonic theory, *The Well-Beloved* would certainly be superficial. However, one of the things Hardy is concerned to show is the limitedness of the hero's insight. His self-awareness is presented by Hardy as accurate as far as it goes, but he shows that it does not go very far. He understands the irrationality of the fascination, especially when he is beginning to feel that his ideal is embodied in the second Avice; he realises it is, "a forsaking of the accomplished and well-connected Mrs Pine-Avon for the little laundress, under the traction of some mystic magnet which has nothing to do with reason".[7] He is dimly aware of the contradictory qualities of his obsession; sometimes he speaks of his well-beloved as a goddess, often emphasising that she is of primitive origin — he calls her, "Aphrodite, Ashtaroth, Freyja";[8] on the other hand, she often seems to embody qualities that are the reverse of divine — he calls her "sprite, witch, troll".[9] Thus, while most of the time seeing the well-beloved "in Platonic phraseology — the essence and epitome of all that is desirable in this existence",[10] he is also aware that she can embody less lofty aspirations, even represent evil itself. These perceptions are presented as dim and transient; Pierston is too preoccupied with each passing embodiment of the ideal to analyse himself or his situation with any real penetration. Hardy stresses Pierston's inability to control his reactions; he has a perpetual feeling of helplessness, since the "Phantom" might at any time "seduce him before he was aware"[11] or he might have to "sit and behold the mournful departure of the well-beloved from the form he had lately cherished".[12]

In these ways, Hardy emphasises Pierston's inability to understand or come to terms with his own nature or that of the beloved. He says right at the beginning of the novel, "God only knows what she really was; Pierston did not".[13] He points out that Pierston never gave much consideration to the idea that she was "a subjective phenomenon" and that her "ghostliness" and "independence of physical laws and failings had occasionally given him a sense of fear".[14] Later, he is aware of "a sudden Sapphic terror of love" and "a fearful lapse from reasonableness".[15]

This fear of his own nature and failure to understand it is never overcome. Hardy treats Pierston's escape from the clutches of his obsession in a wry and cynical way; in his disillusionment he is even less self-aware, and shows less understanding of the nature of things than when he was obsessed with his ideal. He cannot understand the disappearance of his sense of ideal beauty any more than he could understand its presence. With its loss goes also his appreciation of art and natural beauty. The transformation is so extreme that Pierston becomes a destroyer of beauty instead of a creator and seeker of it. He demolishes "the old moss-grown, mullioned Elizabethan cottages" in his native village, substituting modern houses with ventilators. (Hardy's disapproval is made overt only in the Preface.) More significantly still he replaces "the old natural fountains" with hygienic piped water.[16] This ending is quite different from the serial version, published in *The Illustrated London News* in 1892. This ends with Pierston's cynical laughter at discovering that Marcia has become an aged "crone": "He laughed and laughed till he was almost too weak to draw breath . . . 'I — I — it is almost too droll, this ending to my would-be romantic history' ".[17] The changed ending in the final version makes Pierston's failure of understanding and lack of self-awareness far more explicit. The destruction of the natural fountains suggests perhaps that he never understood the deeper springs of his nature and finally denied them altogether.

The central points which I have enumerated here show that there are hints of something besides the search for Platonic ideal beauty in the novel. In a fairly simple way, Hardy here anticipates a number of points in Jung's theory of the anima. Jung developed this theory over a number of years, from about 1916 to 1934 and added further revisions to the 1954 edition of his *Collected Works*; it gradually became more complex and multifaceted as Jung's thinking, especially about the collective unconscious, developed. He tended, each time he mentioned a theory, to add a little more, to develop first one aspect of it, then another, and thus makes it difficult to give an account of his theory that is both brief and comprehensive. Basically, Jung argues that there are masculine and feminine traits in everyone and he gives the name "anima" to "the woman in a man".[18] He says that as long as a man is unconscious of his anima it is frequently projected upon a real woman.[19] He sees the anima not only as an aspect of the individual's unconscious, but also as an archetype of the collective unconscious; thus the animus and anima "have given rise to mythological gods and goddesses".[20] He maintains that men are nearly always unconscious of their anima, and have enormous difficulty in recognising what it is; most men tend to project it on to a real woman, "thus giving rise to magically complicated relationships" and even "pathological consequences".[21] The anima is "instinctive, spontaneous, irrational, even magical".[22] In his later development of the theory, he sees it as "a natural archetype that satisfactorily sums up all the statements of the unconscious, of the primitive mind, of the history of language and religion".[23] From this, Jung argues further, that since human beings are both good and evil, the anima necessarily embodies the extremes of good and evil and is thus naturally seen sometimes as a goddess, sometimes as a succubus or a witch: "Because of their numinous, suggestive power [the animus and anima] have formed since olden times the archetypal basis of all masculine and feminine divinities and therefore merit special attention, above all from the psychologist, but also from the thoughtful layman".[24]

Even such a sketchy summary of Jung's main points about the anima suffices to highlight a number of points it has in common with Hardy's "fanciful" story. An examination of some parallel passages shows that Hardy's thinking is very close to Jung's, though Hardy's points are suggested rather than elaborated. Such an examination of the resemblances between Hardy's treatment of the well-beloved and Jung's concept of the anima indicates that, as Hardy himself said in the *Life of Thomas Hardy*, the serious interest of *The Well-Beloved* lies in its psychological exploration. Though the basic idea of the work is far from new, in its detail and in its theoretical presentation it treats the subject in a new way and frequently anticipates Jung.

Early in the novel, Hardy states quite clearly that Pierston is unconsciously projecting what is really "a subjective phenomenon"[25] on to a succession of women. This exactly corresponds with Jung's statement about projection in *The Integration of the Personality*. While this aspect of Pierston seems plausible, it has both advantages and disadvantages for Hardy as a novelist; the projection of the "subjective phenomenon" means that Hardy can treat it dramatically, and indeed use it as a basis for a conventionally complicated plot; but Pierston's lack of understanding of his own nature means that Hardy must necessarily, if he is going to explore him in any depth, give a good deal of explanatory comment. Unfortunately, Hardy here comments at some length but without convincingly fathoming Pierston's personality, while suggesting that there are depths to be explored.

Another way in which the well-beloved matches the anima is in its conflicting qualities; both embody extremes of good and evil. Pierston sees her sometimes as goddess, sometimes as "witch" or "troll". Jung makes the same point, "The nixie from long ago is an even more instinctive version of a magical feminine being whom I call the 'anima'. She can also be a siren, mermaid . . . she changes into all sorts of shapes like a witch."[26]

These passages also illustrate another point which is central to Jung's conception and mentioned several times by Hardy — the ancient, primitive origin of the anima. Hardy reminds the reader of the history of the island of Ancient Slingers, and of the isolation of the families there "from Norman, Anglian, Roman, Balearic — British times".[27] He emphasises particularly the Roman connection, as well as earlier, more primitive links: "Tradition urged that the temple of Venus once stood on top of the Roman road leading up into the isle; and possibly one to the love goddess of the Slingers antedated this".[28] These passages may seem to show merely Hardy's interest in the past; yet the references to goddesses and elsewhere to "Aphrodite, Ashtaroth, Freyja or whoever the love queen of this isle might have been",[29] and who, Pierston feels, is punishing him, suggest a more subjective connection than mere antiquarianism. Jung's awareness of the relationship between his "anima" and the figures in ancient myth led on to his formulation of the theory of the collective unconscious: "anima and animus . . . live and function in the deeper layers of the unconscious, especially in that phylogenetic substratum I have called the collective unconscious".[30] Hardy does not formulate such a theory in this novel, but much of what he writes implies its existence: Pierston's reference to "that olden seductive one — that Protean dream-creature"[31] combines both the antiquity and subjectivity of his obsession. Since Hardy virtually formulated the theory of the collective unconscious in the first chapter of *The Return of the Native*, it is not surprising that he should make use of it in an oblique way here.

The amorality of the anima, which Jung insisted on, is also a feature of Hardy's well-beloved. Jung describes the anima as "the archetype of life itself"[32] and therefore necessarily including both good and evil. In his summing up of his views in "Aion", he says, "As numina, animus and anima work now for good, now for evil".[33] Similarly Pierston's beloved shifts from Platonic ideal, to "Goddess who pulled the string",[34] to troll. He feels that its embodiment in Mrs Pine-Avon is "unquestionably an awkward thing" and that "the Goddess in her implacable vanity might be punishing him anew".[35]

Hardy does not here amplify or comment on Pierston's bewildered attempts to account for the transitoriness or contradictions of his ideal. He does not show the relationship between this particular aspect of the beloved and the theory as a whole, but leaves it simply as a part of himself which Pierston has not come to terms with.

These contradictory qualities in the anima are, naturally enough, associated with a sense of fear. Jung says that the anima "occasionally causes states of fascination that rival the best bewilderment: or unleashes terrors in us not to be outdone by any manifestation of the devil".[36] Similarly, Hardy describes the "sense of fear" which Pierston experiences. The "sudden Sapphic terror"[37] is part of the whole irrational experience. Pierston is aware of "the fearful lapse from reasonableness"[38] in himself. The changing embodiments of the well-beloved are completely beyond rational control. Each time, he feels "that the Beloved had emerged from the shadows without any hint or initiative from him",[39] that "it was certainly not a wanton game of my own instigation".[40] Likewise, its departure seems to occur as an event outside himself. He describes the change from seeing "a divinity" to seeing "a corpse" as something that simply happens to him; he is either "powerless" in the grip of an idealising passion[41] or he has lost all feeling for the woman who seemed to embody the ideal. The "Phantom" may "seduce him before he was aware",[42] so that the change from "the accomplished and well-connected Mrs Pine-Avon to the little laundress" was "under the traction of some mystic magnet which had nothing to do with reason".[43] This love for the second Avice demonstrates this point particularly emphatically: "while enrapturing his soul, it simultaneously shocked his intellect".[44]

The irrational nature of the anima is given great emphasis by Jung. He reiterates that "the anima is not the soul in the dogmatic sense, not the 'anima rationalis', which is a philosophic conception, but a natural archetype that satisfactorily sums up all the statements of the unconscious, of the primitive mind".[45] He writes of "her irrational elfin nature",[46] but adds that it is "the terrifyingly chaotic things that reveal a deeper meaning".[47] In comparing Hardy's treatment of irrationality with Jung's, the lightweight quality of *The Well-Beloved* becomes particularly apparent for Hardy does not explore but merely hints at deeper meanings. What is striking is that even when he is treating his theme lightly his central preoccupations with psychological complexities, and with using the novel form to explore them in a new way, are still apparent.

Though Jung was, like Hardy, more interested in the anima than the animus, both authors show, by cursory references, that they are aware that the experiences they are describing are not confined to the male sex. Jung admits the existence of the animus, though he does not tell us much about it. Hardy allows the second Avice to be caught up in the same non-rational pursuit of the beloved as Pierston. This is important since, by implication, it enlarges Hardy's scope. He is not writing merely about an obsession characteristic of the artistic temperament, but of a more universal phenomenon. When Pierston explains his predicament to Somers, he says that it is

> a fond superstition that the Beloved One of any man always, or even usually, cares to remain in one corporeal nook or shell for any length of time . . . each shape, or embodiment, has been a temporary residence only . . . Now there is no spiritualistic nonsense in this — it is simple fact put in the plain form that the conventional public are afraid of.[48]

It is characteristic that, through Pierston's words, Hardy indicates his awareness that he is challenging what is conventionally regarded as normal or desirable. Jung suggests the universality of his concept when he defines the animus as "the man in woman" and anima as "the woman in a man".[49] Pierston trembles on the brink of recognising a female element in himself: "The sight of the new moon as representing one who by her socalled inconstancy acted up to his own idea of a migratory Well-Beloved, made him feel as if his wraith in a changed sex had suddenly looked over the horizon at him".[50] Here Hardy seems to be just hinting at something which Jung was to make a fundamental facet of his theory.

It is remarkable that there are so many points of similarity between *The Well-Beloved* and Jung's writing about the anima concept since the aim and tone of their work is very different. Jung makes his points with great weight and emphasis and requires serious and profound contemplation of them from the reader; Hardy treats many of the same points casually, in passing, with little attempt to explore their significance. Perhaps the most marked divergence between them lies in Jung's very emphatic and repeated insistence on the importance of an understanding of the anima: "The degree of unconsciousness one meets in this connection is astounding. Hence it is practically impossible to get a man who is afraid of his own femininity to understand what is meant by the anima."[51] Hardy does not treat Pierston's failure so seriously. If he had wished to explore the theme in the kind of depth with which Jung treated it, he could have made Pierston into a character who was capable of coming to some understanding of his own anima, who was not simply bewildered and bemused by his own emotions. Alternatively, he could have made the failure to understand the cause of far more serious psychological aberrations. But either change would have led him into serious and disturbing areas of consciousness and undermined the comparatively lightweight and "fanciful" quality of the novel. Both versions of the ending are refusals of painful explorations, though the final version does hint at some evaluation of the effects of Pierston's failure in self-knowledge.

It is interesting that both authors' speculations were thought to be immoral. Jung was accused of attaching too much importance to what were really "worthless erotic fantasies". Hardy mentions that some critics "affected to find unmentionable moral atrocities in its pages",[52] and he suggests "a reviewer *himself* afflicted with sexmania might review so".[53] His final comment is, "*The Well-Beloved* is a fanciful exhibition of the artistic nature, and has, I think, some little foundation in fact. I have been much surprised and even grieved by a ferocious review, attributing an immoral quality to the tale. The writer's meaning is beyond me."[54] Hardy's attitude of pained innocence is not wholly justified; in the serial version there is bigamy, and it is made quite clear that the bigamous marriage has been consummated. (*The Well-Beloved* must be unique in having its serial form bowdlerised for book publication, instead of the other way round.) He has also suggested in the book itself that he is writing about something that "the conventional public are afraid of ".

Hardy's modest claim for the authenticity of the psychology in this novel has some justification; at least we can claim for it that an important psychological writer of the twentieth century wrote on very similar lines. This does not, of course, prove that either Hardy's or Jung's speculations were correct, but *The Well-Beloved* does illustrate the searching, even daring nature of Hardy's thought. In this book, in which he was not attempting anything weighty or profound, he casually tossed off ideas about psychology and the nature of love which, more than twenty years later, Jung was to begin to make central in his work. This does not make *The Well-Beloved* a successful novel; it is far from being this, since the speculative psychological theories are not embodied in imaginatively developed, interesting and plausible characters. But it is important in the study of Hardy's work because it reveals perhaps more clearly, because more starkly, the theoretical basis of Hardy's thinking about psychology; the closeness of the parallels to Jung show that he was a pioneer in the kind of thinking about psychology which became common in the following century, and he was one of the first to use the novel as a vehicle for this. The aspects of psychology examined in this novel are largely new to Hardy — his central psychological interests come to a climax in *Tess* and *Jude* — so that it is not surprising that his first experiments in a new area should be tentative and unsure. It is tempting to wonder what he would have produced if he had continued to experiment in a further novel instead of turning to poetry after *Jude*. Proust saw him as a predecessor.

Proust's interest in Hardy, especially in *The Well-Beloved*, and his sense of affinity with him, adds a further dimension to our sense of the psychological interest of the book. It is significant that one of the major novelists of the twentieth century, whose importance derives partly from the way he combines innovation in the novel form with a profound exploration of the way the mind works, should feel he had much in common with Hardy and that Hardy should recognise and acknowledge the resemblance. Proust became aware of the similarities between *The Well-Beloved* and his conception of his own work at an early stage in its development. About December 1909, he wrote to Robert de Billy: "I have just been reading something very beautiful which unfortunately slightly resembles what I am doing (only it is a thousand times better). *The Well-Beloved* by Thomas Hardy. It doesn't even lack that slight touch of the grotesque which is an essential part of all great works."[55] The praise is excessive but it is certainly true that many of the central ideas of *The Well-Beloved* are developed with much greater subtlety and complexity by Proust. Indeed, Hardy's initial idea corresponds almost exactly with the central thread of *A la Recherche du Temps Perdu*. A passage in the *Life* dated February 1889 reads, "The story of a face which goes through three generations or more would make a fine novel or poem of the passage of Time. The difference of personality to be ignored. (This idea was to some extent carried out in the novel *The Well-Beloved*, the poem entitled 'Heredity', etc.)"[56] "A novel on the passage of time" is not quite what we get in *The*

Well-Beloved, but the idea is there embryonically, and the similarity in conception to Proust's work certainly seemed significant
to him.

Beloved, but the idea is there embryonically, and the similarity in
conception to Proust's work certainly seemed significant to him.

In the passage in *La Prisonniere* where Proust writes directly
about Hardy, he comments mainly on the structure — "the stone-
mason's geometry" — of the novels: "the parallelism between *The
Well-Beloved* where the man is in love with three women and *A Pair
of Blue Eyes* where the woman is in love with three men and in short
all those novels which can be laid one upon another like the vertically
piled houses upon the rocky soil of the island".[57] These comments,
apparently on the structure, are closely related to the subject matter
of the novels. Proust chooses to mention two novels concerned with
three successive lovers, and which therefore resemble his own work.
In *Le Temps Retrouvé*, he writes: "I had indeed suffered successively through Gilberte, through Madame de Guermantes, through
Albertine. Successively also I had forgotten them, and only my love
dedicated at different times to different beings, had lasted."[58] Hardy
draws attention to this resemblance: *The Well-Beloved* is based on
"the theory of the transmigration of the ideal beloved one, who only
exists in the lover, from material woman to material woman — as
exemplified also by Proust many years later".[59] Both authors are
particularly interested in the relevance of this theory to the
artist — Hardy applying it to Pierston as sculptor, Proust discussing
it more fully from the point of view of the writer, but also relating it
to artists generally and making a number of references to sculptors
in particular, as if, perhaps, he had *The Well-Beloved* in mind as he
wrote. In *Le Côté de Guermantes* his simile of the artist's work
would seem to imply this:

> When I found myself alone again at home and remembered that I
> had taken a drive that afternoon with Albertine, that I was to
> drive in two days' time with Mme de Guermantes and that I had to
> answer a letter from Gilberte, three women each of whom I had
> once loved, I said to myself that our social existence is, like an
> artist's studio, filled with abandoned sketches in which we have
> fancied for a moment we could set down in permanent form our
> need of a great love.[60]

Similarly, Pierston creates "marble images" of "the Goddess", and "though not a belief, it was, as has been stated, a formula, a superstition, that the three Avices were interpenetrated with her essence".[61] Here we have the three women, the permanent form, the theorising about the nature of the experience; parts of *The Well-Beloved* could almost have been a slight preliminary sketch for *A la Recherche du Temps Perdu*.

This is borne out further by another point raised in Hardy's first mention of *The Well-Beloved* in the *Life*. Referring to "the face which goes through three generations", he says "the differences of personality to be ignored".[62] This corresponds to a sentence in *A l'Ombre des Jeunes Filles en Fleur* where Proust is outlining some recommendations to novelists: "Perhaps he would be stating another truth if while investing all the persons of his story with distinct characters, he refrained from giving any to the beloved".[63] In fact, neither novelist really acts on his own suggestion; the successive women do have individuality, yet they both succeed in showing that what absorbs the central character is his own emotional state rather than the personality of the loved one.

This, of course, is central to the whole conception of both novels. In comparing Hardy with Jung, I have shown the importance of the idea of projection in his theory of the nature of an idealising love. Proust takes the same idea and develops and expands it. "When we are in love with a woman, we simply project into her a state of our own soul . . . the important thing is therefore not the worth of the woman but the depth of the state . . . the emotions which a young girl of no kind of distinction arouses in us can enable us to bring to the surface of our own consciousness some of the most intimate parts of our being".[64] This is an expansion of Hardy's "subjective phenomenon" (which Pierston "never much considered")[65] — an expansion because Proust's narrator is more aware of the subjectivity, which is analysed minutely, whereas Pierston is merely capable of fearing and suffering, with only a superficial grasp of what is happening to him. In noting the resemblance between Albertine and Gilberte, the narrator comments, "They are, these women, a product of our temperament, an image inversely projected, a negative of our sensibility".[66] Pierston's attempts to understand his own reactions to the first two Avices are far more groping and uncertain: "He could not read her individual character owing to the confusing effect of her likeness to a woman whom he had valued too late. He could not help seeing in her all that he knew of another, and veiling in her all that did not harmonise with his sense of metempsychosis".[67] This lack of understanding, both of himself and of the woman he loves could have led on to some interesting exploration of Pierston's personality, but unlike Proust Hardy merely hints at complexities; the complications of the plot are allowed to dominate. Yet Hardy had pinpointed, given in bare outline many aspects of the subject which Proust deals with so minutely. For instance, "the little laundress" corresponds to "the young girl of no kind of distinction"[68] whose significance is so fully analysed by Proust. Pierston's successive loves are the basis of his art; Proust writes, "a writer needs many beings to express one feeling".[69] Most important of all, both novelists are dealing with the same "subjective phenomenon", and it is significant that when Hardy commented in 1926 that, "It appears that the theory exhibited in *The Well-Beloved* in 1892 has been since developed by Proust still further", he chose to quote a phrase which is an almost literal translation of one of his own: "*le caractère purement subjectif du phénomène qu'est l'amour*".[70]

Hardy, Proust and Jung wrote about the same areas of emotional experience. All three are concerned with the subjectivity of love, with the way it is projected on to numerous human beings and with the way the present experience is affected by the past. Both Proust and Jung in their different ways explore these matters with great subtlety and in depth. They were writing more or less simultaneously, *A la Recherche du Temps Perdu* being published between 1914 and 1927 and Jung's major work on the anima between 1916 and 1934. Their work is part of the great explosion of writing concerned with the functioning of the mind and emotions and especially with the part played by the unconscious which occurred during this period in the writings of both psychologists and novelists. Both of them regard their findings as immensely important and are prepared to pursue them in the face of disapproving criticism. *The Well-Beloved* is a pioneer work in the same area, published in its first version in 1892, before any of the major works by psychologists on the unconscious had been written and before novelists had started to focus so much on this aspect of the mind. Obviously, it is much simpler and more tentative than *A la Recherche du Temps Perdu* or Jung's major work but it raises the subjects they later examined more fully, it persists in speculations which challenge conventional views, and it indicates the existence of unconscious drives in its hero, even if it does not explore them adequately. In these ways, even in this admittedly minor novel, Hardy's adventurous, experimental qualities are apparent. In 1886, he wrote, "Novel-writing as an art cannot go backward. Having reached the analytical stage it must transcend it by going still further in the same direction".[71] In the major novels of this period, *Tess of the d'Urbervilles* and *Jude the Obscure* he was doing just this, developing his lifelong examination of the ills which society's demands inflict on the individual and exploring the psychological effects in searching and complex ways. In the contemporaneous *Well-Beloved* he seems to have been on the brink of "going still further" in a slightly different direction. Here he seems, at a cursory glance, to be merely toying with a psychological theory. The weakness of *The Well-Beloved* is that he does not take his theory seriously enough, and, as so often in the minor novels, allows intricacies of plot to obscure the central interest. Yet Proust recognised the significance of the idea and developed it in one of the major experimental works of fiction of the twentieth century. Sue's exclamation, "What pioneers we were!" is everywhere applicable to Hardy himself, even in his slighter works.

4 Boldwood: "a man trained to repression"

Boldwood of *Far from the Madding Crowd* marks an important early stage in Hardy's development as a novelist. The treatment of this character shows an increasing interest, already demonstrated in *Desperate Remedies* and *A Pair of Blue Eyes*, in complex, disturbed personalities; it is, in a tentative way, a study of the development of insanity. The treatment is sometimes clumsy, sometimes inconsistent, and frequently exposes the need for some new technique for presenting the psychological complexities that Hardy has perceived. Nevertheless, this character shows the early interest in psychological theory revealed in the *Notebooks* developing into a capacity to embody that knowledge in psychologically complex characters and even to achieve startling new insights, some of which were later also perceived, through his clinical studies, by Freud. By the time of *Jude the Obscure* Hardy had found more effective ways of exploring in a novel his insights into neuroses; in Boldwood we have a comparatively crude and uncertain attempt at a similar theme. In spite of the obvious struggle with the mode of presentation, the depth of understanding is apparent.

In this early attempt to explore abnormal psychology, Hardy has chosen an extreme case — a murderer, reprieved on the grounds of insanity. He makes sure in quite explicit ways that the reader questions Boldwood's sanity from quite early in the novel. Troy asks "if there has ever been insanity in his family",[1] and Boldwood himself says that he is mad.[2] These suggestions are intensified later by direct comment, ("his unswerving devotion to Bathsheba could only be characterised as a fond madness"[3]), by Bathsheba's fear of him,[4] and her dread that "if I don't give my word, he'll go out of his mind",[5] and by Gabriel's uneasiness about his state of mind.[6] Thus we are clearly concerned with a character who seems to himself and to the people who know him to be hovering on the brink of insanity. Such a character could, of course, be dealt with in a completely superficial way. In spite of his uncertainty about how to explore Boldwood in depth, Hardy is able to go astonishingly far.

This is due to his remarkable understanding of a complex mental state. It is a study of repression. Hardy calls Boldwood "a man trained to repression"[7] and this aspect of him is of central importance to Hardy's whole conception of the character, however tentative and uncertain this may be. He depicts him as a man who has fiercely repressed his sexual instincts; he calls him "the bachelor", "the celibate", and stresses the rigidity of his demeanour as he passes Bathsheba on the road after the market ("The farmer had never turned his head once, but with eyes fixed on the most advanced point along the road, passed as unconsciously and abstractedly as if Bathsheba and her charms were thin air"[8]). He describes him as living in the "atmosphere of a Puritan Sunday lasting all the week".[9] He is "that dignified stronghold"[10] and contains within him "the perfect balance of enormous antagonistic forces".[11]

These descriptions of Boldwood correspond closely to Freud's accounts of repression: "the essence of repression lies simply in turning something away, and keeping it at a distance from the conscious",[12] and "a delicate balancing is here taking place".[13]

Boldwood's failure to notice Bathsheba at the market-place when everyone else was discussing her suggest that he is "turning something away . . . keeping it at a distance". This is reinforced by the description of his passing by silently on the empty road, "with his eye fixed on the most advanced point along the road". The fixity of his look suggests an avoidance rather than a mere lack of awareness of her. He is emphatically keeping her at a distance from his consciousness. Hardy, like Freud, also stresses the precariousness of the internal balance. Though there is no reference to any specific distorted memory of a traumatic experience such as Freud elicited from his patients during analysis, nevertheless Hardy's descriptions of Boldwood's behaviour do suggest that "the ego drew back, as it were, on its first collision with the objectionable instinctual impulse; it debarred the impulse from access to consciousness".[14] Hardy does not put the conception in abstract theoretical terms, but he shows that this is the condition of Boldwood until his defences are broken down. He repeatedly "draws back" from "the objectionable instinctual impulse". He cannot look at a woman; his spontaneous impulses are suppressed.

Hardy's treatment of Boldwood shows, I think, that he was hovering on the point of suggesting that his unbalanced state of mind derives from the burying of a traumatic sexual experience in the unconscious. Admittedly, Hardy does not say this with any clarity or definiteness. He is, rather, groping towards an awareness of this psychological phenomenon; as a result unreconciled contradictions in the character remain. They remain, I think, not simply as a result of carelessness, but because Hardy was intuitively aware of their significance. He clearly saw the relevance of a person's past to his emotional development, but with Boldwood he is indecisive about it, sometimes saying that his early years were wholly uneventful, sometimes hinting at catastrophic experiences. This uncertainty is raised almost as soon as Boldwood makes his appearance, in the inconclusive discussion about him between Liddy and Bathsheba. Liddy says that "he met with a bitter disappointment when young", but Bathsheba replies, "People always say that".[15] From then on the ambivalence about Boldwood's past is maintained. There is a series of suggestions that the valentine awakened in him emotions never felt before:

> "It was the first time in Boldwood's life that such an event [the receipt of the valentine] had occurred."[16]
> "Adam had awakened from his deep sleep . . . to Boldwood women had been remote phenomena".[17]
> "Though forty, Boldwood had never inspected a woman with the very centre and force of his glance".[18]
> "His face showed that he lived outside his defences for the first time and with a fearful sense of exposure."[19]
> "I had never any view of myself as a husband in my earlier days".[20]
> "You are the first woman of any shade or nature I have ever looked at to love".[21]

Interwoven with these suggestions that Boldwood had led all his life cut off from sexual experience are references to his "wild capabilities" which can be guessed at from "old floodmarks faintly visible".[22] Since these phrases occur immediately after a reference to the "hotbed of tropical intensity" on which Bathsheba has "carelessly thrown a seed", there can be no doubt that the "wide capabilities" Hardy refers to are sexual. Yet it seems strange that

Hardy did not notice the contradiction and eliminate it. I think the reason is that he had dimly perceived that the memory of what had caused the "old floodmarks" would have been repressed in such a nature. He does not give the clear evidence of this that Freud obtained clinically, nor has he formulated the theory clearly and rationally, as Freud did; nevertheless, something very like Freud's formulation can be sensed in the background of the portrait of Boldwood. Freud writes "everything that had been forgotten had in some way or other been distressing; it had been either alarming or shameful or painful by the standards of the subject's personality. It was impossible not to conclude that this was precisely why it had been forgotten — that is, why it had not remained conscious".[23] Thus, though Bathsheba feels, after the scene of violence when Boldwood threatens to horsewhip Troy, that, "Such astounding wells of fevered feeling in a still man . . . were incomprehensible, dreadful",[24] Hardy does not leave the reader feeling that it is totally incomprehensible. His perception that this "hotbed of tropical intensity" can coexist with "impassibleness" is based on his tentative recognition of the significance of repression. In "Inhibitions, Symptoms and Anxiety", Freud says "there does undoubtedly exist a correspondence . . . between the strength of the impulse that has to be repressed and the intensity of the resultant anxiety".[25] This, again fits in with the total picture of Boldwood: "his equilibrium disturbed, he was in extremity at once".[26]

I think we can see, in the conception of this character, the idea of repression beginning to come to the surface of Hardy's mind, but, perhaps without being fully grasped by him; he felt no contradiction in leaving in the text mutually exclusive statements about Boldwood's past because he had in mind two ideas that were not incompatible — that the events had occurred, and that Boldwood had completely forgotten them. Hardy's openness to experience, his refusal to force his observations into a formula probably enabled him to reach this insight. He insisted that his novels were "a series of seemings"[27] and claimed that "unadjusted impressions have their value".[28] Perhaps he was more aware that he was postulating the existence of repression than I have suggested; he may have quite deliberately placed the apparent contradictions in the text in order to make readers experience Boldwood's conflicting feelings, to make them see the contradictions in him as they are seen by the other characters, and thus the "series of seemings" embodied in the novel.

Whether they are tentative, intuitive, or fully thought out, Hardy's insights into the neurotic personality he has created are extraordinarily similar to the insights derived by Freud from analysis.

That Hardy had this particular perception seems at first rather surprising. For many years, Freud thought that repression was "a concept which could not have been formulated before the time of psycho-analytical studies".[29] That Hardy should perceive such a thing simply through observation and intuition suggests an unusual insight into the workings of the unconscious. But in 1911 Freud acknowledged that this was after all possible, when his attention was drawn to Schopenhauer's *The World as Will and Idea*. Schopenhauer offered an explanation of madness:

> in that resistance of the will to allowing what is contrary to it to come under the examination of the intellect lies the place at which madness can break in upon the mind. Each new adverse event must be assimilated by the intellect . . . . However the health of the mind can only continue so long as this is in each case properly carried out. If, on the contrary, in some particular case, the resistance and struggles of the will against the apprehension of some knowledge reaches such a degree that the operation is not performed in its integrity, then certain events and circumstances become for the intellect completely suppressed, because the will cannot endure the sight of them . . . thus madness appears . . . . One may thus regard the origin of madness as the violent "casting out of the mind" of anything.[30]

I quote this passage at length because of Hardy's well-known interest in and affinity with Schopenhauer. I am not suggesting that he was indebted to Schopenhauer for his idea of Boldwood, since it is likely that he read *The World as Will and Idea* for the first time when he bought the first English translation, published in 1883. I am suggesting rather that the similarities in the thought of Hardy and Schopenhauer are not limited to their philosophical ideas, but extend to psychological matters, and that they were both forerunners of Freud — a point which Freud acknowledged as far as Schopenhauer was concerned, pointing out "the large extent to which psycho-analysis coincides with the philosophy of Schopenhauer — not only did he assert the dominance of the emotions and the supreme importance of sexuality, but he was even aware of the mechanism of repression".[31] This sentence could apply equally well to Hardy. Freud frequently admitted that "there are many instances

in which laborious psycho-analytical investigation can merely confirm the truths which the philosophers recognised by intuition".[32]
He makes the same admission with regard to imaginative writers.
That Hardy's understanding of psychology had enabled him to
grasp something which Freud had initially thought could only be
revealed through psychoanalysis suggests that his insight was particularly profound.

These hints about Boldwood's past are important, but they are
not presented to the reader wholly effectively. The implications of
the unresolved contradictions have not been fully assimilated into
the novel. They have not been explored enough, so that this aspect
of Boldwood remains more a theory than something we have experienced. Similarly, Hardy's attempts to show Boldwood's mind at
work (after receiving the valentine) are not wholly successful and yet
they are indicative of an unusual understanding of the nature of the
unconscious. Boldwood's waking vision of the woman writing the
valentine "had no individuality. She was a misty shape," but
"whenever Boldwood dozed, she took a form and comparatively
ceased to be a vision".[33] This is the opposite of the popular, traditional view of dreams ("dreamlike" suggesting hazy indefiniteness).
But since Freud, we have become aware that repressed material
sometimes surfaces in dreams ("The dream is a disguised fulfilment"[34]). Hardy, in that brief sentence is showing his profound
understanding of the nature of repression; it is only when the censor
is partially lifted in sleep that Boldwood can allow the idea of a
woman as a being with a body to come to the surface. It is also significant that in the midst of his fantasies about the unknown woman,
Boldwood studies himself closely in the mirror. Hardy always stresses
the characteristic self-absorption of neurotic people; here,
Boldwood seems to be afraid that he is fading away — he sees himself
as "wan", "insubstantial", with vacant eyes. (This is in complete contrast with the simple vanity and delighted enjoyment of her own appearance which Bathsheba shows when she, too, contemplates
herself in a looking-glass). Later, Hardy emphasises Boldwood's self-
absorption more strongly: when he and Gabriel are in despair over
the marriage of Bathsheba and Troy, he shows how a stable, well-
balanced man, even at times of utter misery, is aware of the world
outside himself: "Gabriel, for a minute, rose above his own grief in
noticing Boldwood's";[35] Boldwood remains totally wrapped up in
himself, oblivious of all externals. By this technique of contrast, so
characteristic of Hardy's structuring of his novels, Hardy is able to

stress the neurotic nature of Boldwood's response to suffering. The description of Boldwood's appearance, of "the square figure sitting erect upon the horse, the head turned to neither side, the elbows steady by the hips, the brim of the hat level and undisturbed in its onward glide",[36] recalls the earlier occasion when Boldwood "never turned his head once, but with eyes fixed"[37] passed Bathsheba on the road. By this means, Hardy emphasises the recurrence of the behaviour pattern; Boldwood's characteristic response to unhappiness is self-control, superficial imperviousness, indicative of the tendency towards repression.

This inability to see anything outside himself even includes Bathsheba. On two occasions, by a mixture of bullying and pleading, he extracts promises from her. She is reluctant, agonised, obviously only doing what he asks out of pity and guilt, and, on the second occasion, weeping. Boldwood's reaction to this unhappiness in the woman he so passionately loves, is on both occasions to say, "I'm happy now".[38] Such self-absorption is almost total, but Hardy shows further, through the disaster to his stacks, how the neurosis is gaining hold of Boldwood and restricting his ability to cope with the normal demands of life. Before he became aware of Bathsheba, Boldwood was in control of his precarious mental state, able to respond to the demands of practical, though not of emotional life. Hardy shows that he has been a highly competent farmer. As his balance becomes more and more disturbed, he becomes less able to grapple with external problems; the neglect of the stacks, dramatically contrasted with the sane Gabriel's fight to save Bathsheba's, shows effectively the insidious increase in the neurosis. The world of the neurotic is limited to himself.

This contributes to Boldwood's idealisation of Bathsheba. He treats her as an object for his own satisfaction, without the slightest awareness of her as a person. Since she is totally unreal to him, it is easy for him to idealise her. However, Hardy points out that this is "natural", "natural to the mood and still more natural to the circumstances",[39] possibly thus emphasising the abnormality of the rest of Boldwood's behaviour. Idealisation is too common in Hardy's novels — he sees it as an almost universal component of love — for him to feel that in itself it is a symptom of Boldwood's neurosis. But the swing from idealisation to instant belief in her "dishonour", as Troy calls it, does suggest a more than normal remoteness from the actual woman he thinks he is loving, while also showing how easily he is jolted off balance. Also, his feeling that "no sorry household realities appertained to her"[40] (ironically, at his first call at the house she was busy with springcleaning and covered with dust) develops at the end of the book into his delighted anticipation of "six years of intangible, ethereal courtship".[41] Hardy seems to be suggesting that a remote or fantasy fulfilment of his desires is as much as Boldwood can contemplate. The clothes fetishism is in keeping with this. Hardy does not use the term, nor does he say that Boldwood is using the clothes as a substitute for Bathsheba, but he does emphasise that it is an important manifestation of his condition. He calls it "a discovery throwing more light on Boldwood's conduct and condition than any details which had preceded it".[42] Yet Hardy treats these "unequivocal symptoms of mental derangement"[43] very cautiously. The people who make the appeal for the murder to be treated as "the sheer outcome of madness" are said to have "perhaps too feelingly considered the facts latterly unearthed",[44] and Gabriel doubts whether Boldwood was mad enough to justify a reprieve. These points reinforce our sense of Hardy's serious and well-informed concern for psychological accuracy. Though, in places, the manner of presentation is melodramatic, Hardy's conception of the character is far from being simplified or superficial. His portrait of Boldwood is a tentative, exploratory examination of the manifestations, and, to a much lesser extent, of the causes of neuroses. He repeatedly contrasts normal with abnormal, well-balanced with unbalanced responses to experience, yet at the same time, and especially in the closing chapters, he makes it clear that he sees no clearcut borderline between sanity and insanity, nor any definable point at which a person can be identified as neurotic.

The new insights and subtlety of understanding are not matched by new techniques for expressing them in this novel. Hardy succeeds with the traditional modes. The external expression of inner turmoil is particularly well caught. Tension is effectively suggested in Boldwood's rigid posture and stiff manner. Descriptions of his forced attempts at naturalness and control are vivid, and visual: "If the word 'fun' had been 'torture', it could not have been uttered with a more constrained and restless countenance than Boldwood's was then".[45]

The imagery, as so often in Hardy, plays an important part in establishing in a visual way the nature of the character. The images of "a stronghold", of a man "living outside his defences", of "violent antagonistic forces"[47] help "to make vividly visible" the struggle going on inside Boldwood, and the strength of the barriers he has built around his emotions. With the sudden, unexpected return of Troy, these shattered defences have to be swiftly rebuilt. In a single image, Hardy indicates that this has been attempted: "a voice sounding far off and confined, as from a dungeon . . . 'Bathsheba go to your husband' ".[48]

Associated with these images of defensive walls are images of powerful natural forces uncontrollable by fortifications — high tides, floods, rivers ("stagnant or rapid, never slow"[49]), "astounding wells of fevered feeling", "a hotbed of tropical intensity".[50] The image of Boldwood as being "without a channel for any kind of disposable emotion"[51] suggests both the controlling walls and the danger of their bursting. These images present in concrete terms the Freudian theory that the central feature of neurosis is "the lack of defence against a dangerous perception".[52]

But, though Hardy's methods of presenting Boldwood are successful as far as they go, their inadequacy to match the profundity of his perceptions is clear. The account of Boldwood's night thoughts after receiving the valentine shows an astonishing insight into a disturbed personality, but the method of largely external description of behaviour used later in the chapter does not sustain this insight wholly effectively. Hardy needs, perhaps, the stream-of-consciousness technique to convey his perceptions, but even this would not be adequate for exploring Boldwood's unconscious; something perhaps similar to the Circe episode in Joyce's *Ulysses*, or the rhythmical, powerful suggestive prose of the "Anna Victrix" chapter of Lawrence's *The Rainbow* would be needed. The brief reference to his dream is certainly inadequate. And yet, Hardy does succeed in creating in the reader a sense of what it is like to be Boldwood at this time. He does it largely through describing the scene and creating the atmosphere: "the pale sheen had that reversed direction which snow gives, coming upward and lighting up his ceiling in an unnatural way, casting shadows in strange places";[53] "that preternatural inversion of light and shade which attends the prospect when the garish brightness commonly in the sky is found on the earth, and the shades of earth are in the sky".[54]

In these passages Hardy arouses an emotional, even sensuous response in the reader; he brings home to us the strange, bewildered state of Boldwood, for whom everything, both in himself and outside, seems distorted and unnatural. In this, as in many other ways, Hardy has affinities with Lawrence. Though he does not achieve the intensity or psychological depth of, say, *The Rainbow*, his use of description here functions in a rather similar way to some of Lawrence's descriptive passages, such as Mrs Morel shut out in the moonlight. There is the same vivid accuracy of observation, the same sense of the strangeness of the natural world, and of the characters' emotional states, though Lawrence creates a feeling of greater intensity than Hardy does. Both novelists intend to awaken a sympathetic awareness in the reader; neither allows a detached or analytical attitude to the character, and yet both, Lawrence to a far greater degree, of course, are putting out feelers into areas of the personality which are not fully conscious, are attempting to explore aspects of the characters' being which cannot perhaps ever be wholly known.

The psychological-sexual element in *Far from the Madding Crowd* is, of course, only one facet of the book, but it is an important one which also emerges in other, more indirect ways. The phallic symbolism of Troy's sword-play is well-known, but there are many other similarly erotic images, as R. C. Carpenter has pointed out in an essay where he stresses "their usefulness in getting across to the reader the emotions, if not the explicit content, of erotic situations".[55] Without this sense of strong, complex feelings underlying the action, *Far from the Madding Crowd* would be little more than a pleasant pastoral tale with moments of melodrama. A balanced estimate of the book must give due weight to the psychological insights, while taking care not to overevaluate them in relation to other aspects of Hardy's art. It is conspicuous, for instance, that he attempts no account of Boldwood's state of mind at the moment of committing murder. While this is partly for psychological reasons — he wants to suggest that the action is purely instinctive, a reflex action to Bathsheba's scream — I think it is also because of the importance Hardy attached to telling a good story. He wants suspense, action, drama here, not psychological exploration. In a letter to Mrs Henniker [56] he criticises Meredith for "infringing the first rules of narrative art": "A child could almost have told him that to indulge in psycho-analysis of the most ingenious kind in the crisis of an emotional scene is fatal".

I have focused my attention on Boldwood because this character demonstrates effectively Hardy's early interest in the complexities of disturbed personalities and the problems they pose for the novelist. But I do not want to give the impression that his psychological insight is restricted to the unbalanced, neurotic or mentally ill. Boldwood illustrates this aspect of humanity in a novel in which the structure is specifically designed to highlight the variousness of human beings, and the widely different ways in which they respond to the same experiences (for instance, the reaction of most of the characters in the book to the storm; the contrasting responses of Boldwood and Gabriel to the loss of Bathsheba).

The contrast of Boldwood with Gabriel is particularly striking. Gabriel is perhaps Hardy's most impressive portrayal of a well-balanced personality. He is imperturbable in the face of catastrophe, yet he is highly sensitive — to music, to nature (he can *feel* his whereabouts in the dark by the nature of the ground underfoot, in spite of his farmer's boots — in contrast to Hopkins, who said, 'Nor can foot feel, being shod'), and to other people. He is almost an idealised figure, with his sensitive awareness of all the goings-on of nature, his responsibility and trustworthiness, but Hardy's clear-sightedness about human beings prevents this; he has a carelessness about him which leads to near-suffocation in his hut and to the loss of his sheep. He is like Jude in his resilience, but lacks what Jude, and the other main characters in *Far from the Madding Crowd* have, sexuality. Hardy makes it quite clear why Bathsheba, emotional and spontaneous and adventurous, is excited by Troy and how it is that she feels a fearful fascination with Boldwood's mad passion. Gabriel is "more concerned to do her good" which gives him a dogged, rather paternal quality. Hardy convincingly shows that getting to know one another over a long period by working together has given them a sense of comradeship which, as he says, may well be a sound basis for their marriage; however, it is interesting that at this point, when the hopeful marriage has just begun, the book ends. Like Lawrence in *The Rainbow*, Hardy finds the turbulent relationships the ones that are interesting to explore. *Far from the Madding Crowd* creates a pattern of relationships which, with various modifications, will form the basis of many of his subsequent major novels. But emotional stability will never again be shown to have such strength and warmth, and emotional disturbance will become an increasingly prominent element in the pattern.

5 Henchard: "the unruly, volcanic stuff beneath the rind"

The Mayor of Casterbridge demonstrates this change of emphasis very emphatically. The central figure is a huge, "volcanic" personality, disturbed and disturbing, dominating the book and dwarfing all around him. In creating such a violent, demanding, self-centred character and presenting him in such a way that the reader has to enter imaginatively into his experience and feel what it is like to be Henchard, Hardy is challenging us to broaden our sympathies, widen our experiences, feel with someone who may be totally antipathetic. Here it is the difficult and disturbing character which is the one capable of warmth and vitality; the surrounding, more easily acceptable characters tend to be lacking in one or the other or both. In this way, he involves our sympathies with Henchard, however reluctant we may be. This is central to Hardy's art. He is exploring varieties of modes of being, making discoveries about ways of feeling and behaving, extending our awareness and our acceptance of human diversity.

The treatment of Henchard differs in many ways from that of Boldwood and of the characters I shall be examining below. The difference demonstrates the breadth of Hardy's range in characterisation, even when we restrict our view mainly to characters who could be described as emotionally or psychologically disturbed. First, Henchard is conspicuously oldfashioned, behind the times in his business attitudes and obviously totally unaware of the philosophical problems of the day. In this he is the obverse of the characters which are the central interest of the majority of the novels; these are intellectual, 'advanced' young people — Knight and Angel, Clym and Sue — who were grappling with and suffering because of revolutionary theories about the nature of existence. In

Henchard, Hardy shows that a man can suffer equally for the opposite reasons, because he has remained rigid and fixed in old modes of behaviour and is unable to adjust to new attitudes. Admittedly, there are a number of other reasons why Hardy does not raise the philosophical problems which are important in *Tess* and *Jude* in *The Mayor of Casterbridge*; one is that it is set in the mid-century, before religious doubt had become widespread; another is that none of the characters he has created in this book are people who would be interested in examining such questions (though it is characteristic of Hardy's optimistic view of human possibilities that in Elizabeth-Jane he has created a character who might conceivably, if she continued her self-education, one day read *The Origin of Species*). Hardy is here writing, at least to some extent, an historical novel; he is also, as in most of his other novels, dealing with the problems of a changing society, though looking at them from a different angle in this book, and giving his attention and sympathy more strongly this time to the man who cannot adapt himself to change.

Henchard's oldfashioned inflexibility is presented very vividly in social terms, as many critics have pointed out; the market-place is central — much, perhaps most, of life is seen in terms of buying and selling. Hardy combines this broad view of society with a penetrating analysis of the psychological problems which a certain type of personality — monolithic, rigid, aggressive — would encounter when living in such a society. Here, the character of Henchard is markedly different from the other problematic characters in the novels. The difference underlines the breadth of Hardy's view of human nature. In much of his fiction he is writing about the subjects which were the main interest of the psychological writers of the early twentieth century — mainly in the area of sexual problems — and much of what he says shows that he was thinking on similar lines to Freud and Jung well before they had started their work. In *The Mayor of Casterbridge* Hardy explores a different area of psychological complexity — aggressiveness. This is a subject which did not greatly interest Freud until very late in his career. His account of it as something purely destructive and his association of it with the death-instinct is one of the aspects of his psychological theory that has been most questioned both by his contemporaries and by subsequent psychologists. It was, of course, over the relative importance of the sexual and the aggressive instincts that he and Adler parted. All this is relevant to *The Mayor of Casterbridge* because it reinforces our sense of the breadth of Hardy's perception of human beings. Hardy's treatment of Henchard shows his understanding of many of the characteristics of aggressiveness; some of these were later discovered by Freud; others by Adler; others by psychologists and biologists writing in the second half of the twentieth century. If we also bear in mind the insights into sexual psychology given in the other novels, it becomes clear that Hardy had a far wider view of the nature of psychological problems than any single twentieth-century psychologist.

A close examination of Henchard's nature and the ways in which he changes illustrates Hardy's profound understanding of aggression. He thought of the book as primarily "a study of one man's deeds and character";[1] obviously, there are many other facets to the book, but this one is the most dominant and interesting, with Henchard towering immense over the other main characters, who are relatively small-scale and colourless. This makes him impressive, and the initial impact is due to the vivid visual and dramatic way he is presented. A detailed examination of his acts, attitudes and states of mind reveal a subtlety in Hardy's depiction of his inner life which is perhaps surprising in a portrait which at first sight can seem somewhat crude, though full of vitality.

In the introductory chapters, Hardy highlights those characteristics of Henchard which could lead to disaster either for himself or others. Hardy indicates his sense of thwarted ambition, for which he blames his marriage, his attitude of "dogged cynical indifference" and his rejection of human intercourse implied by his method of walking along trying or pretending to read. Some unpleasantness for the people he associates with is suggested by this behaviour, some danger perhaps from the growing violence as he gets drunk; that he is also a danger to himself is shown in his compulsion to blame somebody for the situation; first, he says that Susan's meekness made him sell her, then, almost immediately he blames himself ("it was of his own making and he ought to bear it").[2] These contradictory impulses are typical of his whole personality. His aggressive instincts are not completely under control and the extreme measures he takes (the vow of total abstinence for 21 years) to ensure this control reveal a sense of insecurity which is characteristic of excessively aggressive personalities.

Hardy's leap across twenty years is interesting and indicative of where he wanted the stress to be — on the destructive tendencies of aggression; nevertheless, he does give weight to the positive value of an aggressive instinct as the source of drive, ambition, the will to live and to excel. This is in line with the thought and discoveries of modern researchers in this area, such as Storr and Lorenz. Though Hardy has passed over the years in which Henchard used his aggressive energies effectively to gain a position of power and importance, he has structured the novel in such a way that his qualities and achievements during the twenty missing years are frequently brought to our attention; in addition, there are repeated reminders that it was his "amazing energy"[3] which got him to the top. But Hardy focuses mainly on the other side of the picture. He concedes the strengths of this kind of personality, and then sets himself to explore its weaknesses.

When he reintroduces Henchard at the height of his power, he shows him "exaggerated in traits" but also "stiffened" and "disciplined".[4] The likelihood of conflict (both within himself and with others) is increased, since his former large-scale emotions, now exaggerated, will require even more powerful controls. Hardy immediately starts to show the instability and impulsiveness of his nature. He states in the description of him at the banquet that, "his goodness, if he had any, would be of a very fitful cast — occasional, almost oppressive generosity rather than a settled, mild and constant kindness".[5] What follows demonstrates this fitfulness vividly and dramatically, and very rapidly. In the dispute about the grown wheat he just manages to control himself but "there was temper under the thin bland surface".[6] The opposite emotion of passionate enthusiasm "almost fierce in its strength"[7] flares up in response to Farfrae; he feeds him enormously, impetuously dismisses Jopp, and then abruptly allows Farfrae to be "eclipsed" by the arrival of Elizabeth-Jane, so that Farfrae wonders at "the suddenness of his employer's moods".[8] But at this stage while still in a position of power and importance, he has a large degree of self-control so that his behaviour can still be regarded as normal; it shows in his "gentle delicacy of manner" to Elizabeth-Jane, his teetotalism, his carefully calculated plans for renewing the relationship with Susan. But the precariousness of this control is hinted at in his rapid return home after the interview with Susan, as if his suppressed energies had to have an outlet in hurried movement.

Up to this point, Hardy has mainly suggested that Henchard's "strong impulses" are more a danger to others than to himself; the selling of his wife, the rejection of the complaints about the wheat, the dismissal of Jopp, all support this impression. He now begins to show that Henchard's view of himself indicates a concealed sense of insecurity — ill-concealed would perhaps be a better term since the forcefulness of his self-assertion implies a desperate need for his importance to be acknowledged. The possibly self-destructive aspect of his aggressiveness shows itself in his "gloomy fits" which he attributes to "the loneliness of my domestic life when the world seems to have the blackness of hell and, like Job, I could curse the day that gave me birth".[9] Hardy gives him these despairing moods even when his position is unthreatened; he seems to have overridden the wheat problem, his domestic troubles are about to be resolved, he has the help and friendship of Farfrae. Hardy's whole study of Henchard's personality is an examination of the close relationship between aggressiveness and self-destruction; with the loss of status, wealth, relations, friends, Henchard's gloom becomes intensified and gradually, in spite of his fitful attempts to reassert himself, swamps all his aggressive tendencies which were the source of his energy and vitality. But even before he "passed the ridge of his prosperity and began to sink"[10] his tendency was to feel that he was not getting his due, that his ambition was being thwarted by forces outside himself. Instead of welcoming the arrival of Susan as a relief from his "domestic loneliness", he "castigates himself with the thorns which these restitutory acts brought in their train; among them the lowering of his dignity in public opinion by marrying so comparatively humble a woman".[11] The ambitious conception of himself inevitably makes him unhappy and excessively vulnerable to any diminution of his position, possessions or relationships.

Hardy shows Henchard's attitude in all his dealings and relationships to be fundamentally self-centred, and this quality persists through all the vicissitudes of his life and the psychological changes he undergoes. His "peremptory" insistence on Elizabeth-Jane taking his name, his domineering relationship with Farfrae, his brutality to Whittle are all designed to increase his feeling of importance and power. The Whittle episode is an emphatic illustration of how very precarious this is. As soon as Farfrae opposes him, he succumbs. This abrupt giving way when defied or challenged in any way is very characteristic. It is as if his hold on his own identity is so weak that any criticism can undermine it. Admittedly, he defends himself ruthlessly when attacked about the wheat, but this is at a time when he has all the trappings of his eminence in the town to support him. With Whittle, he knows he has gone too far and he is very conscious of the men watching the altercation. His capitulation is, characteristically, pushed to its furthest possible extreme: "Ask Mr Farfrae, he's master here".[12] Later, Hardy says, "the momentum of his character knew no patience",[13] but he has already shown this in action several times before he makes this statement. Henchard envisages himself on a grand scale; he cannot tolerate a middle position. He must be the most powerful in his community, or the most abject. His pendulum-like behaviour can be contained in ordinary life provided the swings do not become too violent; if they do, they can lead on one side to murder, and on the other to suicide. Henchard advances to the brink of both of these. This tendency governs his repeated irrational responses to criticism. His dismissal of Farfrae in response to taunts about the failure of his fete is very similar to his attitude to his defeat over Whittle. The impulsive, violent reaction makes him feel powerful for the moment, but on reflection "his heart sunk". Similarly, he dismisses Jopp for saying, "It's a fine warm day" at a moment when gambling on bad weather has brought him disaster. In all three cases, what Henchard resents is that somebody he regards as a subordinate should have an independent life of his own. Taken in isolation, these episodes might seem to be simply indications of a domineering and demanding master, but considered in conjunction with his behaviour in more intimate relationships they suggest weakness rather than strength, insecurity rather than confidence, and an obsessive concern with maintaining his own importance. After the loss of Farfrae, then Susan, then Elizabeth-Jane through the discovery of her parentage, the personality change which is to lead eventually to his disintegration becomes apparent. After reading Susan's letter, "through his passionate head there stormed this thought — that the blasting disclosure was what he had deserved. He remained unnerved and purposeless for near a couple of hours".[14] We have been shown him blaming himself before, but this is the first time he has moved into a negative, depressive state — a state which in its extreme form becomes catatonic withdrawal. He seems on this occasion to be on the edge of such a condition: "he was like one who had half fainted and could neither recover nor complete the swoon".[15] This simile conveys a sense of loss of contact with the external world, and a feeling of helplessness which seems to reflect very accurately the kind of experience suffered by manic-depressives in the depressive stage of their illness. The self-accusations, though fully justified, do not show healthy self-knowledge; as before, they are immediately followed by a shifting of the blame on to something outside himself: "he could not help thinking that the concatenation of events this evening had produced was the scheme of some sinister intelligence bent on punishing him. Yet," Hardy adds, "they had developed naturally."[16]

At this point, the pattern of character development already established, consisting of swings between extremes of exaltation and depression (social as well as psychological) starts to gain momentum. The behaviour pattern is repetitive, but with a fitful downward movement. Hardy shows his awareness that there is no clear dividing line between mental health and mental illness. The aggressive-depressive nature of Henchard's personality makes him very vulnerable but there are many points on his downward course when recovery is still possible. The psychological accuracy of this is important; it is also artistically very effective to have such a character as the main centre of interest in the novel, since the outcome is held continually in suspense and our primitive interest in what is going to happen is effectively sustained, and completely integrated with the psychological interest.

At this stage, Henchard's capacity for recovery is shown to be still active in the revival of his interest in Lucetta, a result of "an emotional void he unconsciously craved to fill".[17] The use of the word "void" is significant here; it underlines Henchard's incapacity to feel he exists unless someone outside himself is telling him so. This, in a moderate form, is not, of course, an indication of mental disturbance; we all need some bolstering up from others. But when Henchard ultimately feels that he himself has become a void, and he expresses the feeling in the terms of his will, his psychological disintegration is complete. At first, his feelings towards Lucetta are "the almost mechanical" result of the loss of Farfrae and Elizabeth-Jane, but with the development of emotion, his usual tempestuousness returns: "To feel that he would like to see Lucetta was with Henchard to start for her house".[18] (This is nicely contrasted with Farfrae, who, when torn between business and Lucetta, after some conflict, allows business to win, thus illustrating that he will never allow himself to be overwhelmed by his emotions; his is one of those "well-proportioned minds" mentioned in *The Return of the Native*.) Initially, difficulties have a revitalising effect: "Henchard's smouldering sentiments towards Lucetta had been fanned into higher and higher inflammation".[19] His "warm gaze" is like the sun compared with Farfrae's moon; his admiration was "so fervid that she shrank";[20] taking tea with Lucetta and Farfrae makes him "well-nigh ferocious". Thus Hardy shows the rapid movement from a state of severe depression through one of extreme but perhaps fairly normal passion to one that is almost manic. Henchard's whole mental life is brought into jeopardy because of this emotional state: "the thus vitalised antagonism took the form of action"[21] and he attempts to "cut out" Farfrae in business if he cannot do it in love. The failure of his reckless business deals cannot be confined in its effects to merely material things because of "the momentum of his character": "the movements of his mind seemed to tend to the thought that some power was working against him".[22] He even contemplates the idea that "someone had been roasting a waxen image of him".[23] Here again we see the repetitive emotional pattern of his response to failure; the feeling that he is not responsible for himself is conveyed in the phrase, "the movements of his mind seemed to tend to the thought . . . ", suggesting that to Henchard what he thinks seemed to happen almost apart from himself. This underlines the point that his aggressiveness and quickly induced sense of failure are related to a feeling of insecurity about his own identity and significance. But "at this time of moody depression", he is not so far gone that he cannot respond to shock-treatment; this is provided by the episode of the wagons. For the moment, he becomes alert, aggressive, self-assertive. Even overhearing Farfrae make his proposal to Lucetta does not subdue him, and he forces her to say she will marry him. But, as always, his triumph is precarious, and the return of the furmity woman suffices to make him feel himself worthless again, at least as far as public affairs are concerned. He makes a desperate attempt to stage a revival in both personal and business matters by proposing to Lucetta; with the failure of his attempt, "Henchard stood as if idiotised".[24]

This the turning point. Hardy emphasises that after the exposure by the furmity woman, "he passed the ridge of his prosperity and began to sink",[25] both commercially and socially; he is also sinking psychologically. Hardy stresses that there are still possibilities open to him; his honesty in response to the furmity woman, and in his bankruptcy his generosity to the poor creditor, his glimpse that he may have wronged Farfrae, all suggest that he is still in touch with reality, that his world is not restricted to the area of his own gloomy thoughts. He is still capable of practical self-preserving action and takes a job as a journeyman. Yet his attempts to reassert himself and prevent the total disintegration of his personality are either excessively violent or excessively foolish, and always totally in-effective. The violence is largely due to drink and disguises the fact that he is sinking into a depressive state. His violence at The Three Mariners when he forces the choir to sing the 109th Psalm is only fitful, "for the volcanic fires of his nature had burnt down".[26] Each attempt at self-assertion suddenly collapses partly because he is still capable of recognising the foolishness or wickedness of what he is doing. At the Royal visit, he claimed, "I am not going to be sat on", but at the crucial moment, "by an unaccountable impulse gave way".[27] He reads Lucetta's letter to Farfrae with the intention of "annihilating" them, but withdraws at the last moment. (Farfrae's comment is that "he's just a bit crazed".[28]) Likewise, in the fight with Farfrae, he withdraws at the moment of victory, shattered by horror at the murder he was on the point of committing. In his remorse, he remains crouching in a stupor in an "attitude unusual in a man, and in such a man. Its womanliness sat tragically on the figure of so stern a piece of virility".[29] This is a more extreme form of the withdrawn state he fell into after Farfrae had pushed him out of the way at the Royal visit, and "Henchard regarded with a stare of abstraction the spot on the lapel of his coat where Farfrae's hand had seized it".[30]

The fight marks the end of Henchard's aggressiveness and he moves into a permanently depressed state which is lit up by little flares of aggressive or self-assertive behaviour. The Skimmity ride and Farfrae's refusal to believe his message complete his degradation; he has lost "his self-respect, the last mental prop under poverty".[31] He feels that all he has left is Elizabeth-Jane; "a great change had come over him" and he feels that with her "life could still be bearable".[32] This temporary tranquillity is destroyed by his behaviour on the arrival of Newson; he is "amazed at what he had done . . . the impulse of a moment . . . telling mad lies like a child",[33] but in fact the act is completely in keeping with his personality. Afterwards, he feels "everybody has left me", that there is "nothing to come, nothing to wait for"[34] and that suicide is his only resource. His manic attempt to murder Farfrae and his depressive attempt at suicide express the two extremes of his personality.

After this he is "denaturalised". His "instinctive opposition" (to Elizabeth-Jane's marriage to Farfrae) no longer "takes shape in action".[35] Hardy briefly sums up the depressive mental state: "this moody view of himself took deeper and deeper hold on Henchard, till the daily necessity of facing mankind, and of them particularly Elizabeth-Jane, became well-nigh more than he could endure. His health declined; he seemed morbidly sensitive. He wished to escape

those who did not want him and hide his head for ever".[36] He sees the
only alternative is for him to be "tolerated" as "an inoffensive old
man" in Elizabeth-Jane's household. That he is prepared reluctantly
to consider submitting to this "humiliation" indicates that he has not
yet reached the state of total apathy characteristic of the most severe
depression. However, the return of Newson obliterates even this
hope of satisfying his hunger for love. His departure from Casterbridge does not signal the end of Henchard as a man with a capacity
for life, though he feels himself that it does: "I outcast, encumberer
of ground, wanted by nobody, despised by all, live on against my
will".[37] But Hardy stresses that he is really in the same position as
when we were first introduced to him, wearing the same clothes,
equipped with the same skills, but now lacking the vital quality, "zest
for doing". Yet he does keep going, and earns his living and thus
copes in a basic way with the bare necessities of life. This makes
plausible his final flare-up of energy, when he decides to go to the wedding. Hardy stresses the exhausting effort required "to initiate this
reversal", and the "curious high-strung condition"[38] he is in. When
Elizabeth-Jane comes to speak to him, he has already felt himself
"supplanted" by Newson, dancing so vigorously in the next room,
and relapsed into a withdrawn, motionless state; "he did not sufficiently value himself"[39] to push his case with her. Hardy presents
this as the ultimate cause of his disintegration. He describes him as
"self-alienated"; with his total loss of all human relationships apart
from the despised Whittle, he does not feel himself to have even the
significance to commit suicide. Whittle's description of his physical
collapse — the bowed posture and "wambling" walk, the loss of ap-
petite and sinking into complete immobility — is almost a replica of
a clinical description of a patient in a state of severe depression; the
only difference is that in the novel the process to this state is speeded
up and compressed.

Henchard's will is a striking illustration of Hardy's insight into
mental disturbance. His welcoming a state of complete nothingness
is the corollary of his drive for position, importance, love. Without
these, he feels he ceases to exist. His will gives complete expression to
his sense of total nullity.

This remarkable presentation of the disintegration of a personality is so powerful because Hardy succeeds in making the reader
feel involved in the shifting, changing, conflicting mental states of
his character. The perceptive, imaginative achievement is almost

wholly consistent with recent work in psychology on the subject of aggression. It is a further example of Hardy's extraordinary modernity. In his sensitive analysis he is closer to our own contemporaries than to Freud or Adler, though he has a lot in common with them too.

A comparison of the work on aggression of some twentieth-century psychologists with Hardy's sympathetic creation of an aggressive character is illuminating because it draws attention to his capacity, not always recognised, for close analysis; it shows that his combination of imaginative insight and clearsighted analytical thought led him to conclusions about aggression similar to those reached by psychologists making exhaustive clinical studies of the subject (and therefore perhaps tends to reinforce our intuitive recognition of his accuracy), and it places him where he wished to be, ahead of his time — in this case about 70 years ahead.

Hardy seems much more at home with this subject than Freud ever did. This is an aspect of psychology where he diverges from Freud more than anywhere else. The latter was very slow to concede the existence of an aggressive instinct; his first positive comments in "Beyond the Pleasure Principle" (1920) and his more fully developed theory about it in "Civilisation and its Discontents" (1930) both represent aggression as purely destructive. For Freud, it is one element in the death instinct: "part of the (death) instinct became directed towards the outer world and then showed itself as an instinct of aggression and destruction . . . . Conversely any cessation of this flow outwards must have the effect of intensifying the self-destruction".[40] There is no suggestion in Freud's work that aggressive drives may be essential for man's functioning in society, or even for his survival. Hardy's portrait corresponds to the latter part of the passage quoted from *Civilisation and its Discontents* but he certainly indicates that outward-directed aggressive drives can sometimes be effective even though they contain destructive tendencies too; for instance, the town council had elected Henchard Mayor because of his "amazing energy" even though his aggressiveness had often "made them wince".[41]

In this way, Hardy's total picture is closer to Adler who sees "the aggression drive" as leading to "sports, competition, duelling, war, thirst for dominance and religious, social, national and race struggles", but also as the source of qualities possibly more beneficial to mankind: "The stronger aggression drive creates and chooses a large number of occupations . . . judge, police officer, teacher, minister, physician and many others are taken up by people with a large aggression drive".[42] Obviously, the Mayor comes into this category. Adler recognises both aspects of the aggression drive and emphasises that when it is present in excess, the destructive or self-destructive aspects of it will be dominant. He shows that "the goal of complete superiority introduces into our life a hostile tendency . . . whoever takes the goal of godlikeness seriously or literally . . . will soon be compelled to flee from real life . . . into art, or more generally, into pietism or neurosis".[43] Thus, according to Adler, the excessively aggressive man has two alternatives; he is either "capable of proceeding along a straight line bravely, proudly, overbearing, obstinate, cruel; or he may . . . prefer, forced by experience, to resort to byepaths and circuitous routes to gain his victory by obedience, submission, mildness and modesty".[44] This sums up some of the stages of Henchard's development, though without bringing out, as Hardy does, the complexities, conflicts and shifting moods and attitudes in the process from the proud, overbearing state to the submissive, mild one. This is to be expected, of course; the psychologist gives us the theory, the novelist gives us the same theory as a lived experience.

Recent developments in the study of the psychology of aggression have led to an increasingly profound and subtle examination of its various components. Modern studies have tended to support Adler's basic original conception, stressing the universality and importance of aggression, whereas Adler, in the face of criticism, modified his original conception by renaming the aggression drive, "the goal of superiority". Nowadays, the stress tends to be on the close interrelationship between the positive and destructive aspects of aggression: "there is no clear dividing line between the forms of aggression which we all deplore and those which we must not discard if we are to survive". Similarly, Lorenz maintains that "with the elimination of aggression . . . the tackling of a task or problem . . . would lose all impetus."[45] Storr sums up the current investigations by saying that

> in the light of the researches of Lorenz and other biologists, we have to recognise that aggression is a drive as innate, as natural and as powerful as sex, and the theory that aggression is nothing but a response to frustration is no longer tenable in the light of biological researches. The aggressive drive is an inherited constant, of which we cannot rid ourselves, and which is absolutely necessary for survival.[46]

Hardy has implied a similar view of human nature. While not showing Henchard's rise from poverty, he has repeatedly stressed the part played by his aggressive energies in making that rise possible and contrasted this with the indolence of the other councillors, who are happy to let him take all responsibility upon himself.[47]

Another major aspect of the aggressive drive is the relationship between aggression and depression. Hardy shows this with great sensitivity and understanding in his treatment of Henchard. It is an aspect of aggression which Freud naturally emphasised, since he associated it with self destruction and death. He argues that when all goes well a man is not self-destructive, but in the face of calamity he, "imposes abstinence on himself, punishes himself with penances . . . adversity means one is not loved by the highest power of all, and threatened by the loss of love, one humbles oneself".[48] This corresponds with the description of the effects of disaster given by Hardy and by Adler, but the suggested causes are not exactly the same. Adler sees "cursing oneself, reproaching oneself, self-torture and suicide"[49] not as manifestations of a death instinct, but as forms of neurotic behaviour designed to reinforce the sense of superiority. Hardy's treatment of Henchard is broadly on these lines. Adler amplifies the point by suggesting that "the tendency of the neurotic is the striving from the feeling of inferiority towards the 'above'. The combination of these moods lead to a neurotic constant back-and-forth . . . at one time the traits of powerlessness, at another the trait of exaltation becomes more prominent. The process is most clearly visible in manic-depressive insanity".[50] In Hardy's account of Henchard's development, the repetitive, pendulum-like swing is very insistent, especially at times when total defeat seems complete, and yet Henchard devises still another means of staging a come-back.

Recent writers on aggression have stressed that "moods of depression are intimately connected with difficulty in handling aggressive feelings".[51] Storr stresses that love is an important source of self-esteem and

failure in a love-relationship is felt as an attack upon the self. The extreme hatred which is mobilised by rejection is actually self-preservative: an attempt by the rejected person to assert himself in spite of the injury to his pride. The more dependent the person is on the love of another, the more he will feel threatened and therefore hostile if this love is withdrawn.[52]

This is similar to Hardy's statement that Henchard was basically unchanged, but "with his sinister qualities, formerly latent, quickened
into life by his buffetings".[53] Here we see Hardy theorising about the
psychology of the character he has created, and also, naturally, he
demonstrates the pattern of behaviour he has described: when Henchard is still mentally and emotionally strong, the loss of Farfrae's
love arouses hatred; the loss of Lucetta's arouses contempt — "Farfrae had married money and nothing else";[54] he is able to return
for Elizabeth-Jane's wedding because he reminds himself that she
did not drive him away, he left of his own accord. After her apparent rejection of him at the wedding, there is no self-preservative
"mobilisation of hatred", but, instead, the neurotic total loss of all
vitality. Henchard has now entered the phase of extreme depression:
"loss of love, failure, bereavement, often causes depression which
unlike simple sadness, is characterised by the inhibition of the aggressive drives towards the external world and redirection of this impulse against the self, with consequent self-reproach and feelings of
unworthiness".[55]

These feelings are treated in a variety of ways by people unable to
handle effectively these aggressive drives — "They may be turned inward and directed against the self". Henchard does this, frequently
blaming himself: "It was of his own making and he ought to bear
it";[56] "It was what he had deserved";[57] "He cursed himself like a less
scrupulous Job";[58] "It was part of his nature to extenuate nothing
and to live on as his own worst accuser".[59] This stage in depression
leads to a frame of mind which is particularly destructive. "Depressed people . . . feel they can only obtain what they need from
others by being gentle and submissive, thereby reducing their
effectiveness and grip on life".[60] Hardy's analysis of Henchard's
thoughts when he contemplates living with Farfrae and Elizabeth-
Jane indicates exactly this frame of mind: "it was terrible to his pride
to think of descending so low; yet for the girl's sake he might put up
with anything; even from Farfrae; even snubbings and masterful
tongue-scourgings. The privilege . . . would almost outweigh the humiliation."[61] The return to Casterbridge for the wedding is an attempt to put himself in just this position. With his failure, "his grip
on life" is completely lost and leads to the wish, expressed in his will,
to eliminate himself from the face of the earth.

At other times, of course, he puts the blame on others. According
to Adler, "the life-plan of the neurotic demands that if he fails, it
should be through someone else's fault".[62] This attitude tends to be

Henchard's immediate response to disaster, especially in his younger days and in the earlier phases of his decline; Susan's meekness had done him "more harm than the bitterest temper" and caused him to sell her; Farfrae is responsible for his failure as a corn-merchant; Jopp is blamed for his gambling on the weather. These moods are violent, but almost always quickly replaced by self-blame, from which he then often attempts to escape by blaming, not another person but some powerful external force. The development of this feeling that "there is some sinister intelligence bent on punishing him"[63] coincides with his movement towards neurosis. The rain which causes his financial ruin makes him feel that "some power is working against him", even that, "somebody has been roasting an waxen image of me".[64] Hardy says that these fears come to Henchard "in time of moody depression when all his practical largeness of view had oozed out of him".[65] Passages of this kind may seem to support the view that Hardy is giving a traditional portrait of a primitive being, with traditional fears and imaginings — and to some extent this is true; but the interesting and original point about his view of Henchard is that such a primitive being is complex. As he insists in "The Dorsetshire Labourer",[66] "Hodge" — the stereotyped figure of the country working man — does not exist. Like D. H. Lawrence, Hardy is well aware that inarticulate and intellectually simple people can have inner lives of great emotional intensity and complexity. Henchard's primitive assumption that disaster is inflicted upon him by an external supernatural force is something which seems to be latent in all of us, and emerges in neuroses and insanity. Freud points out that a common reaction to adversity is to feel that it "means that one is no longer loved by the highest power of all".[67] It is common for paranoid schizophrenics to feel that "they are powerless to resist the evil intentions of others, especially since their persecutors are imagined to possess telepathic, hypnotic or supernatural powers".[68] But as Henchard moves into his depressive state, these attributions of hostility to people and powers outside himself cease to occur, and he blames himself exclusively for his ruin. That the opposite poles of internally and externally directed hostility are intimately connected is shown by Hardy in Henchard's attempts to solve his problems by murder and by suicide. Parallels to this have been recorded in recent studies: "The intimate connection between self-destruction and aggression emerged clearly from the many incidents in which the offender's intentions wavered uncertainly between murder and suicide".[69]

These tendencies are closely linked to the pendulum-like swing from aggressiveness to powerlessness which I have already noted, and this too ties up with the impulsiveness of this type of personality. It has been suggested that individuals unable to come to terms with their aggressive drives may either repress them and turn them inward against the self, or disown them and attribute them to others, or express them in explosive or childish forms. Henchard does all three. The selling of Susan, the "roaring" at Whittle, the dismissal of Farfrae, the shouting in council so that "his voice might be heard as far as the town pump",[70] and many other episodes all have an explosive, childish quality. He even comes to recognise it himself. After his lie to Newson, he is "amazed at what he had done. It had been the impulse of a moment". He had told "mad lies like a child".[71]

Hardy's portrait of Henchard contains all the major elements the aggressive personality as analysed and defined by twentieth-century psychologists. There also seem to be some hints of traits which psychologists would define as schizoid; this is plausible since it is generally recognised that we all to a greater or lesser degree have some schizoid tendencies, and Hardy certainly does not suggest that Henchard is suffering from schizophrenia, which would be unlikely to coexist with some of his other traits.

Henchard's most striking experience of a schizoid kind is his imagining that he has seen himself floating in the weir. Guerard is wrong to call this "macabre absurdity, not macabre neurosis".[72] The fact that Henchard immediately accepts the idea that it is himself is significant. R. D. Laing, commenting on Dostoevsky's story "The Double", points out that Dostoevsky "shows how this 'delusion' (that the character has seen himself) is intimately connected with Golyadkin's own secret intention *not to be himself*".[73] That Henchard has this same wish at this time, though perhaps he is not fully conscious of it, is implied by his plan to drown himself; the wish is eventually fulfilled through the negative statements of his will. However, because of Elizabeth-Jane's intervention, showing him that it was a delusion, and her concern for him, the immediate effect of the experience at the seven-hatches weir is revitalising. His feeling of insecurity and insignificance is overcome by the feeling that this time the supernatural is not against him: "even I be in Somebody's hand".[74] Here we can see that Henchard's schizoid tendencies are not impervious to reason, though, of course, the reassurance he obtains from the episode is only momentary and is inadequate to set at rest in any permanent way his fears and self-distrust.

This schizoid tendency appears also in the way Henchard sometimes seems to feel that his thinking has a separate existence from himself; it is one of his defences against his guilt-feelings and leads him on to blaming an external power for his disasters. After the ruin of his crops, "the movements of his mind seemed to tend to the thought that some power was working against him".[75] When he contemplates telling Farfrae that Elizabeth-Jane is a bastard, Hardy says, "the thought sailed into his ken". Then Henchard asks, "Why should I be subject to these visitations of the devil when I fight so hard to keep them away?".[76] Storr says that, "one characteristic of the adult schizoid is a strong desire for power and superiority, combined with an inner feeling of vulnerability and weakness".[77] This sums up the elements underlying Hardy's conception of Henchard. His attribution of his thoughts to the devil is an attempt to discount his own inner weakness, to push it outside himself, to blame it on the "other".

In several other episodes there are suggestions of a schizoid element in Henchard's personality, for instance in his simultaneous longing for and fear of emotional involvement. "In schizoid people there is an emotional dislocation of such a kind that however powerful and competent a man may be in fact, he still feels at the mercy of any one whom he allows to become emotionally important to him".[78] Henchard creates precisely this situation by telling Farfrae his life story. Hardy stresses that the feeling is entirely onesided; when Henchard mentions that his story had given Farfrae power over him, Farfrae says simply, "I had forgot it".[79] Thus, the feeling of vulnerability is entirely self-induced.

It is arguable that Hardy underplays the importance that sexuality would have in a personality such as Henchard's. However, before making such a judgement it is important to recognise the complexities which Hardy is showing us. First, it fits in with the studies of aggressive-depressive personalities that the sexual needs should be subservient to the supportive ones — "Some object for pouring out his heart upon — were it emotive or were it choleric — was almost a necessity".[80] It is Elizabeth-Jane who is the object on this occasion, and Farfrae also fulfilled this purpose, as well as Susan and Lucetta. Nevertheless, Hardy does not endorse Henchard's claim to a totally detached attitude to sexual relationships; though he tells Farfrae that, "being by nature something of a woman-hater, I have found it no hardship to keep mostly at a distance from the sex";[81] this is clearly an example of his lack of self-knowledge. Though Hardy implies that Henchard goes for long periods without any close relationship with a woman, his sexual feelings are liable to periodic volcanic eruptions, and this convincingly reflects his normal emotional pattern. He could hardly have been as indifferent or even antagonistic to "the sex" as he tries to suggest to Farfrae, or he would never have (apparently impulsively) married Susan, nor embarked on the affair in Jersey. Similarly when his dutiful attitude towards Lucetta on her arrival at Casterbridge is received with coolness, his feelings immediately flare up, and become a "fervid" and "ferocious" passion. Thus, Hardy's analysis of Henchard's mode of loving reveals two main elements; as a man of violent extremes, it is natural that his sexual feelings are also violent and extreme; and also as a man with a desperate need for superiority, any kind of love and admiration, whether sexual, filial or friendly is a necessity to him. Henchard's own account of the way his life has gone shows a rare insight into his own nature: "his attempts to replace ambition by love had been as fully foiled as his ambition itself".[82] Love and ambition are equated because for him both function in the same way.

Hardy's exploration of aggression indicates a point of view similar to Adler's, and even more to present-day psychologists', rather than to Freud's. He sees it as potentially a positive element, contributing to the capacity to love and to achieve, but also as a destructive element when it is too violent for the individual to be able to cope with its demands. These parallels with twentieth-century writing on psychology are important not because they confirm or validate Hardy's portrait of Henchard — our own imaginative response does that — but because the very close and detailed correspondence draws attention to the modernity of Hardy's thinking. The plot and Henchard's psychological development are perfectly fused and as a result a casual reader may easily fail to recognise fully that the novel is an imaginative realisation and a minute analysis of a particular kind of psychological disturbance. Setting Hardy's account of Henchard alongside some clinical analyses draws attention to an aspect of Hardy's complexity as a novelist which has often gone largely unnoticed.

The variety of Hardy's methods of delineating character is to some extent responsible for this, preventing us from ever feeling as we read *The Mayor of Casterbridge* that we are studying a case history. But

in order to highlight the psychological complexity, I have concentrated on the analytical aspects of Hardy's technique. It is interesting that in the year in which the novel was published (1886)
Hardy wrote: "Novel-writing as an art cannot go backward. Having
reached the analytical stage, it must transcend it by going further in
the same direction".[83] As I have shown, he has gone a long way in
The Mayor of Casterbridge and will go further in *Tess of the
d'Urbervilles* and *Jude the Obscure*, but he has not turned the novel
into a theoretical or clinical work. The picture of Henchard is particularly vivid visually and dramatically. The descriptions of his outward appearance are naturally concentrated at the beginning of the
book; later, these first visual impressions are reinforced by the imagery, but Hardy only gives further descriptions when Henchard's
physical appearance has changed. Even in the early descriptions,
hints of his inner nature are always implicit or explicit. Often Hardy
proceeds gradually from the outer to the inner: "the qualities sig-
nified by the shape of his face, the occasional clench of his mouth
and the fiery spark of his dark eyes began to tell in his conduct; he
was overbearing, even brilliantly quarrelsome".[84] Hardy frequently
works in this way, using the appearance as a starting-point for analysis, but of a conjectural kind, thus putting the reader, until he has
become immersed in the novel, in the position of an observer. When
he reintroduces Henchard after twenty years, he first refers to his
"coarse . . . rich complexion . . . loud laugh, large mouth".[85] He
then goes on to discuss the laugh: "Many theories might well have
been built upon it. It fell in well with conjectures of a temperament
which would have no pity for weakness . . . but ungrudging admiration for greatness and strength".[86] When used in this generalis-
ing way, the method is ponderous, like his similar treatment of
Eustacia, but when used more succinctly or more visually, it is very
effective in combing an impression of both outer and inner being.
Phrases such as: "marks of introspective inflexibility on his
features"[87] effectively crystallise several elements in his personality;
"a curl of sardonic humour upon his lip . . . as though contemplating
some terrible form of amusement"[88] makes a strong visual impact
and at the same time exposes Henchard's state of mind. Similarly,
the account of the change in his behaviour after his bankruptcy is
both visual and psychological: "He now gazed more at pavements
and less at housefronts . . . more at feet and leggings, less into pupils
of eyes with the blazing regard which had formerly made them

blink".[89] In these ways, Hardy informs us about mental states in a manner which appeals to our visual imagination rather than to our analytical reason; this makes an important contribution to the vividness of the novel and to the"sense of felt life" in it. It shows Hardy's increasing mastery in fusing the inner and the outer aspects of his characters.

Hardy's use of imagery in *The Mayor of Casterbridge* plays a large part in creating Henchard as a physical being. The pattern of images effectively reinforces what Hardy tells us about him by other means. Throughout the book images are used to suggest his grand-scale, elemental qualities, but in the first part the images are of things active and violent, while in the later parts they are still of large or powerful things, but in a state of collapse or decay. The early images are frequently of storms; "he gazes stormfully";[90] "there stormed through his passionate head this thought — that the blasting disclosure was what he had deserved";[91] his voice is "dry and thunderous";[92] he moves "like a great tree in the wind".[93] There are recurrent fire images; in the earlier parts, he is frequently "blazing"[94] "smouldering"[95] and "inflamed".[96] But after the second encounter with the furmity woman, his face seems "powdered with ashes"[97] and when he has "begun to sink" there is "a film of ash over his countenance".[98] Hardy uses the image of a volcano similarly. In the early part, there was still, "the unruly volcanic stuff beneath the rind",[99] but later, "the volcanic fires of his nature had burnt down".[100] Hardy uses the latter image after the violent scene at The Three Mariners when Henchard has "busted out drinking". The image conveys succinctly, without the need for analysis, the fact that the violence is the result of the drinking and does not really represent a resurgence of his strength and vitality. Animal images function in much the same way; he is "as wrongheaded as a buffalo";[101] his affection for Farfrae is "tigerish"; "Henchard was constructed on too large a scale to discern such minutiae as these (Lucetta's glances at Farfrae) which were to him the notes of an insect set above the compass of the human ear".[102] By these three images Hardy conveys the blundering violence of Henchard's nature, his terrifying qualities, but also something of his grandeur. Later, the images of "the netted lion"[103] and the "fangless lion"[104] aptly suggest the powerful creature subdued, and "the dark ruin",[105] the huge structure disintegrated. Mythological and biblical images work in the same way. The comparison with Faust, "a vehement and gloomy being"[106] reinforces our sense of Henchard's grandeur and of his doom, while showing him at this stage still fighting against it. Later images of "Samson shorn"[107] and Cain[108] are of great figures destroyed and outcast. In these ways, the pattern of images corresponds to the pattern of Hardy's psychological exploration.

The analysis of Henchard's complexities is frequently presented in dramatic terms and this, too, contributes to "the sense of felt life" in the novel. As always in Hardy, there are numerous impressive dramatic scenes which carry tremendous weight and serve to crystallise certain qualities in the characters. It is sometimes claimed that these scenes are melodramatic rather than dramatic, but I think in the context of Hardy's grand-scale view of things, and in particular in the context of Henchard's "volcanic" character, they are wholly convincing and appropriate. The wife-selling, the encounter with the furmity woman in the magistrate's court, the fight with Farfrae, the scene of violence with the choir at The Three Mariners all serve to give the reader a sense of participating in the events of the novel, of living through the experience. This is one of the qualities Hardy has in common with Lawrence; however far he pushes the novel in the direction of analysis, he never evokes a critical detachment. We are involved with Henchard, we know how he feels, we can imagine what it is like to be him. In this way, Hardy extends our sympathies by making us enter in to the emotional life of a character whom most people would have difficulty in feeling sympathy for. The sense of involvement, of living through the experience as we read, is a vital element in our response.

The dialogue in *The Mayor of Casterbridge* is particularly effective in creating this sense of life going on naturally. Hardy's occasional ponderousness, which cannot always be justified, rarely occurs in the dialogue in this novel. In the scene at The Three Mariners, the violent colloquial exchanges, contrasted with the solemn rhythms of the psalm expressing ruthless hatred, are combined with the ruthless action of Henchard, seizing the poker and later bending it across his knee like a twig; the whole effect is powerfully dramatic, and increases our awareness of how uncontrollable Henchard's hatred of Farfrae has become. Also, by showing that the whole episode occurred because he happened to get a glimpse of Farfrae out of the window, Hardy creates a further impression of his irrational impulsiveness and of a rapidly increasing loss of control. Here the visual, the dramatic and the analytical all work powerfully together. As Hardy said after completing *The Mayor of Caster-bridge*, "my art is to intensify the expression of things . . . so that the heart and inner meaning is made vividly visible".[109]

Hardy indicated by title, subtitle (*A Story of a Man of Character*) and in his preface that the book is primarily about Henchard. Looked at not simply as the focal point, but as an element in the total structure, Henchard still dominates, because of his nature, because of the way he is presented and because of his placing in the novel. The other characters highlight his personality. They are the normal, the adaptable, the moderate, and so they emphasise his abnormality and extremism. Farfrae is essentially moderate and well-adjusted to the demands of ordinary life. He has no uncontrollable passions; he loves Lucetta but does not let love interfere with business (in contrast with Henchard who starts by thinking about her money but soon becomes "inflamed"); he treats his workers reasonably but pays them less than Henchard; he sings nostalgically about Scotland but feels no powerful urge to return to his roots; he is ambitious in business, but buys and sells on a small scale; he is concerned about Henchard but does not want to "make a hole in a sovereign"[110] looking for him. He is the epitome of moderation. By nature, he never goes to extremes. Elizabeth-Jane, by deliberation, never goes to extremes. She is wary, self-controlled, carefully protecting herself from excesses in any direction, whether in the choice of clothes or in feeling emotions. She is able to watch the developing love between Farfrae and Lucetta with pain, but without anguish. Henchard proudly says that his sufferings "are *not* greater than I can bear",[111] but Elizabeth-Jane moulds her life so that her sufferings will never become too intense for her to bear. Yet, because of her feeling for Henchard, she never seems cold in her moderation, as Farfrae does. It is not an innate lack of sensibility that causes her restraint but rather a self-protective attitude learnt from bitter experience and from observation of her step-father; in this way, she is like Hardy himself who "never expected much".[112] Lucetta is more emotional and impulsive than Farfrae and Elizabeth-Jane, and in this might seem to resemble Henchard. But Hardy shows her emotions to be of a normal, not particularly deep kind. She romanticises, poses, flirts, is anxious about her reputation and shrinks away from any expression of passionate feeling. Susan's total lack of vitality and her "ghostliness" are presumably meant to put her at the opposite extreme to Henchard's energy and physical solidity, but she is so washed-out and diminished that she is never adequately established as a human being and her impact is too slight for her to complete the pattern of contrasts effectively. The total effect of Hardy's treatment of these other main characters is to make Henchard tower above them all, to concentrate our attention on him, and, above all, to make us experience his mode of being. While reading the novel, we are caught up in his violent emotions. By contrast, the "average" or "normal" characters seem less compelling. In this way, Hardy succeeds in making the "average" reader enter into a mode of being different from his or her own.

Henchard is also the focal point of the novel because he is the focus of attention of many of the other characters, major and minor. The first account of him as Mayor comes from a townsman looking through the hotel window. Elizabeth-Jane watches him constantly and several times the analysis of his personality comes, by implication, from her; it is she who observes his "tigerish affection", his "tendency to domineer" and that Farfrae "bent under his weight".[113] Farfrae notices his moodiness, the councillors and townspeople criticise him, Whittle reveals his gifts of coals to his mother, even a little boy sent with a message reports comments on his temper and intelligence. In these ways we get an all-round view of Henchard and a strong sense of his impact on the community. Thus the "conjectural" method adopted by Hardy to lead us gradually from outward appearances in to the inner life of the character also plays a part in building up our sense of the world in which this life is led.

An understanding of the psychological accuracy and complexity of this huge central figure enlarges our sense of the scope of the novel. We can see *The Mayor of Casterbridge* as a historical novel concerned with the effects on people's lives of changes in agriculture, as a novel about the persistence or destruction of ancient traditions, as a dramatic novel, having affinities with Greek tragedy, as a traditional, ballad-like tale; all these are valid ways of responding to it. This diversity and multiplicity of interests is an important characteristic of Hardy's novels. It is indicative of the breadth of his vision, of his openness to varieties of experience that he should offer to the reader the possibility of so many ways of responding. The parallels with modern psychology add a further dimension. Hardy's great achievement lies in this fusion of old and new ways of looking at character. In form, at least on the surface, his novels are traditional, in that there is much emphasis on telling a story, yet he uses this basic traditional form as the vehicle for expressing perceptions into the nature of human complexities and abnormalities which correspond closely to modern clinical findings and indicate an extraordinary depth of insight, especially into disturbed personalities. Hardy has a more complex conception of characterisation than he is usually credited with. This particularly applies to his treatment of Henchard. Because he is a blustering, oldfashioned person, capable of very little self-knowledge, it is possible to assume that Hardy's conception of him is equally traditional and simple. That this is not so is clearly brought out by the juxtaposition I have made of Hardy's imaginative exploration of his characteristics with the clinical examination of similar personalities made by modern psychologists. Here, too, Hardy is a precursor of Lawrence in suggesting so effectively the complex psychological experiences of an inarticulate and apparently simple person. This exploration of the nature of aggressiveness in the character of Henchard shows how wide Hardy's range is in the understanding of psychological disturbance. The structure of the novel is always designed to draw attention to the varied nature of people and things, to the diversity of modes of experience, to the possibilities of choice, of reacting to a given experience in a variety of ways. In *The Mayor of Casterbridge* our attention is focused on, our emotions are involved with, Henchard himself; we are made to expand our sympathies and vicariously enter into his experiences; simultaneously, we have the simpler task of understanding what it is like to feel his impact on others. So we see him from the inside, from the outside, and in a particular time and place, but we are also made to feel, because of Hardy's profound psychological insight, that we have in him a kind of personality and a way of behaving and feeling which is not limited to Henchard or to Casterbridge in the middle of nineteenth century, but which we might encounter, in others or in ourselves, in any age or place. Hardy maintained that his novels were "a series of seemings"; this is true of *The Mayor of Casterbridge*. The form is an open rather than closed one. Henchard wishes to be obliterated in his death. But Hardy does not end the book here; it ends with Elizabeth-Jane's discovery that "the one to whom such unbroken tranquillity had been accorded in the adult stage was she whose youth had seemed to teach that happiness was but the occasional episode in a general drama of pain". This ending is characteristic and important. It has often been partially quoted in order to give the impression that Hardy is saying that "happiness was but the occasional episode in a general drama of pain", and thus support a theory that Hardy expresses undeviating pessimism. This is a distortion not only of that particular sentence but of the whole attitude of the novel. The final sentence conveys a sense of the variety, unexpectedness and continuity of life and human possibilities. Though the tremendous potential of such a man as Henchard may have come to nothing, Hardy does not end on a note of finality; he ends by making us look forward to future possibilities.

In his novels, Hardy continually created complex characters, many of them psychologically disturbed in a variety of ways. Henchard is his one detailed exploration of the nature of aggression. It is a subject which, in the light of his constant attacks on intolerance and cruelty, we would expect him to feel antipathetic. For this reason, this novel reveals, possibly more than any other, the immense range of Hardy's insight, sympathy and understanding.

6 Grace: "a conjectural creature"

The Woodlanders was published in 1887, the year after *The Mayor of Casterbridge*; it is an immense contrast to it, perhaps because it was the development of an idea Hardy had been considering for many years — in 1874 he mentioned "a woodland story he had thought of (which later took shape in *The Woodlanders*)";[1] presumably, too, he wanted to do something quite different from the previous work which it followed so quickly. Structurally, the contrast could hardly be greater; instead of one huge dominating central character, there is at the centre a very nebulous personality, and she is central in a comparatively limited way. Henchard and Grace, characters utterly different from one another, in novels coming so close together in chronological order, draw attention to the breadth and inclusiveness of Hardy's vision of human nature. Unlike the surrounding characters in *The Mayor of Casterbridge*, the other characters in *The Woodlanders* are not subordinate to the central character, though their function in the novel is in relation to her, either directly or indirectly. Perhaps the biggest difference of all between the two novels is the change from the busy market town to the wood-encircled village. The wider horizons in Casterbridge, the changes in society, the developments in business methods and in agriculture are shown to create problems for people accustomed to a traditional way of life. For the characters in *The Woodlanders* these problems, if they exist at all, are on the periphery of their lives. Fitzpiers is a doctor and a scientist, but his experiments are dilettante; he is fond of quoting Shelley, and his late-night playing around with coloured smokes seems nearer to Shelley's undergraduate experiments than a serious attempt to push out the boundaries of scientific knowledge of the late nineteenth century. Even an actual change in the divorce laws does not appear as an advance by society towards greater tolerance, but merely as a reinforcing of the *status quo*, with one law for the rich and another for the poor. The village is static, enclosed, shut off by the woods from the world where change occurs. Even the characters who have contact with that world endorse without questioning current conventions and attitudes. Fitzpiers sees himself primarily as a gentleman and is very concerned that he has diminished his status by marrying Grace. Mrs Charmond plays the conventional role of a lady of leisure, though unlike the other characters, she does question "the terrible insistences"[2] of society when they thwart her desires. Grace's "fashionable education" has trained her above all to accept convention; it has raised her up the social scale, and made her anxious most of the time to maintain her footing there (her father comes to feel that she is "in mid-air between two storeys of society"[3]), but this only emphasises her conventionality. She is not one of Hardy's "advanced" young people; neither she nor any of the characters are in any way pioneers.

This is in keeping with the setting. The sense of place is more dominant in *The Woodlanders* than in any of Hardy's other novels; even Egdon Heath dominates *The Return of the Native* less because the central characters are stormy and explosive and match these qualities in nature. In *The Woodlanders* the environment is claustrophobic and the characters are subdued and acquiescent, making only muted attempts to change their situation when it becomes unbearable. This inevitably makes the novel less exciting and dramatic than some of the others, our emotions are less violently aroused because the characters are so much more low-key than most of Hardy's major characters. The feelings shown in this novel are subdued, but Hardy is nevertheless continuing to pursue the analytical approach. It was between the writing of *The Mayor of Casterbridge* and *The Woodlanders* that he said: "The novel as an art cannot go backward. Having reached the analytical stage it must transcend it by going further in the same direction."[4]

The analysis of Grace is the focus of the novel because she is torn between the world of the woods and the world outside; her two lovers personify the split. The problems of marriage and divorce, education and the social structure are all related to her. In contrast, all the other characters belong in either the outer world or the woodlands, and only she is involved in all the problems the book raises. For these reasons she is the unifying centre of the book, but because of the nature of the personality Hardy has created, she does not dominate it. The impact of this novel derives more from the vividness of the setting than from the treatment of the characters. Commenting on *The Woodlanders* in 1912, Hardy said, "I think I like it, *as a story*, best of all. Perhaps that is owing to the locality and scenery of the action, a part I am very fond of."[5] This feeling for the scenery is certainly reflected in the book; the woods, and individual trees dominate the lives of the characters and seem to have more vitality than the people themselves. However, in Hardy's development as a novelist, Grace is significant because she shows the almost clinical precision of his analysis of character, even when it is thrown off almost as an aside and is not the central preoccupation of the novel. Along with the consideration of specific social problems, such as education, social mobility and divorce, this analysis gives *The Woodlanders* that concern with "modern" developments which is characteristic of his two subsequent major novels, *Tess* and *Jude*. But it differs from them in that the "modernity" is wholly in the treatment, and not in the views and attitudes of the characters.

A study of the treatment of Grace brings these crucial elements embedded in the novel to the surface. The conflicting elements are brought together in her because she is trying to belong both to the ancient, traditional, isolated world of Hintock and to the mobile, "cultivated", higher class world beyond its boundaries. There is nothing particularly "modern" about this world as depicted in *The Woodlanders*, it is simply the life available to the rich and educated at any time during the previous 100 years or so. Grace is simply trying to adjust to a change in her position in society; in this she differs from Henchard and Angel who are confronted by changes in society itself, and from Jude and Sue who try to initiate change themselves. This is not to say that *The Woodlanders* is unconcerned with changes in society. Hardy makes us aware of the implications for change as it becomes possible for such an ordinary girl as Grace to move from one class to another. But in this novel he concentrates on the effects on the individual of such a move and does not here direct much attention towards the need for society to change in order to make life more bearable for the individual. At the end, some characters have departed, some have died, but Hintock remains unchanged, the woods continuing to be the most vital and dominant form of life there.

The unchanging, claustrophobic hollow in the woods where Hintock lies allows very restricted scope for human relationships; people live in tiny family groups or as isolated individuals. Marty, Giles and Grace are all apparently only children; both Giles's parents are dead, and, before long, both Marty's. The Melbury family is isolated by their feeling of superiority, and really consists only of Grace and her father, since her stepmother, a former servant, is a completely unassertive and colourless personality, conforming always to the moods and wishes of the other two. The lack of strongly developed individual identity characterises most of the people of Hintock to some degree. Giles merges with the background ("Autumn's very brother"); Mr South's life is dominated by a tree; Marty, though initially a strong, distinctive personality, ultimately merges her life with that of a dead man, using his tools, following his craft, and mourning over his grave. Even Mr Melbury seeks fulfilment not in himself but through his daughter, and she reciprocates by conforming most of the way to his wishes. Hardy shows how strong the pressures towards conformity and acceptance are in such a society and that this acquiescence entails some loss of individual identity, which may well lead to neurosis, as with Mr South's tree obsession; he feels he does not exist apart from the tree and so dies when it is felled. Significantly, Giles mentions that, "Others have been like it afore in Hintock".[6] The restricted nature of this environment parallels the closeknit family structures studied by some modern psychologists. The dangers are similar: the failure of the more vulnerable members to develop strong individual identities and the possibility that here is one of the sources of schizoid tendencies.

The portrait of Grace is of an ordinary, basically uncomplicated girl, who, after an unsophisticated childhood in the village and woods has been moulded and shaped into complexity, into a combination of "modern nerves with primitive feelings".[7] The novel shows a clear awareness of the dangers which such parental pressures expose the individual to, but in this book Hardy has chosen to examine a character who is not especially vulnerable, and who has only moments of psychological instability. This is in keeping with the whole tone of the book where extreme behaviour takes the form of extremes of self-abnegation and self-control. Violent passions and behaviour are confined to those who are not natives of Hintock. But just as with more obvious examples of psychological complexity and disturbance in the novels, so here too Hardy shows an insight into mental processes, and occasionally into their more unexpected and neurotic manifestations which parallels modern examinations of personality problems.

Grace is not, of course, a "case", and, unlike most of Hardy's major characters, she does nothing to excess. This is central to his conception of her. She does not have a well-developed and defined personality. Hardy's method of introducing her through her father's eyes emphasises this. Though he worships her footprints, he does not regard her as a being with a volition of her own. He considers marrying her to Giles ("let me get 'em married as soon as I can"[8]) as if he were the only person who had to make a decision about it and discusses it exclusively in relation to himself. Even his pride in her superiority is entirely self-regarding: "Mr Melbury's tone evinced a certain exultation in the very sense of that inferiority that he affected to deplore; for this advanced, refined being, was she not his own?"[9] He regards her as "a gem he had been at such pains in mounting",[10] as a good investment, "If you do cost a great deal . . . you'll yield a better return",[11] and as "good material", which is "sure to be worth while"[12] spending a lot on. Such an attitude, however adoring, runs the risk of undermining the child's sense of her own significance and identity, with, of course, the opposite risk, of a sense of total loss for the parent if the child should indeed assert her own individuality, by whatever means. In the early part of the book, though, before Grace's return, Mr Melbury significantly remarks that she is a "good girl", in other words, she has accepted his concept of her, and plays the role he has created for her.

Our notions of Grace are at first entirely secondhand, but even when she does eventually appear, Hardy presents her as "a conjectural creature",[13] and emphasises how impossible it is to "precisely describe a human being",[14] and especially stresses that her outward appearance told very little about her, "in truth, mainly something that was not she".[15] This introductory meditation on Grace is significant in two ways. It reinforces our impression of the nebulousness of her character, of the "good girl" who unassertively follows the course mapped out for her, without ever having developed any wishes of her own. Secondly, we see briefly suggested here an attitude to characterisation which was to become of immense importance in the twentieth-century novel. This is the idea that characters in novels, like human beings, unless they are extraordinarily limited, cannot be fully known. This was perhaps one of Lawrence's most important contributions to the novel, but it was something already perceived and tentatively developed by Hardy, here with Grace as "a conjectural creature" and later with Sue, "puzzling", "unstateable", and "untranslateable" (echoed by Lawrence is the description of Birkin's "dark subtle reality . . . never to be translated").[16] Even earlier in *The Return of the Native* Hardy had emphasised these enigmatic and "conjectural" qualities by presenting Eustacia through the eyes of some unspecified observer. It is surprising that as late as 1927, Forster said, "a character in a book is real . . . when the novelist knows everything about it. He may not choose to tell us all he knows . . . but he will give us the feeling that though the character has not been explained, it is explicable".[17] Perhaps Forster felt this because in his own novels he locates "the unknown" in the nature of the universe rather than in the nature of human beings. Nevertheless, that somebody as involved in and aware about the novel as Forster should state such a point of view so unequivocally at that date does indicate how rigid the traditional conception of character continued to be and how innovatory Hardy was 40 years earlier.

The Woodlanders is also modern in subject-matter, in that it deals with the problem of children educated above their parents and to some extent alienated from them and their background by this. But Grace has merely learnt to be a conventional young lady of her day. Her fashionable school has given her the refinement her father so much wanted for her, but little more. She has forgotten the different kinds of apples, talks in an affected, "literary" manner, and "avoids everything specially appertaining to her own inner existence".[18] This, combined with her genteel manner and extreme fastidiousness about clothes and surroundings, suggests that there is not any very vivid "inner existence" to talk about. Her excited preparation for the visit to Mrs Charmond (the "six candle illumination" needed to prepare herself again puts the emphasis on externals) also seems to reinforce the impression that she has wholly adapted herself to the "cultivated" life. Hardy describes her on this occasion as "a vessel of emotion going to empty itself on she knew not what",[19] which suggests a curious blankness, an absence of identity, in spite of the presence of emotion. On her return she is in a state of "exaltation" and it is at this moment that Hardy abruptly introduces the conflict between her background and her education. She has been talking to Giles in an affected manner about "Dumas and Mery and Sterne and others", when in response to his implied criticism, she replies "I hate French books. And I love dear old Hintock *and the people in it* fifty times better than all the Continent! But the scheme [of going abroad and writing accounts of her travels in the style of Mery]; I think it is an enchanting notion, don't you Giles?"[20] Here Hardy, at the moment of introducing the conflict, pinpoints not only her inability to reconcile her opposing tendencies, but even to recognise the dichotomy in herself. Her vocabulary and sentence structure reveal the two personalities, just as much as what she actually says. The blunt, straightforward country girl speaks in simple and strong sentences: "I hate French books". Without a break, the society lady replaces her, shifting the language back to the previous elaborate sentence structure and affected diction: "But the scheme; I think it is an enchanting notion". At Giles's party, though she was going cheerfully to "help with the tarts", she allows herself to be prevented, and has to "potter idly" while everyone else is busy, and she gets more and more condescendingly "sympathetic" as chaos develops;[21] she cannot join in the dancing because she has "forgotten" the old dances. Yet "the strangeness of Hintock to her is gradually wearing off"[22] and simultaneously she becomes more and more uneasy at being "the social hope of the family".[23] She at last begins to realise that she may have an existence apart from her father's image of her and complains that he regards her as "a mere chattel".[24] Yet, when it comes to one of the most important decisions of her life, she is prepared simply to accept her father's views: "For myself, I would have married you — some day — I think. But I give way, for I am assured it would be unwise."[25] This apparently unemotional declaration is partly belied by her sighs and pity for Giles, but it shows her still willing to suppress any individuality she has. Hardy sums up the situation: "though mentally trained and tilled into a foreignness of view, as compared with her youthful time, Grace was not an ambitious girl and might, if left to herself, have declined upon Winterbourne without much discontent".[26] Here Hardy is not only contrasting her innate tendencies with her superimposed ones, but also drawing attention again to the absence of any strong desires of her own.

The conflict between Hintock and the "cultivated" world is now sharpened by the developing relationship with Fitzpiers, the opposing lovers embodying the conflicting alternatives. It is not surprising that Grace veers towards Fitzpiers, for her conscious desires, in so far as she has any, are for refinement, and the parental pressure to which she has always submitted is also strongly towards accepting him. But even more important, the hypnotic effect which he exerts over her has a compelling quality which for a girl trained to submission is irresistible. He "exercised an almost psychic influence over her . . . Fitzpiers acted on her like a dram, exciting her, throwing her into a novel atmosphere which biassed her doings until the influence was over, when she felt something of the nature of regret for the mood she had experienced".[27] He shows her without a will of her own, almost without feelings of her own. "The intoxication . . . passed off with his withdrawal. . . . She felt like a woman who did not know what she had been doing".[28] In these ways, Hardy indicates the blank, negative quality of her responses; she exists only as a response to outside influence. Fitzpiers is "handsome, coercive, irresistible",[29] "her ruler rather than her equal".[30] After her timid attempt to break off the engagement, she is "overawed and ever anxious to please",[31] while Fitzpiers "kept himself continually near her, dominating any rebellious impulse and shaping her will into passive concurrence with all his desires".[32] Grace seems to be embarking on a repetition of her family situation, in which opportunities for developing her own personality will be just as slight. But when the situation changes through Fitzpiers's affair with Mrs Charmond, she is confronted with a completely unfamiliar set-up; she is no longer simultaneously adored and coerced. Her reaction is very plausible; she hardly reacts at all. This is in keeping with both her lack of positive feelings about anything most of the time, and with her very muted, confused emotions about Fitzpiers at the time of the marriage. Her jealousy is "a controllable emotion".[33] At the same time, the discovery of his infidelity is a kind of release for her. On meeting Giles, appearing to her "like Autumn's very brother", "her heart rose from its late sadness like a released bough; her sense revelled in the sudden lapse back to Nature unadorned . . . and she became the crude country girl of her latent early instincts".[34] Here, Hardy is again stressing that the "training" and "tilling" have distorted her original nature and that the cultivated lady is a false persona, but the one that had always met with approval and been confirmed by her father and by people generally, apart from Giles.

Her discovery that there is nothing wrong with Suke's teeth hastens her development, and she realises that "her acquiescence in her father's wishes had been degradation to herself . . . she should have obeyed her impulse".[35] In her revulsion against Fitzpiers she is "appalled" to find her early interest in Giles had become revitalised", and she rejects culture in favour of "honesty, goodness, manliness . . . ".[36] Then she looks back at the past and asserts that she disliked her fashionable schools and hated going back after the holidays, "and left you all in the wood so happy".[37] This is the most emphatic indication so far of the violence of the conflict Grace suffered in childhood. Until this point, the impression has been that she found it quite easy to become the superior "fastidious miss" of her

father's ambition. Here, Hardy makes it clear that her removal from
her familiar surroundings and assumption of a new personality, was
painful, if not traumatic. But at the time, she simply accepted it
without complaint. Now she has, for the moment, stood up to her
father and criticised his treatment of her, though not in a way which
enables her to resolve her inner conflicts or to develop a stronger
identity or to react in a normally wholehearted way to experience.
For instance, Mrs Charmond's revelation of the nature of her affair
with Fitzpiers gives Grace only a momentary shock: " 'O my great
God', she exclaimed . . . 'He's had you! . . .'. After the moment of
energy, she felt mild again".[38] For a moment, in Grace's unusual
bluntness of expression, "the crude country girl" makes her appearance, but immediately afterwards, she returns to her usual state
of not feeling anything with any intensity. Yet after this and with the
realisation, after Fitzpiers's fall from the horse, that both Mrs Charmond and Suke actually feel love for him, Grace faces "a critical
time in her emotional life".[39] She thinks, "How attractive he must be
to everybody", and Hardy adds, "The possibility is that, piqued by
rivalry, these ideas might have been transmuted to their cor-
responding emotions by a show of the least reciprocity in Fitzpiers".[40]
This is appropriate for this girl whose emotions have apparently
never been strong, who has always been mild and undemanding, accepting whatever has been offered to her. This submissiveness — to
others and to convention — is the guiding force of her nature. The
delayed emergence of her hatred for school, which she had never expressed at the time, shows that in childhood she could feel, but even
then, never expressed her feelings; continual suppression has caused
feelings to dwindle away to almost nothing. But at last, confronted
by her husband's total unconcern for her, she begins to question the
attitudes which have been fed to her. Though she becomes ill as a
result of her uncertain state, neither married nor divorced, and
leaps out of bed in terror when she hears that Fitzpiers is coming, yet
she is "an elastic nerved daughter of the woods" and soon recovers.
Nevertheless, Giles feels that her experiences have made an impact
on her and she is "a new woman . . . a creature of more ideas and
dignity, and above all, more assurance". While this shows itself in
some of her actions (encouraging Giles to kiss her for instance) she is
not free from conflicting inclinations: "While craving to be a country
girl again . . . to put off . . . the fastidious miss . . . completely, her
first attempt had been beaten by the unexpected vitality of that fastidiousness".[41] Similarly, she is both glad she got Giles to kiss her,

and at the same time is living the "existence of a self-constituted nun",[42] and the shock of discovering the impossibility of divorce turns her love into "an ethereal emotion that had little to do with living or doing".[43]

Thus the comparatively surface conflicts about choice of husbands and ways of life are the outward expression of a deeper division. But when Hardy says that she "combined modern nerves with primitive feelings" and that she was "doomed by such co-existence to be numbered among the distressed and to take her scourgings to their exquisite extremity", we may perhaps question how far this statement corresponds with what he has shown us and is about to show us. He has, after all, indicated that her emotions are usually half-hearted and has called her "elastic nerved". Her spells of "nervousness" are shortlived. As for her "primitive emotions", if by this Hardy meant violent passion regardless of the consequences, one would be justified in denying that there was any trace of this in Grace. She shows herself adaptable, willing to love Fitzpiers again after his infidelity, eager to love Giles when divorce seems possible, but able to "etherealize" her love when that hope fails, and able to revert to her husband after the death of his mistress when that seems to be the socially desirable thing to do. Her insistence on "propriety" is primarily part of her "modern nervousness", but this wish to be "correct" is not strongly challenged by her emotions.

But, as I have indicated, there is a profound, though not apparently violent conflict in Grace, and it is this that Hardy was identifying in the phrase "modern nerves and primitive feelings". He clarifies the kinds of effect her upbringing is likely to have on her in a passage describing her state of mind when she is in Giles's hut. In the stormy night, she feels entirely alone; "She seemed almost to be apart from herself — a vacuous duplicate only. The recent self of physical animation and clear intentions was not there".[44] Some similar descriptions in twentieth-century psychological writings are simply another way of putting Hardy's conception. The resemblance is so close that Grace's feeling that she is "a vacuous duplicate" of herself is echoed in almost the same language in *The Divided Self* and *The Self and Others*; Laing describes the various forms of "ontological insecurity" which are the basis of schizoid tendencies: "the individual may come to feel he is merely a vacuum",[45] "that form of self-division which involves a split of the person's being into a disembodied mind and a de-animate body".[46] The similarity between the ideas and language in *The Woodlanders* passage and those from Laing is remarkable. Hardy here in his fictional analysis has anticipated by many years the insights derived from clinical studies. This is not the first indication of schizoid tendencies in Grace. She found a way of coping with her thwarted love for Giles by making it an "ethereal" emotion that had little to do with living and doing".[47] Laing sees this kind of disembodying as "a *modus vivendi* with some forms of anxiety and despair".[48] Of course, there are "'ordinary' people who feel in moments of stress dissociated from their bodies",[49] but Hardy seems to me to be exploring in Grace something rather more marked and deepseated than this. In one of the case histories in *The Divided Self*, that of Julie, the parallels with Grace's early life are striking. Julie said she had "no self". "I am only a response to other people. I have no identity of my own". She blamed her mother: "I was merely her emblem." Like many schizophrenics, and like Grace, she had been an exceptionally "good" child, never any trouble, never making any demands, never asserting herself, and never apparently feeling anything strongly.[50] I am not suggesting that Hardy saw Grace as a potential schizophrenic, but rather that he saw in her certain tendencies, probably present in all of us to a greater or less degree, which would now probably be described as schizoid; these are intensified by her upbringing and the situation in which she finds herself. Under stress, these tendencies temporarily increase. Grace's early experience is of a kind almost specifically designed to create a sense of "ontological insecurity". The abrupt loss of her identity as "a woodland girl" when she went to school, and the elaborate confirmation by her father of the new superimposed identity almost inevitably have a disorienting effect, given the absence of an assertive personality. With her almost permanent habit (still persisting after considerable evidence to the contrary) of "reverently believing in her father's sound judgement and knowledge as good girls are wont to do",[51] her chances of acquiring an identity of her own are rather remote. The apparent absence of feeling that goes along with this does not mean that she does not suffer. The emotion which recurs in accounts of schizophrenia is terror — terror of disintegration; in extreme cases, patients cling desperately to their various personae because, if they regained their sense of being a whole, single person, they would run the risk of disintegrating again, and the experience of this process is too terrifying to contemplate. I think it is true to say that Hardy suggest only twice in the whole of *The Woodlanders* that Grace is experiencing really violent emotions; once is at the death of Giles, when she is "wild with sorrow", and the other is the occasion when Hardy refers to her "modern nerves", when she crouches in a corner of the room in terror at the possible return of Fitzpiers: "from a corner a quick breathing was audible from this impressionable creature, who combined modern nerves with primitive feelings, and was doomed by such co-existence to be numbered among the distressed and to take her scourgings to their exquisite extremity".[52] The day following this she has the experience of being a split personality; the two experiences, of extreme terror and of being a divided self are related to one another and are in keeping with Grace's nature. If we are not aware of her schizoid tendencies, we are likely to feel that Hardy's phrase, "doomed . . . to take her scourgings to their exquisite extremity" is incongruous with her previous modes and levels of feeling. Yet, the combination of a very low level of feeling with a capacity for terror is a common schizoid trait.

Grace has been almost conditioned into schizophrenia; in moments of stress she totters on the brink of it; but she is resilient, "elastic nerved", and does not succumb. But Hardy indicates that the return of Fitzpiers may well be dangerous for her. Mr Melbury spells out very clearly the likelihood of Fitzpiers's continuing unfaithfulness. At a psychological level she is similarly at risk. As we have seen, the main source of Grace's emotional problems is that her original self has not been confirmed by her parents, and a new identity has been superimposed upon it. Laing has identified a similar pattern:

> The characteristic family pattern that has emerged from the studies of families of schizophrenics does not so much involve a child who has been subject to outright neglect . . . but a child who has been subject to persistent disconfirmation, usually unwittingly. For many years, the lack of genuine confirmation takes the form of actively confirming the false self, so that the person whose false self is confirmed and real self disconfirmed is placed in a false position.[53]

Just this situation, already acted out between parent and child, is about to be repeated between husband and wife. At the time of her marriage, Fitzpiers had seemed, "her ruler rather than her equal".[54] Now, "his suave deference to her slightest whim . . . was a trait in his character as unexpected as it was engaging. If she had been his empress and he her thrall, he could not have exhibited a more sensitive care."[55] Grace's delight in this *volte face* shows again an uncertainty about her own personality. She wants to be confirmed in an "empress" role which is remote from her own personality and can hardly be conceived of as lasting many months. Indeed, her attempts at playing "empress" — getting Fitzpiers to burn his books and narrow his life down to her conceptions — are fraught with danger for their relationship. Her basic insecurity about her own nature has not been overcome. Though she has challenged her father's conception of her, she ends where he had wished to see her — resident in the most expensive hotel. Hardy leaves us appropriately uncertain about the kind of future she faces. Her lack of love for Fitzpiers may enable her to weather his inevitable future infidelities comparatively unmoved. His almost certain failure to continue to confirm her in her false identity as "empress" may lead to her psychological deterioration. This ending resembles most of Hardy's novels in the way it combines a sense of finality (with Marty mourning for ever over Giles's grave) with a sense of continuity. The invitation to speculate about the future is particularly emphatic here, though Hardy felt that he had not made it clear enough: "the ending of the story — hinted rather than stated — is that the heroine is doomed to an unhappy life with an inconstant husband. I could not accentuate this strongly in the book . . .".[56]

Ian Gregor says, "I see the significance of Grace to lie in the fact that she provides Hardy with an opportunity to do a first sketch for Sue Bridehead".[57] While I agree entirely with his analysis of Grace's "divided self", I cannot see her as a forerunner of Sue, except in so far as all Hardy's psychologically complex characters are this. Sue's free and independent, even naughty, childhood ("move on Aunty, this is no sight for modest eyes") is quite different from Grace's prim and proper behaviour. Sue's acquisition of education is entirely self-propelled and never regretted; Grace's superimposed and eventually deplored. Most important of all, Sue's psychological problems are sexual in origin, while Grace's are schizoid. This means that they differ from one another in most of their responses to human relationships, and in themselves. Sue has a clearly defined, though complex, personality, not a divided one; her *volte face* after the deaths of the children is, as I shall show below (Chapter 9), an intensification of earlier attitudes, not a divergence from them. In contrast, Grace's sexual instincts, though uncertain in the choice of object because of her lack of secure identity, seem to be quite strong and fairly uninhibited (though of course Hardy emphasises that she has not the passion of Felice Charmond or the sexiness of Suke Damson). The hypnotic effect Fitzpiers has on her is partly because of his "handsome coercive being"; she encourages Giles to kiss her, enjoys his long, passionate embrace, and even when it turns out to have been "wrong" because the divorce is unobtainable, she is still glad to have had it; nor does she have any problems about sex when she finally goes to the hotel with Fitzpiers; her problems are merely about appearances and the lack of a brush and comb. Sue's psychological complexities are of a totally different kind, and even where they do overlap, the differences are more marked than the similarities. A grasp of these differences seems to me to be absolutely vital to an understanding of Hardy's characterisation. That such a perceptive and accurate critic as Ian Gregor sees Grace as "a first sketch" for Sue confirms my sense of the value of looking at the resemblances between Hardy's works and those of writers on psychology; to do this illuminates the subtlety of Hardy's conceptions. An awareness of the psychological detail which constitutes the character of Grace will prevent the reader from assuming that because Hardy has referred to her "modern nerves" (though he has also called her "elastic nerved") he is giving us a simpler version of Sue. To see Grace as just one in a series is to lose all the complex insights which have gone into her creation. It is perhaps worth mentioning here that Hardy said, "Sue is a type of woman which has always had an attraction for me",[58] whereas he found Grace irritating. These differences between the two characters provide further evidence of the vast range of Hardy's psychological insights. *The Woodlanders* falls into place as one of the novels concerned with, among other things, the analysis of personality, and with exploring ways of treating character in fiction.

Grace is central, but she does nòt dominate the book because of her nature. This is not a weakness, if Hardy wanted other things to be dominant, but he was dissatisfied with her: "he was provoked with her all along. If she could have done a really self-abandoned thing . . . he would have made a fine tragic ending to the book, but she was too common-place and straight-laced, and he could not make her."[59] This sounds more like a criticism of her as a person than as a character in a novel, but the feeling that a heroine needs to have something intense and daring about her is echoed many years later in his comments to Mrs Henniker on her novel *Our Fatal Shadows*: "Of course, *I* should not have kept her respectable, and made a nice, dull, decorous woman of her at the end, but should have let her go to the d _ _ _ _ for the man, my theory being that an exceptional character alone justifies a history (i.e. a novel) being written about a person".[60] This theory is also stated in more general terms:[61] "A story must be exceptional enough to justify its telling. We tale-tellers are all Ancient Mariners and none of us is warranted in stopping Wedding Guests (in other words, the hurrying public) unless he has something more unusual to relate than the ordinary experiences of every average man or woman." Hardy's dissatisfaction with Grace as a heroine reveals itself in the novel. His desire for a heroine who is more vital, more intense, and with a mind of her own has probably had some effect on the structure of the novel, since it begins and ends with Marty. Yet the fact that Hardy did not force Grace into his preferred shape shows how his concern for psychological truth and his confidence in the accuracy of his analysis carried so much weight with him that they overrode a long-held theory of the novel.

At the same time, it has to be admitted that the personality of the heroine does lead to a low-pulsed quality in *The Woodlanders*; the most vivid parts are the life of the woods. Some of these passages are frequently selected as illustrations of Hardy's pessimism. A particular favourite is: "Here, as everywhere, the Unfulfilled Intention, which makes life what it is, was as obvious as it could be among the depraved crowds of a city slum. The leaf was deformed, the curve was crippled, the taper was interrupted; the lichen ate the vigour of the stalk, and the ivy slowly strangled to death the promising sapling."[62] When these two sentences are taken out of context, they do suggest a totally despairing view of the universe, in keeping perhaps with the low-key, subdued atmosphere which is the total effect of the book. But in fact, Hardy gives a balanced, realistic picture of the Hintock world. Though some of the trees are diseased or damaged, it is a fertile world, and nature is particularly bountiful at one stage in the story:

> The earth this year had been prodigally bountiful, and now was the supreme moment of her bounty. In the poorest spots, the trees were bowed with haws and blackberries; acorns cracked underfoot, and the burst husks of chestnuts lay exposing their auburn contents as if arranged by anxious sellers in a fruit-market. In all this proud show, some kernels were unsound as her own situation, and she wondered if there were one world in this universe where the fruit had no worm and marriage no sorrow.[63]

In this way, the setting embodies a view of life as neither wholly good nor wholly bad, a view that seems reasonable rather than pessimistic.

Though the lives of those who are completely at one with their surroundings are in some ways narrow and limited, Hardy creates a sense of their stature and significance and relates them to a wider world than the cultivated people with their social aspirations can attain. Marty and Giles going to work in the early morning are "part of the pattern in the great web of human doings then weaving in both hemispheres from the White Sea to Cape Horn".[64] At times, their total self-abnegation, the utterly negative quality of their lives as far as human relationships are concerned makes them seem dwarfed by the setting. On other occasions, they appear as great, impersonal figures, almost forces of nature themselves. Giles as "Autumn's very brother" is perhaps conventionally idealised by Grace in her forlorn state, but Marty at the end is "almost like a being who had rejected with indifference the attribute of sex for the loftier quality of abstract humanism".[65] Structurally, Marty, appearing in the opening and closing scenes, forms a framework to the book, as the woods enclose the characters. But Grace is central in the sense that she unites all the main threads — the inner and the outer worlds, the problems of education, marriage, psychology. As a central character, she is not gripping. We can take an interest in her psychological makeup, but her inability to live with any intensity, accurate and illuminating though it is, means that our emotional involvement is slight. To end with Grace worrying about her toilet accessories in the expensive hotel (while rejecting Fitzpiers's offer to go to a less "imposing" one) would diminish the book. Marty's eulogy over the dead Giles takes us into a world of stoical acceptance of love and loss and death. Grace is the structural, but not the emotional, centre of the book.

It is for these reasons that the insights into Grace's psychology seem almost casually thrown off, along with the penetrating treatment of Mr Melbury and the swift sketch of Mr South's tree obsession. Hardy's lack of emotional involvement with Grace is exceptional. With nearly all his other major characters one of the most striking qualities is his ability to sympathise, and to extend the range of the readers' sympathies.

The subtle detail and convincingness of his analysis of an unsympathetic character is evidence of his effortless responsiveness to human complexities. Just as his ear was attuned to the different sounds the wind makes in different kinds of tree, so his mind was open to the variousness of human beings. In *The Woodlanders*, as in most of the novels, the characters sometimes seem dwarfed by the physically overpowering surroundings, but those who work with nature also share in its elemental qualities. The interplay between that unchanging natural life, the characters who accept it as the only mode of life, and those whose lives are uncertain and divided, shapes the novel. Though the woods and woodlanders evoke the most vivid imaginative response, Grace's "divided self" is the focus of all the conflicts explored by the novel.

7 *The Return of the Native*: the psychological problems of modern man and woman (I)

All Hardy's novels deal to some extent with the problems both of adjusting to changes in society and of coping with its failure to change in response to the individual's needs. His treatment of character emphasises that individuals as well as society are in a process of change and that novelists' methods of exploring character must change in order to reflect this and to take into account new insights. This is the area of Hardy's most important innovations in the novel. Clym, Knight, Angel, Sue and Jude are all examples of the problems of "advanced" thinkers (or those trying to be advanced) in a world which, while accepting industrial change (sometimes reluctantly) resists adamantly any challenge to its attitudes and preconceptions. For the individual, it is not merely an external problem. The "advanced" thinkers are themselves hampered by these same preconceptions and prejudices which they share, often unconsciously, with the society they criticise. Up to this point, I have examined a number of characters which reveal the complexity and subtlety of Hardy's psychological insight; I now come to some novels which demonstrate these qualities even more fully, because in these he is creating characters who are themselves interested in new ideas. In them he finds scope for examining the psychological effects of being ahead of one's time while at the same time attacking "the inert mass of crystallised opinion",[1] which he tried to undermine in all his writing.

In *The Return of the Native*, Clym and Eustacia illustrate in a number of ways the exploratory nature of Hardy's writing. In this novel the experimentation is of a fairly rudimentary kind. In Clym, we have an early example of the "advanced" young thinker; in the treatment of both of them, we see Hardy's increasingly complex and searching examination of the nature of love, and with Eustacia there is some grappling with the technical problems of exploring a character in depth in a novel.

From *Far from the Madding Crowd*, or even earlier, to *Jude the Obscure*, we can see Hardy's interest in complex, tormented, maladjusted beings (often set alongside comparatively stable and uncomplicated characters). In his book on Hardy, Howe suggests that in *The Return of the Native*, "a new kind of sexuality, neurotically wilful but also perversely exciting makes its appearance".[2] This vividly describes the quality of Eustacia's passions, but it is not true to say that such passions appear here for the first time; the sentence could be applied to Boldwood, and even to Miss Aldclyffe's brief Lesbian encounters in *Desperate Remedies*. In this respect, *The Return of the Native* is not a new departure, but a continuation in the line of Hardy's development which was to culminate in *Jude the Obsure*. Howe continues: "A thick cloud — the cloud of modern, inherently problematic consciousness — falls across the horizon of Wessex".[3] It is certainly true that Hardy sees Clym as "a modern problematic consciousness", but I would deny that this is an innovation for Hardy since we see glimpses of similar problems in Knight in *A Pair of Blue Eyes*. In *The Return of the Native* Hardy is following up some lines of thought about psychology and about sexual relationships which he has already tentatively introduced in earlier novels.

This development in the kinds of personality portrayed is accompanied by definite changes and experiments in the methods of depicting them. Hardy's technique in presenting Eustacia is unusual in that there is less analysis and a higher proportion of observation of externals than in most of the other novels. This, inevitably, at some points in the story leads to a concentration on action rather than on mental processes or emotional states, but there are times when the external method becomes an instrument for exploring the subconscious. The choice of a viewpoint largely outside the character is partly the result of the immense significance of Egdon Heath in the novel. In the first chapter, Hardy describes the heath as "the hitherto unrecognised original of those wild regions of obscurity which are vaguely felt to be compassing us about in midnight dreams of flight and disaster".[4] This unequivocal identification of the heath with the unconscious at the beginning of the book establishes its significance in Hardy's portrayal of the human psyche. Through his use of the heath, he is able to suggest great depths in his characters, without much close analysis; the unconscious remains unknown, though we are aware of its existence. Eustacia's affinity with the heath, which coexists with her antagonism to it, gives a sense of enlargement to her character. Whole areas of her thinking and feeling remain mysterious, unanalysed, but we are made aware that they exist. In this, as in so many other things, Hardy is going in the same direction as Lawrence, who said he was trying, "to make new feelings conscious".[5] In *The Return of the Native*, Hardy has not gone as far as this. He has drawn attention to the existence of the unconscious, but he has not attempted to make its nature known.

The importance of Egdon Heath in the novel lies mainly in the way Hardy uses it to enlarge our concept of human nature, and yet it is probably Egdon Heath above all which has given rise to the theory, popular until quite recently, that Hardy's characters are puppets, totally insignificant against an overwhelming background. This view implies that the characters are purely physical beings and disregards the importance Hardy gives to their inner existence. Certainly, Hardy saw man as dwarfed by the size of the universe, but simultaneously he showed him as a central feature of it; he describes Eustacia as "the pivot of this circle of heath country".[6]

It is for these reasons fitting that both characters and landscape are subjected to the same delicate, sensitive scrutiny; there is the same minute observation of the wind in the heather bells and the sigh of Eustacia. Though it might seem that this method would lead Hardy right away from the psychological examination of character, it does not do so entirely. By observing so meticulously every outward manifestation of emotion, Hardy is able to suggest that these observable "expressions" reveal only the surface, and that there are vast depths of emotion, invisible to the outsider; he is thus moving towards the view that human beings are inexplicable — a view further developed in the treatment of the "conjectural" Grace and the "puzzling and unstateable" Sue Bridehead. This is the beginning of Hardy's tentative exploration of that aspect of human beings which Lawrence felt was his own central concern as a novelist. Even by the time of his last novel, Hardy is still only hinting at the existence of "a strange dark continent that we do not explore".[7] Hardy made a small, cautious advance to the edge of an area into which Lawrence boldly plunged.

In Eustacia we have this rather surprising combination of a wild, tormented personality, presented largely from an external viewpoint, and yet conveying an impression of considerable depth. Hardy uses the external, descriptive method on a grand scale (but never again in such a lengthy and elaborate manner) with occasional passages of analysis and together they create an impression of a passionate, fascinating, yet neurotically maladjusted personality. She is first seen from a distance on top of the Rainbarrow, looking like "an organic part of the entire motionless structure".[8] Even when she is seen in close-up, it is stressed that the view is that of an outsider only able to guess at what is taking place in her mind: "What she uttered was a lengthened sighing, apparently at something in her mind".[9] Yet, while emphasising that the view of her is external, Hardy creates an intense interest in what is going on in her mind: "There was a spasmodic abandonment about it, as if, in allowing herself to utter the sound, the woman's brain had authorized what it could not regulate".[10] Emphatically refusing the stance of omniscient author, Hardy not only implies the existence of unseen, unknown depths of feeling, but also emphasises that these emotions may be too powerful for conscious control. In this way, even while using the technique of an external observer, Hardy has been able to suggest "a strange dark continent" in human personality, and in Eustacia's in particular.

This method is used in its most elaborate form in "The Queen of the Night".[11] The view of her is at first a distant one, and the sense of detachment is here increased by Hardy's irony; she would have done well as "a model goddess . . . with a little preparation",[12] he says and at once reminds us that his opinion of goddesses is a low one. He spends many paragraphs creating an impression first of strange, smouldering beauty, gradually becoming more and more extravagant, associating her with "Bourbon roses, rubies and tropical midnights", until he again brings the whole picture into question: "In a dim light, with a slight rearrangement of the hair, her general figure might have stood for one of the higher female deities".[13] This is characteristic of his ambivalent attitude to Eustacia. He encourages us to take her at her own evaluation, to see her as a sublime, exotic creature, and then shatters the illusion, bringing home to us all the more sharply because we have been persuaded to share her own view of herself, the true nature of the situation. In his "Study of Thomas Hardy", Lawrence sees Eustacia as a natural aristocrat, but in doing so he is recreating her as one of his own characters. Hardy is much more uncertain about the value of aristocracy. He stresses how she often, and often consciously, deludes herself in her longing to escape from the world as it actually is. (At one moment, Wildeve is "some wondrous thing she had created out of chaos": minutes later, he arrives and she tells him, "You are not worthy of me".[14]) After comparing her (with reservations) to goddesses, Hardy says that, "at times she was not altogether unlovable".[15] This places in an even more satirical light a sentence two pages earlier: "To be loved to madness — such was her great desire".[16] In these ways, one facet of "The Queen of the Night" is shown to be a romanticising adolescent dreamer, living in a fantasy world of which she is the heroine. Hardy creates a sense of her psychological complexity largely through describing her outward appearance and behaviour, but also towards the end of "The Queen of the Night" chapter by giving some account of what is habitually going on in her mind, while at the same time he retains a position of critical detachment. Even the description of her thinking and feeling is given in generalised summary form rather than following the ebb and flow of her mind and this lends itself to critical, even ironical commentary.

The experiments in method tried out in "The Queen of the Night" are not really successful and, since Hardy did not repeat them, he was probably dissatisfied with it. It was an attempt to convey in an excessively elaborate way the impossibility of completely knowing anyone. The ambivalent effect of the partly ornate, partly satirical commentary seems to have been deliberately intended. It does succeed in creating mixed feelings about Eustacia in the reader, and contributes to our sense of her tortured and conflicting emotions, but its weakness is that in its elaboration it tends to focus attention excessively on technique, which is especially unfortunate in the more grostesque passages (such as the one about mouths like muffins). In a retrospective view, the chapter contributes to our sense of the "nocturnal mysteries" of Eustacia, and mingles with her own wish-fulfilment dreams, but under close scrutiny it seems too long and ornate for the amount of insight it gives us. It is primarily interesting as a crude first attempt to find a method which will enable the novelist to suggest the existence of unconscious and impenetrable areas of the mind without in the process eliminating the element of the unknown.

This chapter is in keeping with Hardy's general scheme of allowing the contradictions in Eustacia's nature and in his own attitude to her to emerge. His general comments have the same effect of emphasising contradictions: "The fantastic nature of her passion which lowered her as an intellect, raised her as a soul";[17] "To an onlooker her beauty would have made her feelings almost seem reasonable".[18] Here again, the wry, onlooker's view is used as a way of bringing out her inner contradictions and of underlining the fact that she cannot be explained or summed up. Here, long before he had clearly developed new ways of looking at character, Hardy is already anticipating the refusal of the twentieth-century novelists to pin down and define characters. Hardy also uses the simple device of observers with opposing views to help reinforce this impression; Charley wholeheartedly accepts her view of herself as a goddess, while Susan Nonsuch sees her as a witch; to Clym's mother she was "not a good girl", to Clym she was a goddess (and then "no longer a goddess").

Although he relies so much on observation of externals and manages, through his suggestive approach, to achieve also considerable depth, Hardy acknowledges the inadequacy and possible inaccuracy of this method of portraying character; he describes how, when dancing with Wildeve, Eustacia's "soul had passed away from and forgotten her features, which were left empty and quiescent as they always are when feeling goes beyond their register".[19] He compensates for this, at this point, by describing her thoughts and feelings, and using imagery which suggests their elemental and uncontrollable quality: "she had been steeped in arctic frigidity by comparison with the tropical sensations here"; the dancing was "like riding upon a whirlwind". His use of her dreams of Clym would seem also to be a move in this direction, a way of exposing her subconscious drives. But, in fact, Hardy's treatment of the dream does little more than amplify the impression we already have of her adolescent imagination; her wish-fulfilment dream images of Hollywood glamour and Clym as her knight in shining armour mainly serve to increase our ironical attitude to her romantic fantasies rather than to give us further insight into her psychological complexities.

The shifting to and fro from an external observer to a view of the inner workings of Eustacia's mind persists throughout the novel. There are times though, when the situation demands some insight into her thinking, but we are kept outside, watching her for clues as to what is going on in her mind, as, for instance, when "she remained in a fixed attitude for nearly ten minutes",[20] looking at her grandfather's pistols. This is, of course, dramatically very arresting, but at this point in the story, a more subtle, inner directed view might have been more rewarding. In much the same way, just before her death, Hardy moves far back, right away from her consciousness. All we know of is the distant splash heard by Clym. Again, from the point of view of psychological penetration, this seems a missed opportunity. But it is deliberate on Hardy's part. He feels that at crucial moments the action is all-important and overrides other considerations, as his criticisms of Meredith indicate.[21] Eustacia's state of mind has already been suggested in the description of her despairing, almost demented condition as she wanders through the storm. Just as Boldwood's murder of Troy and Tess's murder of Alec are treated dramatically, so as to create suspense, so here Eustacia's drowning is a dramatic occurrence, shown from a distance in a scene of great dramatic power. In this episode, Hardy combines the psychological and the dramatic, without using the analytical method at all, but its effectiveness derives from the explorations of her tormented mental state which lead up to this moment. All we know of the fall into the water is what Clym knows. We are left to speculate whether it was accidental or suicidal. But Hardy creates a vivid impression of her state of mind before this final moment in his account of her journey from her grandfather's cottage to Rainbarrow "where she stood to think".[22] He uses in a compressed form all the various methods of exploring her consciousness found elsewhere in the novel. He conveys the confused and fluctuating nature of her thoughts even though at a conscious level she thinks her mind is made up. On opening the door and seeing the rain, she pauses, "But having committed herself to this line of action there was no retreating for bad weather. Even the receipt of Clym's letter would not have stopped her now".[23] When she stands thinking on Rainbarrow she suddenly realises that she is penniless and that she must either ask Wildeve for money, which she is too proud to do, or become his mistress, which now comes to seem equally impossible: "Can I go, can I go?" she moaned. "He's not *great* enough for me to give myself to — he does not suffice for my desire! .... If he had been a Saul or a Buonaparte ...."[24]

Intermingled with these confused and tormented feelings are descriptions of how she appeared to various observers. There is Susan Nonsuch's terror of her witchcraft and her attempt at a counterattack with wax figures, there is Diggory Venn's awareness of a mysterious weeping woman passing his hut in the dark and there is a hypothetical observer who, if present, would have been able to observe her outward appearance and make deductions about the mental state it expressed: "Any one who stood by now would have pitied her .... Extreme unhappiness weighed visibly upon her. Between the dripping of the rain ... from the heather to the earth, very similar sounds could be heard coming from her lips".[25] The same delicate observation which earlier in the novel distinguished the different sounds of the wind coming from different kinds of heath bells is again being applied to human nature. This seeing human beings in the same way as the natural world is central to *The Return of the Native*. The different kinds of affinity which the characters have with their surroundings is particularly important for Eustacia. She is simultaneously identified with the heath and in violent revolt against it. This is emphasised right from the beginning of the novel, when she "seemed like an organic part"[26] of the Rainbarrow, and continues through to the end: "Never was harmony more perfect than that between the chaos of her mind and the chaos of the world without".[27] It is this, far more than the elaboration of "The Queen of the Night" which makes Eustacia at times a figure on a grand scale; it shows her inner world to be as storm-swept and mysterious as the heath itself: "She had imbibed much of what was dark in its tone".[28] We are reminded again of the opening description of the heath as "the original of those wild regions of obscurity which are vaguely felt to be compassing us about in midnight dreams of flight and disaster".[29] By the end of the novel this world of "flight and disaster" and "choas" has wholly filled Eustacia's inner world. Her identity seems assimilated into the storm-swept heath and her death inevitable.

Without this identification with elemental and unconscious forces, Eustacia would have been a fairly slight study of a maladjusted girl — interesting, but without the strangeness and power of Hardy's conception. This is the most effective of the methods with which he is experimenting here. The use of the point of view of some unidentified "onlooker" who can only conjecture about the inner life from its outward manifestations is used rather clumsily, and would seem to work against any profound exploration of the inner life. Yet the intermittent use of such a viewpoint is consistent with Hardy's continually developing interest in analysing psychological complexities, because his very awareness of these complexities makes him particularly conscious of those areas of human personality which recede beyond human consciousness. In this way, as in so many others, his affinity with Lawrence is striking. He has the sense, developed so much further by Lawrence, of pushing out the frontiers of consciousness, of looking into unconscious processes, while always acknowledging that a human being cannot be wholly known. The imagined onlooker is a clumsy device, and Hardy does not use it again. Nevertheless, enigmatic Eustacia is a forerunner of his later "conjectural creatures" and of Lawrence's. Her nature is of the tormented, complex kind which always absorbed Hardy as a novelist. By relating her so closely to the most vividly imagined part of the book, the heath, he makes her mysteriousness convincing.

Similar complexities and contradictions confront us in the character of Clym. In conception, he is another of Hardy's psychological problem characters. Hardy states clearly that Clym's mind was not "well-proportioned", that it was not the kind of mind which will "never cause its owner to be confined as a madman".[30] In the course of the story he shows how he veers towards madness on several occasions — during his nervous breakdown, after his mother's death, when he is overwhelmed by guilt feelings, in his insane rage with Eustacia after discovering about the closed door, and in his obsessional, possibly therapeutic, preaching at the end.

But Hardy does not present Clym simply as an unbalanced personality, but as a representative of the problems of "modern" man's difficulties in adjusting to new ways of thinking and feeling, especially those arising from the loss of religious faith. This sense that anyone who is aware of contemporary philosophical problems is bound to have some difficulty in adjusting his emotions to his intellectual insight occurs in *A Pair of Blue Eyes*, where Knight's intellectual development is seen as emotionally inhibiting, and later in Angel, Jude and Sue. Hardy is not, I think, very successful in handling this aspect of Clym, which he treats in a theoretical way, giving it a good deal of prominence in passages of commentary, but not really embodying it in Clym's character, or in the story. He describes the ravages of profound thinking on his outward appearance: "an inner strenuousness was preying upon an outer symmetry . . . he already showed that thought is a disease of the flesh".[31] But this introduction is followed up only by further abstract statements about him: "In Clym Yeobright's face could be dimly seen the typical countenance of the future", and it is said to express "the view of life as a thing to be put up with".[32] The idea of Clym as a modern man who "would not stand still in the circumstances in which he had been born",[33] is several times stated and discussed and we are told that "he was in many points abreast with the central town thinkers of his date",[34] yet this aspect of his mind is never presented to us in a concrete way (we do not know what books he reads so doggedly — unlike Jude and Sue — nor do we have any clear idea of the nature of his educational theories). It never seems to be a driving force in his character. He does on one occasion feel that there is a specific wrong to be righted; this is when Susan Nonsuch pricks Eustacia in church and says she is a witch. "Do you think I have turned preacher too soon?"[35] Clym asks his mother, but this can hardly be classed as a novel, modern way of looking at the situation. Clym's dissatisfaction with the diamond business, his hope of improving the minds of heath dwellers and some of his conversations with his mother do suggest a philosophical turn of mind; but there is nothing in his behaviour or his thinking to support Hardy's suggestion that he is one of those whose disillusion-ment has grown as they "uncover the defects of natural laws and see the quandary that man is in by their operation".[36] None of his diffi-culties in coping with his emotional experience are derived from a conflict between a traditional education and modern ideas, as those of Angel and Sue are, at least in part, and so Clym's modernity re-mains theoretical and abstract, on the periphery of the story.

The real conflict is between the impulse to do something original ("he would not stand still in the circumstances amid which he was born"[37]) and his affinity with his native setting ("he was inwoven with the heath"[38]). Clym maintains he wants to bring about changes on Egdon Heath but the only occasion when he seems to feel any real necessity for change is the pricking of Eustacia. Otherwise, the heath-dwellers are presented as tolerant and good-humoured and Clym's own readiness to become one of them and to merge with the heath is presented by Hardy as wholly admirable under the circum-stances. Eustacia's snobbish feeling of being degraded by this is shown as alien and self-centred. Clym was quite content to be "a brown spot in the midst of an expanse of olive green grass and nothing more".[39] All his schemes for change and improvement are qualified by his delight in the ancient, unchanging nature of the place: "he could not help indulging in a barbarous satisfaction at ob-serving that, in some attempts at reclamation from the waste, tillage, after holding on for a year or two, had receded again in despair, the fern and furze-tufts stubbornly reasserting themselves".[40] Admittedly, Clym's plans are for purely intellectual change, but his delight in things as they are, and his ready acquiescence in a life of manual labour do not suggest overwhelming singlemindedness in the pursuit of change. Though he appears to be attempting to convey a message at the end, it is presumably significant that his preaching appears to be vague, grandiose and understandably ineffectual.

Though Hardy as commentator tends to lay the blame for Clym's predicament on modern man's clearer understanding of the nature of things, Hardy the novelist relates it much more closely to his personal relationships. Even here, the conflict is sometimes presented in an excessively schematic and theoretical way: "Three antagonistic growths had to be kept alive: his mother's trust in him, his plan for becoming a teacher and Eustacia's happiness. His fervid nature could not afford to relinquish one of these, though two of the three were as many as he could hope to preserve".[41] Though this method of stating Clym's problems simplifies and limits them, the actual presentation of the personal relationships probes his personality at considerable depth. It is in this area that we see the effects of the "not well-proportioned mind".

Hardy's treatment of Clym's relationship with Eustacia explores some aspects of his mental and emotional problems as well as hers. As "the first blinding halo kindled about him by love and beauty" is rapidly extinguished, "sometimes he wished that he had never known Eustacia, immediately to retract the wish as brutal".[42] Immediately, Clym is in a state of conflict over Eustacia, partly because of his mother, but also because of his own attitudes and desires. His "distrust of his position as a solicitous lover"[43] suggests a similarity to Sue, who was "unfitted . . . to fulfil the conditions of the matrimonial relationship . . . with scarce any man".[44] Unlike so many lovers in Hardy who delude themselves about the nature of the loved one, Clym is quite clearsighted about the absence of affinity between himself and Eustacia and knows that "her tastes touched his own only at rare and infrequent points".[45] Though he does say that "she would make a good matron of a school", this is in the heat of an argument with his mother, and is an illustration of the outrageous points people will make when quarrelling, and not intended to be taken as an honest statement of his opinion — there is nothing to suggest he deluded himself as much as this. Of course, he does delude himself about her in his assumption that she will easily abandon her longing for Paris (and she reciprocates by assuming she can easily persuade him to return there). Yet, his decision to marry Eustacia seems to be due to his sensitivity, to his feeling of owing it to her since he has encouraged her to hope he will, rather than to love. She was "no longer a goddess",[46] though his original passionate feelings are reawakened in the early days of the marriage. None of this suggests lack of balance or neurosis in Clym, but his "firmness in the contrary intention" to Eustacia's and his "undeviating manner" perhaps indicate a dangerous rigidity, rather like Angel's.

It is from his relationship with his mother that violent, unbalanced emotions arise. Hardy depicts very powerfully the intensity of their relationship and the close affinity between their minds. Especially moving and convincing is the way they are able to communicate without using words. This gives their exchanges, whether affectionate or hostile, a sense of great depth of feeling: "The love between the young man and his mother was strangely invisible now. Of love, it may be said, the less earthly, the less demonstrative. In its absolutely indestructible form it reaches a profundity in which all exhibition of itself is painful. It was so with these".[47] Even though they are at loggerheads most of the time, either over Clym's career or over Eustacia, they understand one another completely. Mrs Yeobright is really entirely at one with him about the diamond business and in agreement with him on his moral and philosophical position. When she is criticising his abandonment of his job in Paris when he was "doing well", his question, "Mother, what is doing well?"[48] silences her because she fully understands the implications of his question, and really agrees with him. The dissension between them is entirely on account of Eustacia, and Mrs Yeobright's possessive jealousy is such that she would have been antagonistic towards any woman who interested her son. Clym's response to this is very violent: "whenever any little occurrence had brought into more prominence than usual the disappointment he was causing her it had sent him on long and moody walks; or he was kept awake a great part of the night by the turmoil of spirit which such a recognition created".[49] When she finally tells him, during a particularly violent quarrel, to leave the house, he replies, "'I beg your pardon for having thought this my home. I will no longer inflict myself upon you: I'll go!' And he went with tears in his eyes".[50] He returns only to pack and leave. He makes no move to give her the opportunity to say that she had spoken in the heat of the moment, nor does she attempt any approach to him, but simply sits downstairs, listening to him packing overhead. They are both equally inflexible and "undeviating". As Mrs Yeobright tells Eustacia, "He can be as hard as steel".[51]

Clym's emotions about his mother are more extreme and more shattering than anything he experiences in relation to Eustacia apart from his frenzied rage about her failure to go to the door when Mrs Yeobright pays her visit. Because of the quality of their relationship, Clym's breakdown after his mother's death is almost inevitable. Just as Sue Bridehead is shown to be precariously balanced and is then exposed to a traumatic experience which undermines her delicate equilibrium, in a similar way Clym is given his traumatic experience and is shown succumbing to it. After his mother's death he, too, tortures himself with guilt. But the fact that Clym's guilt is to some extent justified (in that he had been as inflexible as his mother) makes his delirious self-accusations seem a little more rational than Sue Bridehead's — his are at least directly related to what has occurred, and his guilt is of a much more conscious kind than hers. Nevertheless, his remorse is extreme, and his claim that "it has not upset my reason"[52] seems hardly justified. Chapter 2 of Book Fifth is entitled, "A Lurid Light breaks in upon a darkened intellect", and reason is said to have "now somewhat recovered itself".[53] His week-long delirium, followed by obsessive preoccupation with his mother, provokes Eustacia's "Other men's mothers have died",[54] which, in spite of its callousness, arouses a certain sympathy in the reader; by making us experience the irritating, obsessional harping on the single theme, Hardy evokes a response to her plea for rationality, and emphasises how remote from normal thinking Clym's frame of mind is. This phase is a very plausible development from Clym's "undeviating" and highly moral behaviour in the past, and from his extremely close and intense relationship with his mother. Hardy very effectively indicates that this mind, which he stated in his earliest descriptions was prone to madness, has now become grossly disturbed, and is on the edge of insanity.

Clym's temporary recovery of control is shown to be precarious, "he sank into taciturnity",[55] but his obsession, though no longer voiced, still possessed him, completely blotting out all other thoughts: "How to discover the solution to this riddle of death seemed a query of more importance than the highest problems of living".[56] It is characteristic of the subtlety with which Hardy handles this stage of Clym's mental disturbance that he shows him, after he has heard the story from Johnny Nonsuch, though "blank" and "icy", as yet sufficiently conscious of things outside himself to be aware of

the imperturbable countenance of the heath, which, having defied the cataclysmal onsets of centuries, reduced to insignificance by its seamed and antique features the wildest turmoil of a single man . . . . A consciousness of a vast impassivity in all which lay around him took possession even of Yeobright in his wild walk towards Alderworth.[57]

This ability, at least for the moment, to perceive the world outside himself is a very important feature of Hardy's conception of Clym; it is what saves him from collapsing permanently into neurosis or even madness; other neurotics in Hardy's novels, Boldwood and Sue, for example, are totally self-absorbed at moments of acute mental suffering (and at other times quite often) and they do not make a recovery as Clym does. After this moment of awareness of the heath, he shuts his mind to it, and going into the house to accuse Eustacia, he seems to become temporarily demented. She sees that he is capable of killing her now, but instead he vents his frenzy in smashing her desk. His accusation that she has been making a trade of prostitution, his idealised account of his mother, his self-righteousness are, as Eustacia sees, almost inevitable counterparts of his previous guilt and remorse. All these attitudes are in keeping with his extremely severe and demanding conscience.

Hardy is creating a picture of an obsessional neurotic, not a madman. After Eustacia has left him, he regains his normal state, still obsessed with his mother ("it had become a religion with him to preserve in good condition all that had lapsed from his mother's hands to his own"[58]) but he is prepared to admit that his enraged accusations of Eustacia were unjustified. In the latter part of *The Return of the Native*, Hardy's treatment of Clym consists of exposing him to a series of shattering experiences, showing his collapse, and subsequent slow return to sanity, followed by another blow and another painful recovery. After the third and final blow, the drowning, he returns to a more extreme form of the guilt and remorse which overwhelmed him after his mother's death. He is more vulnerable now, after his only partial recovery, but he is not so frenzied and is not delirious; Hardy's description of his relatively quiet reaction effectively suggests an even deeper and more settled state of neurotic self-blame. He says quietly, "with a wild smile", "She is the second woman I have killed this year".[59] From this point onwards Hardy depicts an obsession with guilt which is clearly neurotic and also fully in keeping with Clym's always severe and rigid personality. That he now becomes wholly taken up with the idea of his mother as "a sublime saint whose radiance even his tenderness for Eustacia could not obscure",[60] is an authentic development under these particular circumstances, from the original relationship with its suggestions of Oedipal intensity. Hardy even describes him as looking like Oedipus after hearing Johnny's story.[61]

Clym's personality shows many of the qualities which Freud associated with the Oedipus complex. In *Civilisation and its Discontents*, Freud emphasises the part played by the "severe superego", which is one of Clym's driving forces, leading him to abandon diamond-dealing in favour of helping his fellow men. A neurotic element in this is perhaps suggested by his "sitting *slavishly* over his books"[62] (unlike Jude who either studies them enthusiastically or abandons them), and by his eventual blinding himself through overstrain, almost as if it were an unconscious way of escape from the powerful demands of his conscience. It is interesting that Hardy says of him when furze-cutting, "A forced limitation of effort offered a justification of lowly courses to an unambitious man, whose conscience would hardly have allowed him to remain in such obscurity while his powers were unimpeded".[62] Hardy here describes precisely the workings of the superego; this "naturally unambitious" man's conscience "will not let him remain in such obscurity" because the dominant influence of his mother, pushing him towards ambitious goals, has been absorbed and become an inner drive. Though he rejected her goal of financial and social advance in favour of more apparently altruistic objectives, the drive towards effort and achievement is a fundamental element in his personality.

Another feature which, according to Freud, is related to the Oedipus complex is a strong sense of guilt. Clym obviously has this. Further, Freud points out a parallel between the demands of the individual's superego and the demands made by systems of ethics on the community. The superego can make excessive demands on the individual:

> In our investigations and our therapy of the neuroses, we cannot avoid finding fault with the superego of the individual on two accounts; in commanding and prohibiting with such severity, it troubles too little about the happiness of the ego, and it fails to take into account sufficiently the difficulties in the way of obeying it . . . in our therapy we often find ourselves obliged to do battle with the superego and work to moderate its demands.[64]

Similarly, the "cultural superego" or system of ethics can demand more than human beings can achieve: "even in so-called normal people the power of controlling the id cannot be increased beyond certain limits. If one asks more, one produces revolt or neuroses in individuals".[65] Hardy's analysis of Clym illustrates this point exactly; not only does his superego make demands on him as an individual which he is unable to fulfil, but also his theories about the nature of society make excessive demands and Hardy defines the nature of this precisely:

> In passing from the bucolic to the intellectual life the interme-
> diate stages are usually two at least, frequently many more; and
> one of these stages is almost sure to be worldly advance. We can
> hardly imagine bucolic placidity quickening to intellectual aims
> without imagining social aims as the transitional phase . . . . To
> argue upon the possibility of culture before luxury to the bucolic
> world may be to argue truly, but it is an attempt to disturb a se-
> quence to which humanity has long been accustomed.[66]

When Hardy leaves Clym at the end of the novel "lecturing on morally unimpeachable subjects"[67] he is not presenting this as a sat- isfactory fulfilment of his ideas. Though he says that Clym has "found his vocation", he also suggests that the preaching is at least partially therapeutic. The text he quotes[68] indicates that Clym is using the sermons at least in part as outlets for his continuing obses- sion with his mother. The final sentence of the novel hints that he appears as an ineffectual, though amiable, teacher: "But he was everywhere kindly received, for the story of his life had become gen- erally known".

In these ways, Hardy's treatment of Clym corresponds closely to Freud's formulation of his theory of the Oedipus complex and of the relationship between the id, the ego and the superego. This is nothing new in imaginative writing, as Freud's name for his theory and his many references to literary examples of it clearly acknowl- edge. But this parallel between Hardy and Freud does throw some light on the kinds of interest Hardy took in characterisation. Clym is one example among many of his interest in problematic, dis- turbed personalities and illustrates his clear understanding of their complexities. With Clym he attempts to deal with a number of interrelated psychological problems. The imaginative and vivid treatment of his relationship with his mother is wholly successful. The other elements are less imaginatively conceived, in particular the very theoretical and abstract handling of Clym as representa- tive of the problem of the modern, thinking man. Yet in some ways this failure is revealing. In the opening chapter and in the intro- ductory descriptions of Clym, where Hardy is formulating his theories about the nature and problems of modern man, we can clearly see his struggle to shape the novel so that it can be a vehicle for his theories. That the theories are not fully integrated with and embodied in the characterisation of Clym is a weakness, but it is interesting because it reveals that Hardy was working out, painfully and clumsily sometimes, a theoretical basis for his conception of character and for the changes which he felt were occurring in contemporary man. Hardy, in a theoretical as well as an imaginative way, was concerned with the psychological effects of "civilisation and its discontents", but in a way which is not limiting or restrictive. His attempts to fuse so many different elements in a single personality show his awareness of the complex nature of human beings which he never reduces to make them fit a theory.

Hardy then is showing what happens to a mind which is not "well-proportioned" when it is exposed to a series of overwhelming experiences. Though he examines the processes of disintegration and partial recovery at some depth, he does not allow this to dominate the telling of the story. This is one of the reasons why Clym is sometimes shown, as Eustacia is, silently brooding without any clear impressions of the precise nature of his thoughts being given. This creates a very powerful impression of painful and intense emotion which might be lessened by a more clinical attempt to formulate the thoughts in words. Just as Lawrence often creates somewhat inarticulate characters (Will and Anna in *The Rainbow* or, more extreme examples, the characters in "The Fox") and then explores by a variety of means their passionate responses to experience, so Hardy too was conscious of the problems of verbalising the characters' emotions. He states the problem in *The Return of the Native*; in the course of Clym's disagreement with his mother, "it was almost a discovery to him that he could reach her by a magnetism which was as superior to words as words are to yells".[69] Sometimes he did not speak because "the current of her feeling was too pronounced to admit it".[70] But though it would be true to say that Lawrence found brilliant and original ways of solving these problems, in *The Return of the Native* Hardy does little more than show his awareness of them. Even in the later novels he does not go far in developing a technique for this purpose.

The fact that Clym survives his repeated ordeals and finds himself a role which is not totally remote from his original plan to do something for the good of mankind, however ineffectual it turns out to be, is partly due to his sense of belonging to and being part of the heath. In the first chapter, Hardy says, "to know that everything

around and underneath had been from prehistoric times as unaltered as the stars overhead, gave ballast to a mind adrift on
change, and harassed by the irrepressible New". This sentence has
significant bearing on Clym's later development. He can merge with
the heath as a furze-cutter and find it "soothing". Even at the height
of his anguish and frenzy, he is conscious of the heath's hugeness,
permanence and antiquity. On the night of the eclipse, while
waiting for Eustacia, as he watched the moon,

> his eye travelled over the length and breadth of that distant coun-
> try — over the Bay of Rainbows, the sombre Sea of Crises, the
> Ocean of Storms, the Lake of Dreams, the vast Walled Plains and
> the wondrous Ring Mountains — till he almost felt himself to be
> voyaging bodily through its wild scenes, standing on its hollow
> hills, traversing its deserts, descending its vales and old sea bot-
> toms or mounting to the edge of its craters.[71]

This capacity to move outside himself is an important aspect of
Clym's character. The sense of himself as part of the universe,
whether he is feeling at one with "winged and creeping things"[72] as
he cuts furze, or recognising for a moment that the heath "reduced
to insignificance by its seamed and antique features the wildest turmoil of a single man",[73] or feeling he is actually exploring the moon
"gave ballast" to his mind and enables him to survive, without being
completely and permanently overwhelmed by his individual personal troubles; these only temporarily seem to engulf his whole
world.

This relates closely to some of the points made by Jung about the
collective unconscious and man's relation to the cosmos; Hardy
stresses that Clym can feel a sense of being in touch with the cosmos
through being "inwoven with" and "permeated by" the heath; Jung
says that the

> cosmos and man in the last analysis obey common laws; man is a
> cosmos in miniature and is not divided from the great cosmos by
> any fixed limits. The same laws rule for one as for the other, and
> from the one, a way leads into the other. The psyche and the cos-
> mos are related to each other like inner and outer worlds. There-
> fore man participates by nature in all cosmic events and is inwardly,
> as well as outwardly, interwoven with them.[74]

In *The Return of the Native* the passages on the relationship

between man and the heath parallel remarkably Jung's statements
on the relationship between man and the cosmos. Hardy says of
the heath: "It was at present a place perfectly accordant with
man's nature — neither ghastly, nor hateful nor ugly; neither commonplace, unmeaning nor tame: but, like man, slighted and endur-
ing; and withal, singularly colossal and mysterious in its swarthy
monotony".[75]

Similarly, Jung says:"All the mythological processes of nature,
such as summer and winter, the phases of the moon, rainy seasons.
and so forth . . . are symbolic expressions of the inner unconscious
drama of the psyche, which become accessible to man's consciousness by way of projection — that is mirrored in the events of
nature".[76]

Hardy gives a single example, Jung generalises, but they are both
making the same point. Hardy emphasises the extreme antiquity of
the heath: "with the exception of the aged highway, and a still more
aged barrow . . . themselves almost crystallised to natural products
by long continuance — even the trifling irregularities were not caused
by pickaxe, plough or spade, but remained as the very finger-touches
of the last geological age".[77]

Similarly Jung stresses the primeval contents of the unconscious:
"The unconscious psyche is . . . immensely old . . . it moulds the
human species and is just as much a part of it as the human body,
which, though ephemeral in the individual is collectively of immense
age".[78] and: "so far as the collective unconscious contents are concerned, we are dealing with archaic or — I would say — primordial
types, that is, with universal images that have existed since the re-
motest times".[79]

Both authors see that there is conflict between this primeval element and civilisation. Hardy says, "The untameable, Ishmaelitish
thing that Egdon now was, it always had been. Civilisation was its
enemy."[80] At the same time, modern man needed it: "it gave ballast
to a mind adrift on change and harassed by the irrepressible New".[81]
Jung elaborates this more fully:

> Our European ego-consciousness is inclined to swallow up the un-
> conscious, and if this should not prove feasible, we try to suppress
> it. But if we understand anything of the unconscious, we know
> that it cannot be swallowed. We also know that it is dangerous to
> suppress it, because the unconscious is life and this life turns
> against us if suppressed, as happens in neurosis.[82]

Clym illustrates this conflict; he is interested in new ideas, and from the little Hardy tells us about his educational theories, we get the impression that in his efforts to achieve "high thinking" he is prepared to "suppress the unconscious" — his disregard for material advancement suggests this unconcern about man's primitive, instinctive needs. Yet his own instinctive rapport with the heath ultimately saves him from the effects of such an attitude.

Egdon Heath is a Jungian archetype. Jung says that archetypes have their "immediate manifestation in dreams and visions",[83] (this manifestation being "less understandable and more naive than in myths"). Here, finally, we have an exact parallel between Hardy's thought and Jung's: "it was found to be the hitherto unrecognised original of those wild regions of obscurity which are vaguely felt to be compassing us about in midnight dreams of flight and disaster".[84] The phrases "hitherto unrecognised original" indicates that Hardy is quite consciously formulating a new psychological theory 50 years before Jung. It is the formulation of the theory that is new in the novel. As Jung says, the theory finds expression indirectly in myths, dreams and visions, and many writers, especially poets, have embodied the concept in their work. It is Hardy's statement of it as a theory which shows his affinity with Jung. The actual statement of the theory is not of vast importance in *The Return of the Native* itself — it is the imaginative expression of it which creates the feeling of a powerful and timeless relationship between man and nature — but as a further instance of Hardy's recurring ability to give expression to ideas which were further developed in the psychological theories of the twentieth century, it is obviously significant. The frequent recurrence of these similarities in Hardy's works suggests that his exceptionally acute sensibilities which made him aware of the minutest natural objects and the subtleties of human emotion also made him unusually sensitive to new ideas which were just beginning to stir in the consciousnesses of people at the time; his alertness and sensitivity enabled him to use these ideas creatively earlier than most people.

Though the statement of the theory of the collective unconscious is important mainly as evidence of Hardy's tendency to be ahead of his time, the way he used the theory in the novel makes it fundamental to his whole conception and significantly related to his treatment of character in all the novels. Clym's affinity with the heath keeps him in touch with the primitive instinctive aspects of his nature in spite of his conscious drive towards "high thinking", which, if he soared too far, might well detach him completely from them. His modern "disease of the flesh" is shared in an even more extreme form by Knight, Angel and Sue who, with their high evaluation of the intellect, regard anything physical as "gross" and risk the atrophy of their instincts. Their lack of any real sensuous contact with nature makes them even more cut off than Clym; unlike him, they have already committed themselves to one side in "the war between flesh and spirit". Clym, with his intellectual aspirations on the one hand, and on the other, his link, through his ability to merge with the heath, with the "wild regions of obscurity" of his own nature, looks forward more to Jude, who embodies more completely and effectively Hardy's realisation that the "war between flesh and spirit" need not be fought.

8 Knight and Angel: the psychological problems of modern man and woman (II)

Knight in *A Pair of Blue Eyes* (1873) and Angel in *Tess of the d'Urbervilles* (1891), from near the beginning and near the end of Hardy's novel-writing years, are characters which reveal this continuing interest in the psychological difficulties faced by educated, thinking people and his awareness of the disturbance caused by, or perhaps consisting of, a conflict between reason and emotion. These intelligent characters which he creates are, of course, particularly open to the problem which he sees as an essentially modern one. He explores the nature of their disturbance and shows that both Knight and Angel, while being gravely handicapped by their failure adequately to come to terms with their difficulties, are not driven mad by them. In this, they differ from Clym and Sue, who are struggling with some of the same problems but with these two, he considers more extreme personalities who succumb at least temporarily to the pressures and retreat into mental illness. Sue, without the "ballast" that Clym derives from the Heath, is Hardy's most extreme example of this kind of vulnerable personality. Knight and Angel are only moderately neurotic, but through them Hardy explores psychological problems which he felt were beginning to emerge in his day, and which were to become central in the work of the major psychological writers of the next century.

A Pair of Blue Eyes is not a particularly successful novel; it shows Hardy struggling with the conflicting demands of his art, especially of plot and structure. In his treatment of the characters Hardy is similarly uncertain, embarking on complexities and then dropping

them instead of exploring them, or, alternatively, letting a character develop and then awakening to the realisation that it is
psychologically interesting. Yet, in spite of clumsiness and uncertainty, *A Pair of Blue Eyes* shows that as early as 1873 the interests
which were to culminate in *Tess of the d'Urbervilles* and *Jude the
Obscure* were already of central importance to Hardy. In this novel
we have the first tentative examination of "modern" man, his complexities, his inhibitions, his problems in finding a balance between
his instinctive drives and his intellect; we also have, more clearly
than in his two earlier works, Hardy's critical attitude towards contemporary views on sexual matters, especially on the conception of
purity and innocence. Though in this book he says nothing which
could conceivably shock his most conventional reader, he does here
indicate some of those areas that he later examines so searchingly
and outspokenly.

Knight is Hardy's first attempt to look in some detail directly at
the psychological problems of a character. Inevitably, the attempt is
rather a tentative one, and the problems are not faced with his later
boldness. But his treatment of Knight is an early indication of his
interest in the emotional difficulties which he felt confronted modern people and could lead to psychological disturbance. These difficulties he sees as arising primarily from the effects of education
and of the loss of traditional beliefs on people's instinctive, spontaneous responses, especially in sexual relationships. In differing degrees,
Knight, Clym, Angel and Sue, all of them educated and intelligent,
suffer because of their psychological makeup. Angel in particular is
a mature re-examination of the problems first presented in the character of Knight. The situations, the attitudes, the emotional difficulties are all very similar, though their treatment is much less explicit
in the earlier book.

Hardy's conception of Knight shows that the psychological problems he was particularly interested in exploring were inhibitions and
inner conflicts, especially of a sexual nature. Knight is first introduced as an intellectual, a writer who prides himself on taking a
detached, bird's-eye view of humanity, observing the crowds from
his upper window and actually comparing his attitude to that of a
crow. Of women, he says, "I have never formed a deep attachment.
I have never found a woman worth it."[1]

This is Hardy's starting point, the premise on which the character
is based. He does not explore, or even hint at, an earlier history
which might explain his extremely detached attitude to people,

especially women, but instead he uses this given position as a basis for Knight's subsequent behaviour. Similarly, his taste for "untried lips" is presented, at least initially, as an attitude which he has adopted in a fairly arbitrary fashion. Where Hardy's psychological interest reveals itself is the way in which these attitudes are gradually shown to be of the essence of his character, the outward manifestation of his inner, inhibited and self-centred personality. It would not be true to say that Knight displays Hardy's most profound insights into neurotic personalities — none of his psychological foibles is developed enough for this — but the characterisation does show that almost from the beginning of writing novels he was concerned with the kind of personality which has difficulty in adjusting to normal personal relationships. The idea that this difficulty is increased with the development of the intellect is implied in Knight and explicit in Clym, Angel and Sue (there are, of course, characters in Hardy who survive education without disturbance, but these usually carry their learning more lightly). In seeing it as a problem, Hardy is in agreement with Freud's view that, "Our civilisation is, generally speaking, built upon the suppression of instincts".[2] Much of the writing of both Hardy and Freud is concerned with the effects of this. Knight is one example of "the abstinent young savant",[3] who finds it comparatively easy to suppress sexual instincts but nevertheless suffers as a result, and is unfitted because of it for marriage ("complete abstinence in youth is often not the best preparation for marriage"[4]). As Hardy's awareness of human complexity develops, he sees this kind of person as more and more vulnerable, and likely both to suffer and inflict suffering, but even with Knight he is perceiving problems which Freud was to pinpoint some 40 years later. At this stage in his development, Hardy is examining in Knight the effect of "mastering (the sexual instinct) by sublimation, by deflecting the aim to higher cultural aims".[5] But while Freud, in his later work suggests that such behaviour is likely to result in neuroses (as Hardy himself does in his later books), in this novel Hardy shows Knight's "robust intellect which could escape outside the atmosphere of the heart".[6] He suffers, but he is not damaged by his suffering. Hardy does not attempt in this novel to explore the more extreme forms of psychological disturbance.

Nevertheless, there is considerable complexity in Hardy's conception of Knight. The initial qualities that are stressed — the detachment, the lack of any emotional experience, the patronising attitude to Stephen and Elfride make a convincing foundation for the personality he is to develop. Knight's sense of effortless superiority over Elfride shows in his treatment of her novel, in the games of chess, in the discussion of the relative merits of music, books and earrings. The contemptuous attitude to women generally emerges very strongly; not only has he never found a woman "worth" "a deep attachment",[7] but he has "never met a woman who loves music as do a dozen or ten men I know".[8] This makes more plausible his apparently arbitrary "taste for untried lips". Hardy shows as he develops the character that the superiority is more precarious than it seemed at first, that he wants the woman to be "bungling" in her first kiss so that his own inexperience and incompetence will not be shown up. When he learns of Elfride's previous lover, it is "as much wounded pride as sorrow" that he feels: "How childishly blind he must have seemed to this mere girl".[9] Hardy is suggesting a deeper, less conscious reason for Knight's sexual abstinence; there is a certain fear hinted at from time to time: "he almost trembled at the possible result of this new force among the nicely adjusted ones of his ordinary life".[10] After Elfride's partial confession, Hardy makes this point more explicitly, and thus emphasises that the apparently arbitrary insistence on total inexperience is an essential part of the personality: "Perhaps Knight was not shaped by Nature for a marrying man. Perhaps his lifelong constraint towards women, which he had attributed to accident, was not chance after all, but the natural result of instinctive acts so minute as to be undiscernible even by himself".[11] This indication of Hardy's awareness of the significance of unconscious motives is an interesting pointer to the underlying complexity of his conception of Knight, even if this complexity does not emerge adequately in the novel.

Hardy sees Knight's attempts to make Elfride play the role of his ideal woman — totally innocent and inexperienced — as the disastrous idealising which in his view tended to endanger most sexual relationships. We see this theme running through many of his major novels, and made the central element in *The Well-Beloved*. The affinities with the Jungian concept of the "anima" are apparent here too: "It belongs to the nature of the anima that a man can project his image upon the woman with whom he is in love — he will then attribute to her qualities quite different from those she really has".[12] Hardy's creation of a "bachelor by nature" who at the age of 32 had kissed only his mother and sister fills the role of idealiser very plausibly. Hardy stresses the unreality of his love: he did not fall in love with her by looking at her but "by ceasing to do so . . . . Not till they had parted and she had become sublimated in his memory, could he be said to have ever attentively regarded her . . . he appeared to himself to have fallen in love with her soul."[13] This is a simplified version of the Jungian theory; it is significant that a possible translation of "anima" is "soul". Interesting too is Hardy's use of "sublimated", not in the Freudian sense of transferring erotic drives to cultural or intellectual ends, but suggesting an elevating and refining of the loved one (and therefore "attributing to her qualities quite different from those she really has"); Knight's love for Elfride is for a disembodied being with no previous existence. He delights in seeing her in rather the same way as Sue Bridehead sees herself, as an ethereal, Shelleyan being, completely free from the "grossness" of a body. This idealising attitude makes him reject her spontaneous advances to him; when she rushes into his arms after the rescue on the cliff, he does not kiss her because, "Knight's peculiarity of nature was such that it would not allow him to take advantage of the unguarded and passionate avowal she had tacitly made".[14] When, much later, he at last kisses her, he does it "with the carefulness of a fruiterer touching a bunch of grapes so as not to disturb the bloom".[15] This extreme restraint is not the expression of a wholly gentle and tender nature. Freud points out that, "the occurrence of . . . excessive tenderness is very common in the neuroses . . . . We now thoroughly understand the origin of this tenderness. It occurs whenever, besides the predominant tenderness, there exists a contrary but unconscious stream of hostility . . . the hostility is then cried down by an excessive increase of tenderness which is expressed as anxiety".[16] Hardy certainly gives glimpses of such crosscurrents in Knight. There is a hint of sadism in, "he keenly enjoyed sparring with the palpitating, mobile creature, whose excitable nature made any such thing a species of cruelty".[17] His enjoyment of the games of chess is of the same kind, though Hardy here puts it down to "his inexperience of the nature of young women".[18] Hardy's characteristic way of discovering, as he creates, layers of complexity and contradiction shows very clearly here. Knight's later stern rejection of Elfride after she has confessed about Stephen makes these conflicting impulses more evident. He is "stern", "sharp" and "peremptory" with her; the extreme tenderness has been replaced by "the keen scrutiny and logical power which Knight, now that his suspicions were awakened, would sooner or later be bound to use against her".[19] The underlying hostility which reveals itself in apparently trivial ways earlier, now comes to the surface. This shows an understanding of the springs of contradictory behaviour which is very subtle for such an early novel, not otherwise markedly conspicuous for its subtlety.

At the end, Hardy emphasises again the inhibitions and capacity for sublimation which were shown as the controlling elements in Knight's character from the beginning. Even before he has more than a suspicion about Elfride's past, he is beginning to turn again to his former mode of life and feeling: "Though Knight's heart had so greatly mastered him, the mastery was not so complete as to be easily maintained in the face of moderate intellectual revival".[20] Thus, in spite of a good deal of pain, Knight is able to carry out the rejection of Elfride without real damage to himself: "Lengthening time . . . strengthened the mental ability to reason her down".[21]

Hardy's conception of Knight shows an awareness of psychological complexities, an understanding of the nature of emotionally limited but intellectually powerful personalities who are able for this reason to respond to the demands of the superego without psychological damage (apart, that is, from the damage already present; the attenuated nature of Knight's emotions indicates that Hardy's starting point is an already damaged, or at least psychologically limited, personality). The use of these Freudian terms to sum up the central characteristics of such an early character is appropriate because Hardy is here anticipating Freud's diagnosis of some of the problems facing "civilised" man. This is not to suggest that the correspondence with Freud necessarily gives extra validity to Hardy's perceptions, but we can see from this parallel that even Hardy's very early thoughts about human nature, and in particular about the psychological problems of his contemporaries, were developing on very similar lines to those expressed by Freud some 50 years later. The pioneering quality he shows in *A Pair of Blue Eyes* makes Knight a forerunner of later complex characters in the novels. He is less interesting than the later characters because his inner conflict is less intense and less fully explored.

These perceptions underlie Hardy's understanding of the ways in which personality may change. He is often considered to be primarily a master of the stable, static character; it is certainly true that he depicts such characters as Gabriel Oak and Giles Winterbourne with great power and sensitivity. But it is also true to say that throughout his writing of fiction he was deeply concerned with the kinds of change that take place within a character. In *A Pair of Blue*

Eyes he shows some very marked and wholly convincing changes in Knight. (There are some aspects of Knight which are not entirely plausible, but these are unrelated to the changes in his personality). His gradual transformation from the cool, detached intellectual to the tender but still inhibited lover is perceptively treated; the jealous rejection of Elfride, shown to have both conscious and unconscious motivations which are integral to his character, is a partial reversion to his original condition, but he does not regain his unemotional detachment. At first the conflict is violent and he is uncertain "whether he should rush back again upon the current of an irresistible emotion or whether he could sufficiently conquer himself".[22] By showing him torn between conflicting impulses Hardy underlines the change from his original detached stance. The change is not a major one. Knight's efforts to suppress his sexual instincts are characteristic and habitual, as his excessive restraint in expressing his love has shown. Yet Stephen considers him "a changed man" and this view is endorsed by Knight's resurgence of feeling when he realised that his rival was "only Stephen" and "he allowed the fever of his excitement to rage uncontrolled".[23] This is the first time that Hardy has indicated any real lack of control and it is appropriate that it should come after the prolonged attempt to suppress all erotic feelings. It is also interesting that his "Narcissistic self-regard", which makes him insist on being "a first-comer" with a woman, emerges again here. Since it is "only Stephen", whom he despises, who was Elfride's previous lover, he no longer fears unflattering comparison and so no longer needs to suppress his sexual feelings for her.

Though Hardy's conception of Knight shows such a sensitive awareness, his methods of presenting him are not always equally subtle. As I have suggested, his insistence on being a "first-comer" seems at first an arbitrary posture, and is only presented as an integral part of his character late in the book. This is further evidence that Hardy was gradually enlarging his understanding of Knight's personality as he went along. In the later novels the developments are presented more coherently, because he is exploiting his awareness that human nature is not wholly explicable and making this an essential element in his presentation; with Eustacia, Grace and Sue he is exploring the possibilities of this way of seeing character in a manner which leads straight to Lawrence's experiments in characterisation. But here with Knight the idea is not used in this way and the explanatory passages seem merely to occur rather late in the day.

The descriptions of outward behaviour as a means of revealing inner complexities are not markedly successful in Hardy's treatment of Knight, but there is one episode which is extremely effective in this way. This is Knight's purchase of the earrings. His sense of uncertainty and embarrassment are beautifully conveyed, his ashamed refusal to return to the same shop a third time, and his final recovery of his habitual sense of superiority because he feels he has "the profoundly experienced eye of an appraiser" are sensitively realised and add another dimension to our understanding of him.

The episode on the cliff is obviously a crucial one as a turning-point in the relationship of Knight and Elfride. It is a curious passage, epitomising many of the strengths and weaknesses of the book, with its elaboration of topographical and geological detail, its somewhat ludicrous practical complications of the rescue, combined with a powerful picture of man's insignificance in relation to Nature and Time. As far as the character of Knight is concerned, the episode is both penetrating and disappointing. His meditation on evolution while suspended over the abyss is surprising yet authentic and characteristic. The scene illustrates in a striking way that loss of spontaneous feeling which Hardy usually sees as a danger for those who develop the mind out of proportion to the body and the emotions. But the very qualities which make Knight's emotional life so inadequate are in this situation a source of strength, just as they are when he has destroyed his relationship with Elfride. The pedantry of his thoughts when facing imminent death gives him a strength and detachment that prevents panic. At the same time, the descriptions of his physical sensations are very vivid and the suspense, though long drawn out, is effectively maintained.

When Knight comes to face the apparent certainty of death, instead of seizing this as an opportunity for exploring his consciousness under stress, Hardy ostentatiously withdraws: "Into the shadowy depth of these speculations we will not follow him".[24] The method of making this point is clumsy, but it does throw stress on the importance of the unconscious, and in this it is consistent with his practice in the later novels. Suggestions of an undefined "shadowy depth" take us further imaginatively into Knight's state as he hangs on the cliff-face than an attempt to treat it analytically. Hardy ironically highlights this with Knight's platitudes about death which he offers to Stephen and Elfride in the vault. The platitudes are perfectly in keeping with Knight's conscious, intellectual modes of thinking and they presumably spring from the experience on the cliff, but they convey nothing of its intensity. There is a further layer of irony in that Knight's remarks are given some stature by their juxtaposition with the embarrassed monosyllables of Elfride and Stephen who are involved in a little matter of deception, in contrast to Knight's preoccupation with life and death.

In this novel, the comments both on technique and on character and situations often have the rather obvious, stark quality seen in the refusal to examine Knight's consciousness. Explanatory passages that probe deeper into the characters' motives than they can see themselves are combined with others which are more detached and critical, designed to reveal the author's own view of the character's attitudes. Of Knight's attempt to bring "understanding" into passion, he says unequivocally, "It may as well be left out".[25] This is a crude and dismissive way of treating a theme which was to occupy Hardy for the rest of his novel-writing years. He was to grasp it later with a complexity not realised here. But it is not surprising to find him already acknowledging the greater strength of the instinctive drives in comparison with the intellectual ones; in so doing, he gives us another example of the affinity of his thinking with Freud's.

On Knight's reactions to Elfride's confession, Hardy comments that "it is a melancholy thought that men who at first will not allow the verdict of perfection they pronounce upon their sweethearts or wives to be disturbed by God's own testimony to the contrary, will, once suspecting their purity, morally hang them upon evidence they would be ashamed to admit in judging a dog".[26] Similarly, as a further comment on Knight's reaction to his new image of Elfride, Hardy says, "With him, truth seemed too clear and pure an abstraction to be so hopelessly churned in with error as practical persons find it. Having now found himself mistaken in supposing Elfride to be peerless, nothing on earth could make him believe she was not so very bad after all".[27] These generalisations are ponderous, but they are an important element in Hardy's portrayal of Knight, because they show an awareness of the exact nature of his psychological weaknesses, which make him unable to have satisfying human relationships. His critical attitude towards Knight's excessive and idealistic demands anticipates the views of twentieth-century psychologists. When Elfride says, "where the lover or husband is not fastidious or refined and of a deep nature things seem to go on better, I fancy",[28] she is endorsing the points made by Hardy in his own voice in that novel. She is also defining the basic traits of a type of character whose complexities were to become a central feature in the later novels. Widow Edlin's view of the relationships of the central character in *Jude the Obscure* is much the same.

The character of Knight is an important landmark in Hardy's development as a novelist. In it we see a growing awareness of the subtleties, complexities, mixed motives and unconscious drives of human beings, and also some indication of a realisation of the kinds of qualities which make for mental health. In the paragraph added to the Preface to *A Pair of Blue Eyes* in 1912, Hardy says, "it exhibits the romantic stage of an idea which was further developed in a later book". This clearly refers to *Tess of the d'Urbervilles*. Plot and theme are very close, and there are many parallels between the characters of Knight and Angel. Obviously, *Tess* is much more outspoken; by taking the theme of virginity (which, of course, is what is coyly hidden behind the obsession with "untried lips" in *A Pair of Blue Eyes*) Hardy is able to be much more challenging to conventional views. Minor details of the plot recur; both heroines fear to confess their pasts, offer substitute confessions (Elfride about her age, Tess about her ancestry) and when the truth is discovered, both are rejected. The parallels between the characters of Knight and Angel are particularly interesting. They are both patronising, idealising, very tender and very hard. They both reject the women they love, for basically identical reasons. The treatment of Angel, though it has its flaws, is more searching, the origins of his psychological development are given some weight, and his conflicting feelings are much more intense than Knight's. A study of Angel will show to what extent Hardy has developed in his treatment of the psychological problems of this particular type of personality in twenty years of novel writing.

Hardy's extraordinary achievement in the creation of Tess, with her warmth, vitality and attractiveness, has been at least partly the reason for a feeling that the other characters in the novel are markedly inferior conceptions. Some contemporary reviewers often simply disliked them as unpleasant human beings, others regarded them as clumsy or incredible. William Watson's review was exceptional in its recognition of the complexity of Angel:

Perhaps the most subtly drawn, as it is in some ways the most perplexing and difficult character, is that of Angel Clare, with his half-ethereal passion for Tess . . . many readers . . . will be

conscious of . . . anger against this intellectual, virtuous and
unfortunate young man . . . . It is at this point (the confession),
however, that the masterliness of the conception and its imaginative validity are most conclusively manifest, for it is here
that we perceive Clare's nature to be consistently inconsistent
throughout.[29]

Obviously, Angel cannot be so developed as to compete with Tess
for our attention; the essence of *Tess of the d'Urbervilles* lies in its
feeling for and attitude to the heroine. Inevitably, some aspects of
Angel are dealt with perfunctorily; it is a weakness in the structure of
the book that something as crucial as his change of heart in Brazil
should be dealt with so cursorily. Nevertheless, the character of
Angel survives as a subtle and complex conception. Hardy described
him as "cruel, but not intentionally so. It was the fault of his fastidious temperament. Had he not been a man of great subtilty [sic] of
mind, he would have followed his brothers into the church. But he
had intellectual freedom in the dairy. A subtle, poetical man, he
preferred that life to the conventional life."[30]
      Hardy, unlike some of his readers, is not so engrossed with Tess
that he cannot view Angel imaginatively and sympathetically.
He shows Angel as torn between opposite extremes from the start.
Even on the slight occasion when he is first introduced, the possibility of conflict is raised. He is contrasted with his brothers in his
"uncribbed, uncabined, aspect",[31] and in his dancing with the village girls, yet he runs after them in order to discuss "A Counter-
blast to Agnosticism". We next see him shocking his father about
a book, and refusing to enter the Church. However, at this stage it
looks as if the conflict is largely external, and as if taking up farming
has solved his intellectual and emotional problems: "he became
wonderfully free from the chronic melancholy which is taking hold
of the civilised races with the decline in a belief in a beneficent
Power".[32] In introducing Angel, Hardy has emphasised his escape from the pressures of family and the Church; but he has
called him Angel and given him a harp; he shows him fluctuating
between the extremes of rigid puritanism and relaxed unconventionality.
      Hardy makes his uncertainty very real by giving numerous little
examples of his conflicting state of mind. His defiantly "unsab-
batarian" clothes are typical of "a dogmatic parson's son",[33] osten-

tatiously abandoning his conventional upbringing. Similarly, the episode of Mrs Crick's black puddings and "drop of pretty tipple", is used to show that the conflict between the opposing pulls is not resolved. When the gift of puddings is given to the poor and the "pretty tipple" locked away in the medicine cupboard, he feels that his parents are "right in their practice if wrong in their want of sentiment",[34] "though he could not accept his parent's narrow dogma, he revered his practice".[35]

Hardy shows that Angel's attitude to life is based on unresolved conflicting views. Intellectually, he has rejected his father's dogma, but emotionally he is torn between austerity and sensuousness, rigidity and spontaneity. As long as this remains a more or less abstract position, it seems a manageable one. But when strong feelings begin to be involved, the conflict ceases to be abstract and theoretical, and the whole personality is exposed to opposing forces.

He feels that returning from home to Talbothays is "like throwing off splints and bandages",[36] but Hardy shows that his mental and emotional state is more complicated than Angel imagines. When carrying Tess across the flooded lane, he nearly kisses her but thinks, "suspension at this point was desirable now".[37] A little later, he does act on impulse and embraces her; but though the emphasis is on their ecstatic acceptance of each other, Hardy reminds us that this simple, spontaneous act of Angel's is in opposition to his normal mode of behaviour: "Resolutions, reticences, prudences, fears fell back like a defeated battalion".[38] Even now he does not kiss her, and though she has responded to him with "an ecstatic cry", he says, "Forgive me . . . I ought to have asked — I did not know what I was doing".[39] Hardy shows that he can act on impulse when deeply moved (unlike Knight) but the inhibitions which "fell back like defeated battalions" have not been annihilated and he is conscious that "his heart had outrun his judgement".[40] Even in the first flow of acknowledged love, he is "disquieted" by the "novelty, unpremeditation, mastery of circumstance".[41] Though "he was driven towards her by every heave of his pulse",[42] Angel was "a man with a conscience",[43] and he decides to leave the dairy temporarily while he weighs questions of career, money and respectability against love. In this we see his attempts (similar to Knight's) to bring in reason to deal with instinctive drives. At this stage, it only serves to make spontaneity and sensuousness seem all the more attractive. When Hardy speaks of "the aesthetic, pagan sensuous pleasure in natural life and lush womanhood which . . . Angel had lately been experiencing",[44] it perhaps seems a rather exaggerated account of events which include a single passionate embrace, but, seen from Angel's point of view, in the light of his customary restraint, the feeling of sensuous, pagan lushness is understandable. In contrast with his brothers, he had indeed seen "life . . . felt the great passionate pulse of existence".[45]

Thus, up to his return from Emminster, Hardy has continually kept before us the two central conflicting impulses in Angel's character: his capacity for intense feeling and his fear of it getting out of control. Hardy makes the dichotomy quite explicit; the underlying conception is similar to that developed by Freud in *The Ego and the Id*. Angel is shown from the beginning to be the kind of personality which has a demanding superego (in this resembling Knight) while at the same time having powerful instinctive drives (unlike Knight). Having decided that he may allow himself to think of Tess as a possible future wife, Angel, his superego temporarily placated, is able to respond to her in a markedly sensuous, physical way, impulsively embracing her at a moment "when the most spiritual beauty bespeaks itself flesh; and sex takes the outside place in the presentation".[46] He holds her "still more greedily close", sucks the cream off her fingers and "passionately clasps her in forgetfulness of his curdy hands".[47] Unlike Knight, who fell in love with Elfride's soul, Angel loves Tess's "soul, her heart, her substance".[48] Hardy creates an impression of Angel transformed by love into a sensuous, impulsive being, far more capable of feeling intensely than Knight, but he soon qualifies this impression: "he was in truth more spiritual than animal; he had himself well in hand and was singularly free from grossness . . . it was a fastidious emotion which could guard the loved one against his very self".[49] The final phrase of this passage is echoed in Angel's anxiety about the danger Tess exposes herself to when she comes in her nightie to waken him in the mornings; so he presumably is not entirely "free from grossness" or he would not feel she ran a risk through being visible to him through a crack in the door.

In these ways, Hardy creates a sense of genuine and profound conflict. This makes Angel more interesting than Knight, whose sufferings about Elfride's past, at least in the earlier parts, seem superimposed and unnecessary; the later, valid psychological explanation hardly serves to erase the impression first created. With Angel, the conflict is seen to be fundamental to his nature from the start and therefore inescapable. It makes his character psychologically more interesting and truer to the springs of human behaviour.

One factor in Angel's makeup, which makes his response to Tess's confession inevitably one of rejection, is his strongly idealising conception of her. In his interesting and sympathetic analysis of Angel, Arnold Kettle says that "he is in a philosophical sense an idealist".[50] This is certainly true, but I think we can add that the term is also applicable in a psychological sense. Hardy says that he loved her "fancifully and ideally",[51] that to him "she was no longer a milkmaid but a visionary essence of woman — a whole sex condensed into one typical form. He called her Artemis, Demeter".[52] Again, as with Knight, we see the close resemblance to Jung. She is his anima: "A collective image of woman exists in a man's unconscious, with the help of which he apprehends the nature of woman".[53] According to Jung, so long as men are unconscious of their "anima", they project this image on to various women they are attracted to, with disastrous results since they are projecting their own picture on to some one who is very different: "Every mother and every beloved is forced to become the carrier and embodiment of this omnipresent and ageless image which corresponds to the deepest reality in man".[54] Jung stresses the importance of recognising that the 'anima' is subjective. Only by doing this does it become possible for a man to love a woman objectively and not for the qualities he superimposes on her. Neither Hardy nor Jung thought this happened very often; Jude perhaps achieves it, perhaps Gabriel Oak. In *The Well-Beloved*, Pierston, of course, epitomises the man unconscious of his anima. Jung sums up: "Since the image is unconscious, it is always unconsciously projected on to the person of the beloved, and is one of the chief reasons for passionate attraction or aversion".[55]

The reasons Angel gives for rejecting Tess are quite explicit; they are a direct admission that he has been idealising her in very much the way Jung describes and that the image of untouched purity which he had been superimposing on her had been shattered: "You were one person: now you are another".[56] "The woman I have been loving is not you",[57] "She was another woman than the one who had excited his desire".[58]

Hardy raises the possibility of an eventual reconciliation in Jungian terms: "With these natures corporeal presence is something less than corporeal absence; the latter creating an ideal presence that conveniently drops the defects of the real".[59] Characters of this

kind always interested Hardy; Angel, Knight, Clym to a lesser
degree, and Pierston as the most extreme example, all exemplify
Jung's theories. This does not, of course, imply that until Jung,
Hardy was the first person to suggest the existence of such a psychological phenomenon. Jung, in fact, took many of his examples from
literature. What it does show is that Hardy was exploring the same
aspects of human nature as the psychological writers of the twentieth century. Whether or not we accept Jung's theory of the "anima",
we have to admit that Angel is an excellent illustration of the theory
which was central to Jung's thought and plays a very important part
in Hardy's.

There is also an interesting parallel to Angel's idealising attitude
to Tess discussed at considerable length by Freud. It is a short story
by the Danish novelist Jensen, called "Gradiva", in which the hero,
like Angel, calls his beloved by a classical name, but, going further in
his delusion than Angel, actually believes that she is a girl who lived
at Pompeii. But he is luckier than Angel in that his girl understands
the nature of his malady, interprets his dreams and is eventually able
to persuade him to face actuality and to recognise herself as the real
flesh-and-blood creature he loves. The two stories are comparable
in that both heroes have a deluded view of their loved ones, and try
to distance them from reality, at the same time being very possessive
in their attitudes: "He could almost have wished that the apparition
might remain visible to his eyes alone and elude the perception of
others: then, in spite of everything, he could look on her as his own
exclusive property".[60] This parallels Angel's horrified rejection of
Tess when he finds she is not "his own exclusive property". The
stories are comparable in their use of dreams, though in "Gradiva"
these are more prominent. While commenting on this, Freud sum-
marises his theories on dreams as giving us "our best access to a
knowledge of the unconscious part of the mind".[61]

He states that "the dreamer knows in his unconscious thoughts all
that he has forgotten in his conscious ones, and that in the former he
judges correctly what in the latter he understood in a delusion".[62]
This corresponds to Angel's expression of his love for Tess when he is
sleepwalking; the love, rigorously repressed in his waking thoughts,
is allowed to emerge in the dream; but in the dream he sees her as
dead because at this stage, even in a dream, he cannot contemplate
the possibility of accepting her as she really is. The dream "censor" is
at work, allowing through only as much reality as he can bear. He
can contemplate the idea that his idealised symbol of rustic inno-

cence is dead, but not that his ideal could be replaced by a real, living woman. The whole conception of Angel up to this point tallies with Freud's commentary, on "Gradiva": "Every disorder analogous to Hanold's [the hero] delusion, what in scientific terms we are in the habit of calling "psychoneuroses", has as its precondition the repression of a portion of the instinctual life, or, as we can safely say, of the sexual instinct".[63] Hardy expresses very similar ideas in scattered analytical passages: asleep he uttered only "words of endearment severely withheld in his waking hours";[64] awake, "he had himself well in hand", "his small compressed mouth indexing his powers of self-control".[65]

The major point of contrast between the two stories is also interesting. In "Gradiva", the hero is helped by the intelligent, educated heroine to analyse his dreams and gradually to come back to reality. Hardy stresses the point that Angel in his conscious mind knows nothing of his sleepwalking behaviour. But Tess, unlike the girl in "Gradiva", will not tell him about the dream because she feels it would be taking advantage of him "when reason slept".[66] This is completely in keeping with her character, with her self-abnegation, her refusal to demand that anyone should be other than he is (the exact opposite of Angel in this) or to put any kind of pressure on anyone, and one certainly cannot imagine her playing amateur psychiatrist to Angel. Nevertheless, she is aware of what is wrong with him, and tells him so clearly: "It is in your own mind what you are angry at, Angel: it is not in me",[67] so that for the reader there is an anguished sense of missed possibilities here (just as there is when she will not work on his feelings by making a scene at the moment of parting). In these ways the sleepwalking episode effectively deepens our insight into Angel. Most critics have felt this scene to be one of the weakest in *Tess*, largely on the grounds of implausibility; but it corresponds to the findings of psychoanalysis and it throws important and revealing light on the two characters. The fact that the whole event is told from Tess's point of view heightens the tension and focuses our attention on the external and physical, but the underlying psychological truth prevents it from becoming merely a melodramatic episode.

Hardy makes Angel's rejection of Tess psychologically convincing by relating it to his idealisation of her. First, he shows him neurotically withdrawing from reality by refusing to admit that she is the woman he loved. Then the fact that he despises her begins to emerge, but again this new emotion is closely related to his previous attitude to her; though he disguised it from himself, he has in fact treated her in a slightly contemptuous, patronising way throughout their relationship. When she expresses an embittered view of life, he thinks that "such a daughter of the soil could only have caught up the sentiment by rote".[68] He treats all references to her "experiences" with gentle satirical humour, and tells her, "you are a child to me",[69] and thinks she needs to be improved by contact with him before she is fit to meet his parents. The inconsistency of then attacking her for being "childish" is deliberately placed by Hardy and wholly credible; even the brutality of, "you are an unapprehending peasant woman",[70] is not altogether surprising. He now admits that he thinks he has married beneath him: "I thought that by giving up all ambition to win a wife with social standing, with fortune, with knowledge of the world, I should secure rustic innocence",[71] but this was true of his attitude from the start. With the loss of what, as it turns out, he considered to be her one virtue, the way is open for total contempt. Angel's love has clearly been of the narcissistic, self-regarding kind; Freud refers to "the narcissistic rejection of women by men, which is so mixed up with despising them".[72] This kind of male love, according to Freud, also displays "marked sexual overvaluation".[73] Hardy shows clearly these opposing tendencies, to contempt and to overvaluation, in Angel's development. Freud offers an explanation of these contradictory tendencies:

> If the sensual impulses are more or less effectively repressed or set aside, the illusion is produced that the object has come to be sensually loved on account of its spiritual merits, whereas, on the contrary, these merits may really only have been lent to it by its sensual charm.
>
> The tendency which falsifies judgement in this respect is that of idealisation . . . the object is treated in the same way as our own ego, when we are in love a considerable amount of narcissistic libido overflows on to the object. It is even obvious in many forms of love-choice that the object serves as a substitute for some unattained ego idea of our own. We love it on account of the perfections which we have striven to reach for our own ego, and which we should now like to procure in this roundabout way as a means of satisfying our narcissism.[74]

Many aspects of Angel's personality correspond quite closely to this. The repressed sexual impulses, the idealisation and falsification in valuing Tess for the one attribute which she has lost are all there in Hardy's account of him. That he feels guilt over his earlier liaison is suggested by his fear of Tess rejecting him if he tells her before the wedding, and in the way he minimises the whole affair, though Hardy's earlier reference to it had suggested it was a matter of some importance to him; given Angel's habitual restraint and self-control, it is hardly something he would have entered into lightly. The "narcissistic self-regard" also shows itself in the way he thinks that he will "secure rustic innocence" for himself by marrying Tess — significantly, an abstract idea, not a human being. Thus, Hardy seems to have two motives in giving Angel his previous affair. First, it gives a psychological basis for his idealisation and rejection of Tess; because of his guilt feelings he needs her to be the embodiment of the purity which he feels he has lost; when he finds he cannot "procure (it) in this roundabout way", his rejection of her is inevitable, since she has lost all value for him.

Hardy's second motive in making Angel's situation an exact parallel to Tess's is social rather than psychological. By this means, he highlights the injustice of society's attitude to women. That an intelligent and sensitive man such as Angel should not merely fail to make the connection but even deny that there is one is a stumbling block to most twentieth-century readers' credulity, even when the psychological factors are taken into account. But it was more credible at the time and that attitude which Hardy was attacking was embedded in the law; though a man could divorce his wife for adultery, a woman could not divorce her husband for it. In maintaining that his own affair is utterly insignificant, while Tess's is an insurmountable moral outrage, Angel is merely following an accepted pattern of behaviour. Even Schopenhauer wrote in "The Metaphysics of Love":

a man is always desiring other women, while a woman always clings to one man, for nature compels her intuitively and unconsciously to take care of the supporter and protector of future offspring. For this reason, conjugal fidelity is artificial with the man but natural to a woman. Hence, a woman's infidelity, looked at objectively on account of the consequence, and subjectively on account of its unnaturalness is much more unpardonable than a man's.[75]

Von Hartmann in *The Philosophy of the Unconscious* (1884) says in a milder way much the same thing. These were both "advanced thinkers", so it is perfectly plausible that an "advanced and well-meaning, young man ... was yet the slave to custom and conventionality when surprised back into his early teaching".[76] Angel's attempts to justify the rejection are largely concerned with "what people will think". He is even conventional when defying convention (as with his Sunday clothes); his offer to Izz is seen by him as a spurning of "the pedagogic rod of convention" and "wrong-doing in the eyes of civilisation".[77] This inconsistent behaviour is absolutely characteristic. He imagines that his stereotyped gesture of bitterness is unconventional. The episode also highlights his self-absorbed nature, especially when he tells Izz to forget "his momentary levity". But Hardy does not intend Angel to be totally wrapped up in himself, he is sensitive and imaginative too; Izz's reply: "Never, never! O, it was no levity to me",[78] strikes home.

Angel's method of attempting to grapple with his problem is through purely intellectual means: "He was becoming ill with thinking; eaten out with thinking; withered by thinking".[79] He fiercely represses all instinctive impulses; Tess was "appalled by the determination revealed in the depths of this gentle being she had married — the will to subdue the grosser to the subtler emotion, the substance to the conception, the will to the spirit".[80] His final decision is based on his determination to exclude everything except reason: "he knew that if any intention of his, concluded overnight, did not vanish in the light of morning, it stood on a basis approximating to pure reason ... Clare hesitated no longer".[81] Hardy emphasises the "hard logical deposit" in Angel over and over again. He shows how strong the mind and the will must be to conquer the instinctive feelings which were revealed in the sleepwalking scene. Freud makes, abstractly, the same point: "the passions of instinct are stronger than reasoned interests. Culture has to call up every possible reinforcement ... hence the restrictions on sexual life".[82] Angel is represented as having been conditioned to repression by his background and by the things which enabled him to escape from it — his intellectual development and over-reliance on it. Here thought is seen as "a disease of the flesh" in a rather different sense from that intended in *The Return of the Native*. His inadequacy to cope with emotional problems is dramatically embodied in the story; Hardy has gone far beyond the simple "it may as well be left out" of *A Pair of Blue Eyes*.

In these ways Hardy makes Angel's rejection of Tess an act in keeping with the not wholly unsympathetic personality he has created up to that point. Though after her confession, the emphasis is mainly on his rigidity, hardness and obduracy, he retains his sensitivity and continues to be torn between reason and emotion. His attempts to act solely by reason are presented in such a way that we are almost as conscious of his suffering as of Tess's. The "fury of fastidiousness",[83] "the incoherent multitude of emotions",[84] the exclamation, "She is spotless"[85] to his mother, all contribute to our impression that however hard he tries to exclude emotion from his reactions, he will be unable to do so. He comes across as a "suffering, erring human being" even in those scenes where our sympathies are wholly with Tess. This is a point in the book where for many readers Angel becomes merely "an insufferable prig";[86] for them, Hardy has been so successful in making them identify with Tess that they become antagonistic to Angel and so miss some of the subtlety and feeling with which Hardy has presented him.

Hardy's essential quality as a novelist emerges if we recognise the sensitivity of his treatment of Angel here. The main theme is, of course, Tess's suffering and undeviating love and loyalty in which he makes us feel intimately involved; but for a full apprehension of Hardy's art, we must be aware of the minor theme too and capable of entering into Angel's experience, even though this demands of us an emotional response to him which is in direct contradiction to the feelings evoked by our sympathy for Tess. Hardy is on the one hand challenging the conventional views of his contemporary readers, in asking them to accept Tess's "purity", and on the other, suggesting that this acceptance does not justify condemnation of Angel who, for psychological and social reasons, cannot grasp this idea. This breadth of sympathy is particularly striking in this novel, since the whole story is a plea for a change in just those attitudes held by Angel.

For the rest of the book Angel is treated hastily and perfunctorily. His change of heart in Brazil is perfectly plausible and adequately prepared for earlier; the widening of his horizons through his discussions with his travelled and enlightened acquaintance, followed by the emotional impact of the man's death gives sufficient grounds for such a change. Angel had always *wanted* to be unconventional; now he feels he has an intellectual basis for being so. But the episode is unsatisfactory, because it is simply summarised and our emotional involvement is elsewhere — with Tess. Once he has returned to

England, he is significant mainly because he is necessary to Tess's fulfilment. It is sometimes questioned whether having jibbed at an illegitimate baby, he would be prepared to disregard Tess's spell as a "kept woman" and the committing of murder. It is in fact credible enough that having once overcome his "block", he can accept almost anything. The same tendency to act in direct opposition to views that he previously held adamantly is shown in the invitation to Izz. The situation now, with Tess's capture imminent, makes a swing back to his previous position impossible, but Tess foresees that, if there were a future for them, this could happen. The awareness, on the part of the reader and of the characters of the transitoriness of their renewed love makes the final section of the novel profoundly moving. The suffering which has preceded the scene in the woods has been so intense that the reader wants avidly to believe in the moment of happiness. The imagination, tenderness and compassion with which the brief honeymoon in the empty house is presented persuades us into accepting this momentary wish-fulfilment. Our awareness of its inevitable end reinforces our "willing suspension of disbelief" because it corresponds to our awareness of the brevity of such ecstatic peak experiences. Hardy has created a situation in which wish-fulfilment is realistic. Its ephemeral nature is stressed not only by the harsh society waiting to pounce on them, but also by the features of Angel's character that are permanent, however much of "a changed man" he is in some ways. His refusal to comfort Tess at this moment with hopes of life beyond the grave recalls the "hard logical deposit" in his makeup and reawakens our ambivalent attitude to him.

Hardy's chief method of presenting Angel is through analysis and commentary, which give insight into his psychological complexities without allowing them to dominate the book, which might result from a more dramatic approach; the various other techniques serve mainly to give body to Hardy's conception. One of these is the use of contrast, always a prominent feature of Hardy's novels. The main contrast, of course, is with Alec, not only between a sensual, self-indulgent man and an ascetic, self-controlled one, but between a devil with a pitchfork and an angel with a harp. The symbolism is excessively obvious but treated with irony and not much insisted on (Angel is called "misnamed" at one point). It is interesting that the name Angel was actually used in Dorset and there is a memorial to an Angel at Stinsford Church. Knowing this makes the name a little more ordinary and somewhat reduces the symbolic connotations.

This is fortunate since a stark opposition between Angel on the one hand and Alec as Satan on the other would be utterly misleading, weakening all the complexities and ironies created in the novel. The various other contrasts are also designed to show the possibilities of varying angles of vision; if in contrast to Alec, Angel seems priggish, in contrast to his brothers he seems spontaneous and relaxed.

The use of dramatic, visually conceived scenes is important with a character like Angel, who tends to reduce his experiences to abstraction, but as he is not the central character, there are not many scenes which focus entirely on him. Our first picture of him as he tosses off his pack and goes to dance with the village girls makes him immediately attractive and points to his spontaneity which will later be in conflict with opposing tendencies. When he carries the milkmaids across the flooded lane, we get a similar picture of attractiveness and vitality; these impressions of these aspects of his nature are very important in preventing his inflexibility from seeming too easy and too dominant. In most of the scenes with Tess, the setting and all the other elements are seen in relation to her, and Angel is subordinate; this happens when she listens in the garden to his harp and when they walk in the fields on Sunday evenings. But there is one scene where they both have equal prominence; this is the evening of the confession when the two figures are seen "walking very slowly, without converse, one behind the other, as in a funeral procession", and later "again in the same field, progressing just as slowly".[87] Here the image of shared anguish and despair when otherwise they are in a state of antagonism is very telling. (The scene is recreated in "Beyond the Last Lamp",[88] where two "loiterers, wan, downcast" are seen first in the early evening, and then again hours later: "Moving slowly, moving sadly/That mysterious tragic pair".) These scenes play an important part in our picture of Angel, because they include him in the tragic experience and give him solidity and an actuality which is needed when there is so much emphasis on his ethereal brightness and his abstract philosophising.

The use of dialogue should have a similar effect, and sometimes it does. His teasing of Tess about her claim to experience, his playing with literary allusions, his somewhat self-conscious use of new learnt turns of speech ("a drop of pretty tipple"), his earnest, cautious conversation with his parents, his blunter treatment of his brothers all show Hardy's ear for nuances of speech. Perhaps, too, one can believe that under stress he would become excessively polysyllabic, as so many of Hardy's characters do; but "such a grotesque prestidigitation" is taking the theory a bit far, even if it is meant to represent "the perfunctory babble of the surface while the depths remained paralysed".[89] This way of reacting has something in common with Knight's preoccupation with geology while hanging on the cliff-face, though in this instance, Knight is rather more convincing.

The various external and dramatic methods of presenting Angel contribute to our sense of him as a solid, knowable being, but the accompanying almost continuous author's comment and analysis is vital to our understanding of him, and through this of Hardy's criticism of the attitudes of his time. Hardy repeatedly insisted that he was offering "a series of seemings", [90] "unadjusted impressions",[91] in his novels. Thus he enables us to experience what it is like to be Angel as well as to be Tess. At the same time he is in this novel obviously and consistently arguing a case in defence of his heroine, and we are certainly justified in attaching a good deal of weight to his comments. With Angel, he not only analyses him in depth, as I have shown, but also comments on the analysis in a very interesting way. He says, "Some might risk the paradox that with more animalism he would have been a nobler man. We do not say it".[92] This evasiveness shows Hardy's awareness of being too far ahead of his time in suggesting such a view. However the point is made, and it is a point which was to become central to Freud's theories. A comparable passage reads: "Experience teaches us that for most people there is a limit beyond which their constitution cannot comply with the demands of civilisation. All who wish to be more noble-minded than their constitution allows fall victim to neurosis; they would have been more healthy if it could have been possible for them to have been less good".[93]

Here, then, Hardy not only shows an insight into psychology as profound as Freud's, but also defines the nature of the problem in the same way as Freud does. Hardy had already made the same point when he spoke of "the great passionate pulse of existence, unwarped, uncontorted, untrammelled by those creeds which futilely attempt to check what wisdom would be content to regulate".[94] Hardy is not only interested in the same psychological problems as Freud, but his comments and suggested remedies are remarkably similar to Freud's. Both challenged current views, both asked for toleration and sympathy.

Hardy does not always sustain this level of honesty, when writing on this subject. When he describes Angel's earlier sexual relationship, he says, "Luckily he escaped not greatly the worse for the experience".[95] This rather conventional comment fits in suitably with Angel's further development, but it is not clear why such an experience should be "a liberal education" for Tess and not for Angel.

On the subject of virginity, we have seen that the conventional nineteenth-century view was the one Angel adopted. Surprisingly, we find Freud in 1917 expressing an identical view:

> The high value which the suitor places on a woman's virginity seems to us so firmly rooted, so much a matter of course, that we find ourselves almost at a loss if we have to give reasons for our opinion. The demand that a girl shall not bring to her marriage to a particular man any memory of sexual relations with another is, indeed, nothing other than a logical continuation of the right to exclusive possession of a woman, which forms the essence of monogamy, the extension of this monopoly to cover the past.[96]

I have already quoted Freud on the disadvantage of celibacy as a preparation for marriage (of course, he was thinking of men then) so that his inconsistency here is clear. So we see that Hardy was not only more tolerant than his own time, but also more tolerant than Freud in his views on relations between the sexes. This is just one instance of Hardy's greater sympathy with and understanding of women than Freud and is one of the many ways in which he anticipates later twentieth-century thinking.

The characterisation of Angel not only shows an ability to understand and analyse a personality full of conflicts and contradictions, but also to diagnose the causes of his emotional tumult, while at the same time creating for the reader a real sense of a suffering human being who also inevitably inflicts suffering on others. In the comparison with Knight, what ultimately stands out, after one has noticed the similarities, is the development of feeling; though the basic psychological types have much in common, in Angel, Hardy has created a much more intensely experiencing sensibility; as a result he is able to convey much more fully what it is like to be such a person as Angel.

Hardy called him "a sample product of the last twenty-five years";[97] the conflict between his "advanced ideas" and his tendency to be "surprised back into his early teachings"[98] have produced a "fractured consciousness". In this, he is the opposite of Tess. In her, Hardy has created a character capable of achieving perfect harmony of being, but thwarted by the attitudes of the society in which she lives. Thus the novel is a vehicle for his profound psychological insights into both disturbed and balanced personalities, for his comments on the society of his day, and for his plea for the acceptance of the whole human being — soul, mind and body.

Tess calls herself a victim, and she is — a victim of men and of society, rather than a "product" as Angel is. She suffers, not because of inner divisions in herself, but because of society's unwillingness to accept the complete human being that she is. Of course, the conventional view of her as an unmarried mother troubles her, affects her thoughts, makes her think she is an "anomaly", but it does not affect her in any profound way, or cause deep psychological disturbance: "Most of the misery [of having the baby] had been generated by her conventional aspect and not by her innate sensations".[99] After the baby's death, "she became what would have been called a fine creature; her aspect was fair and arresting; her soul that of a woman whom the turbulent experiences of the last year or two had quite failed to demoralize".[100]

These lines are not refuted by that much-quoted phrase, "the ache of modernism". Unlike the words I quoted in the previous paragraph, this is not an authorial comment, but it occurs in a description of Angel's thoughts on discovering Tess's fear of "Life in general"; also, the idea is half retracted almost as soon as it is expressed. The whole passage reads:

> She was expressing in her own native phrases — assisted a little by her Sixth Standard training — feelings which might almost have been called those of the age — the ache of modernism. The perception arrested him less when he reflected that what are called advanced ideas are really in great part but the latest fashion in definition . . . of sensations which men and women have vaguely grasped for centuries.[101]

In the following paragraph, after pointing out that Angel did not know of her past experiences, Hardy adds, "Tess's passing corporeal blight had been her mental harvest".[102] Thus, the implications are that she has gained rather than lost by her experience: "But for the world's opinion those experiences would have been simply a liberal education".[103]

For these reasons, I find it impossible to accept Ian Gregor's view, persuasive though he is, of her "fractured consciousness", unless the emphasis is very strongly on the conscious nature of the division; conventional views of her situation, of course, especially Angel's after her confession, affect her thinking and her happiness, but not her fundamental self. This inner confidence shows itself even when she is most threatened and most vulnerable; she is able to say, "It is in your own mind what you are angry at, Angel; it is not in me".[104] The total lack of any neurotic self-centredness at this time is further evidence that there is no inner "fatal dislocation".[105] Her sympathy for the dying pheasants and her recognition of "the relativity of sorrows and the tolerable nature of her own, if she could once rise high enough to despise opinion. But that she could not do, so long as it was held by Clare,"[106] shows her sustaining an impressive mental balance and sensitivity to others which is so characteristic of her.

Thus I most emphatically reject Gregor's statement that Clare's "splintered consciouness divides himself against himself very much, in a way, as Tess herself is divided".[107] He also says, "She is to be a true inheritor of the modern world and to receive what was for Hardy its distinctive legacy, that interior conflict which he describes as the mutually destructive interdependence of flesh and spirit".[108] I think that Hardy is expressing in *Tess* the exact opposite of this. In the early mornings, she seems to Angel to be "the abstract essence of woman", but by midday she is an ordinary milkmaid; the exalted, ethereal being can coexist happily with the woman from whom "Clare learnt what an impassioned woman's kisses were like upon the lips of one whom she loved with all her heart and soul, as Tess loved him".[109] It is society's disapproval of the flesh which is destructive. By the end of the book, even Tess's resilience is worn away. She begins to feel that "in inhabiting the fleshy tabernacle with which nature had endowed her she was somehow doing wrong",[110] and finally that harmony between mind and body which had been her great strength is indeed dislocated; "his original Tess had spiritually ceased to recognise the body before him as hers — allowing it to drift like a corpse upon the current, in a direction dissociated from its living will".[111] To suggest that this had been even approximately her state of mind from the beginning falsifies the whole book, undermines Hardy's plea for a change of attitudes and also makes incredible the serenity of her acceptance of her end. Somebody suffering from "a fatal dislocation of consciousness" could hardly be capable of the "I am ready" with which she accepts her capture at Stonehenge.

Tess resembles not Angel but Jude. Like him, she is faced by "the war between flesh and spirit"; like him, she shows that such a war need not exist. Her way of showing it is different for she is "a vessel of emotions rather than reasons".[112] She shows it at Talbothays, and at the house in the wood where Hardy's description of the honeymoon, with the passionate absorption with one another of the husband and wife, and the isolation, and forgetfulness of the outer world bears strong resemblance to the first days of the married life of Will and Anna in Lawrence's *The Rainbow*.

Both Tess and Jude need the combination of sensuality and spirituality which their society denies. Tess's insight into her situation is not as clear as Jude's; she is more prepared — at an intellectual level, though never emotionally — to accept society's judgement than he is. She marks an important stage in Hardy's development, both from the point of view of his psychological insight and of his criticism of society. Already, he is implying that the war between flesh and spirit need not be fought. Tess could have "mind and body in harmony"[113] if society would allow it, but in the end her endurance and resilience are defeated. But even the acceptance of life with Alec is not a neurotic gesture; her despair in the circumstances is justified. In *Tess* Hardy raises the problem of society's disapproval of "the flesh" and pleads for a change. In *Jude*, the "pioneers" have a faint glimpse of a possible future in which the complete man and woman will be accepted.

9 Jude and Sue: the psychological problems of modern man and woman (III)

In *Jude the Obscure* Hardy develops in a still more experimental way some of the central interests of *Tess of the d'Urbervilles*. The further exploration of psychological problems and unconscious motivation is concentrated mainly in the characterisation of Sue. With Jude, Hardy takes very much further some of the ideas about the nature of a balanced personality and its relation to society which had arisen in the course of the creation of Tess. The pattern of *Jude the Obscure* is similar to the previous novels; "all is contrast — or was meant to be",[1] and the central contrast is between well-balanced, resilient Jude and neurotic, vulnerable Sue. One of Hardy's earlier ideas for a title — "The Malcontents" perhaps, or even "Hearts Insurgent" — would have more adequately conveyed the central concerns of the novel than the actual title, which is related more closely to the original conception of "a story about a young man who could not go to Oxford";[2] this is not surprising since the final title was "one of the earliest thought of".[4] The theme of thwarted hopes of education, though vitally important, is not central to the novel as it finally developed: "Christminster is of course a tragic influence in one sense, but innocently so and merely as a cross-obstruction".[4] Some of the most interesting innovations are in the treatment of Sue, because with her Hardy's creative imagination takes to their furthest point his exploration of complex, psychologically disturbed personalities. But with Jude, too, in a less extreme way, Hardy is experimenting and exploring. Like Tess, Jude, though hypersensitive and with many conflicting impulses and at loggerheads with society, is not really psychologically disturbed. In this he differs from Knight, Angel, Clym and, of course, Sue, because he is inwardly fairly well balanced, in spite of not being well adjusted to the world around him. Hardy's interest in him as a victim of society is sustained throughout, but in the central parts of the novel, where the focus is mainly on Sue, his complexity and inner conflicts are less fully created than the external problems. One of the purposes of *Jude the Obscure* is to show that society imposes unnecessary suffering on its members, that "whatever may be the inherent good or evil of life, it is certain that men make it worse than it need be".[5]

The characterisation of Jude demonstrates Hardy's ability to depict complex characters who are not neurotic, who contain contradictory elements within them, who are continually struggling with these conflicting tendencies, yet who are not damaged psychologically by the conflict. It is important to recognise this. Jude has too often been interpreted as a weak character, an easy victim of society and of rapacious women. In fact, until close to the end, he copes with both his own strong passions and ideas and with the external world in a resilient and tenacious way. He never uses "the flight into neurosis" (Freud, *passim*) as a protection from the hardships of life. His loss of the will to live at the end seems a fairly reasonable reaction to the loss of everything that makes life meaningful to him. His disintegration is more the result of external pressures than of inner disturbance.

In this novel Hardy for the first time pays considerable attention to childhood experiences. This new attention to the significance of the characters' early lives is in keeping with the increased psychological awareness and analytical treatment found here. Jude is shown in circumstances and states of mind that might well have led to neurosis or psychosis later. Yet Hardy persuades us of his resilience. He shows him an orphan in a dreary, renovated North Wessex village with a reluctant aunt. The departure of the schoolmaster leaves him without any emotional ties; for though Aunt Drusilla's rejecting remarks are made with "pleasantry", Jude feels her glances and those of her friends "like slaps on the face".[6] Hardy stresses his sensitivity; he was "a thoughtful child who has felt the pricks of life before his time"[7] and his sympathy for the birds is partly because they "seemed like himself to be living in a world which did not want them".[8] Meditating on the responsibilities of growing up, he becomes aware of the cruelty of life, but Hardy adds, "Then like the natural boy, he forgot his despondency and sprang up".[9] Hardy is here making explicit a point about Jude's personality which runs right through the book. He has well-developed natural instincts; he is also exceptionally thoughtful and sensitive. With Jude, Hardy is exploring how a nature like this, and with no secure roots, can survive. As a boy, Jude is clearly not engulfed by the miserableness of his situation; though he is sensitive and aware about it, significantly he is also sensitive, perhaps hypersensitive to the sufferings of others, going to immense pains to avoid treading on earthworms and mourning for trees that are cut down or lopped. His sensitivity is not a self-absorbed kind; his awareness of things outside himself is a strength and forms a marked contrast with characters whom Hardy depicts as neurotic. Hardy indicates the Jude is strong as well as sensitive especially effectively in the encounter with Farmer Troutham, for Jude persists in explaining his philosophical position even while actually being beaten, and afterwards, when he wants to cross the now forbidden field in order to look at distant Christminster, he reminds himself that "the path was a public one" and defiantly follows it. This persistence in the face of adverse external circumstances is to be characteristic of his future behaviour. It shows an ability to trust to his own judgement and to continue in a mode of behaviour he feels to be right; his later defiance of conventions arises from these qualities. At the same time, he has a flexibility, a capacity to adjust to changing circumstances which can, at least sometimes, be a strength. Orphaned and rejected, "it had been the yearning of his heart to find something to anchor on, to cling to",[10] and he finds it in his vision of Christminster.

This is the first of many cycles, moving from despair to hope. Many times his aspirations are crushed; he repeatedly recovers himself, finds a new aim and moves towards it with renewed determination. All his drives are powerful; his ultimate failure is not the failure of a weak man. His life is a series of cyclical movements from aspiration to defeat to renewed efforts. After finding in the "anchorage" of Christminster a substitute for secure human relationships, he embarks resourcefully on his attempt to acquire an education. The failure to obtain books through Vilbert leaves him "crying bitterly" and an "interval of blankness" follows, succeeded by new hope when he thinks of appealing to Phillotson. When he realises that the books are practically useless, he wishes "that he had never been born". Hardy's comment that somebody might have helped him, "But nobody did come because nobody does",[11] seems to suggest a totally despairing attitude, both on Hardy's part and on Jude's. But this is immediately qualified in the next few lines by Hardy's leap across three or four years to the time when Jude reads Greek as he drives the baker's cart. After his initial disappointment with the books, he realises the vastness of the effort ahead of him, and is stimulated by the realisation: "To acquire languages, departed or living, in spite of such obstinacies as he now knew them inherently to possess, was a herculean performance which gradually led him on to a greater interest in it than the presupposed patent process".[12] Simultaneously, "He had endeavoured to make his presence tolerable to his crusty maiden aunt by assisting her to the best of his ability".[13] Hardy's account of Jude's adolescence shows this hypersensitive, imaginative boy grappling with tremendous problems in a sensible, practical way. At the same time, Hardy is already indicating the intellectual conflicts that will take years to resolve. In a moment of "impulsive emotion", he chants Latin hymns to the moon, then realises he has been immersing himself in pagan literature inappropriate for a budding bishop. His psychological strength lies partly in his capacity for extremes of feeling of an impersonal, aesthetic kind. His conflicts are largely theoretical or external, not unconscious and repressed. He is "a man born to ache a good deal" but this is in some degree because he faces adversity realistically.

Jude's sexual awakening is another instance of his strength and vitality. He is nineteen and up to this point has appeared to be the "abstinent young savant"[14] immersed in his "dream of learning", but he has had to be tough and resourceful in a way that had not been necessary for Knight or Angel. It is not at all implausible that he should be so abruptly awakened and that immediately the instinctive drive should be so powerful. He has shown his capacity for intense feeling; it is not surprising that his sexual feelings should be equally intense. At the same time Hardy beautifully suggests his naivete when he fails to grasp Arabella's intentions, even when she drags him down to the ground on the hillside. (No doubt Hardy had Jude in mind when he wrote in reply to a magazine questionnaire about the desirability of sex education for girls, "Innocent youths should, I think, also receive some instruction . . . for it has never struck me that the spider is invariably male and the fly invariably female".[15]) So begins the next cycle, which takes Jude through the phases of the excitement of the first experience of sex, through disillusionment with it, and the doggedly determined fulfilment of his duty to the supposedly pregnant Arabella, to despair as he discovers that powerful though sensuality is, by itself it does not provide a fulfilling relationship, at least not for him. Their violent quarrel over the pig-killing and the discovery of his mother's suicide and the renewed reminder of the traditionally unhappy marital relationships of the Fawley family lead him to see suicide as the only way out of what appears to him to be a permanent situation. Hardy's deadpan treatment of this episode is curious. Perhaps he felt that having established the cyclical pattern of Jude's behaviour, he could now demonstrate it a third time without needing to enter into Jude's emotional state. He describes only his physical actions — his walk out to the middle of the frozen pond, his jumping on the ice, his return to the bank, and then Jude's very detached comment: "It was curious, he thought. What was he preserved for?"[16] This factual treatment keeps the whole episode in a fairly low key. Hardy presents the suicidal state as something that a sane and rational man could experience. One does not feel that "the balance of his mind is disturbed", but simply that for the moment he has reached the limits of his endurance, perhaps not surprisingly. Then he remembers that it is possible and normal to drown one's sorrows in drink, and proceeds to do so. The whole episode has a deliberately tentative air. Jude, still immature, is seeking in a fairly theoretical way "for a solution to his problems". When one remedy does not work, he experiments with another, and returns home to find Arabella has solved the problem with a third. Hardy shows Jude as dazed by unhappiness about his future, rather than deeply disturbed psychologically. The suicidal act is more like playing Russian roulette than a serious attempt at self-destruction. The discovery of Arabella's departure opens up the possibility that life may again become liveable. He is confused, "he could not realise himself",[17] but soon "the spark of the old fire" is lit.

Once Jude has become involved with Sue, the chances of continuing this pattern of survival and renewal after disastrous events are considerably diminished, not because of his character, but because of hers. She damages or destroys all the men she encounters; there is nothing in Jude's personality or in the way he responds to or is fascinated by her to suggest that he should be an exception. Hardy stresses that he could have weathered the blow of his exclusion from Christminster, but "deprived of the objects of both the intellect and the emotions", he temporarily succumbs. What follows is an expression in imaginative terms of a statement of Freud's: "Life is hard, we cannot do without palliative remedies — (a) powerful diversions of interest, which lead us to care little about misery, [Sue] (b) Substitutive gratifications which lessen it, [Christminster] (c) Intoxicating substances which make us insensitive to it".[18]

The academic rejection alone does not undermine Jude's basic confidence in his own ability; he writes, "I am not inferior to you" on Biblioll gates. But this, combined with the assumption that because of his marriage, Sue can never be his, and that soon she is likely to be doubly removed from him because of her relationship with Phillotson, leaves him with no resource but to desensitise himself with drink. His drunken display of learning and his arrival at Sue's house in a helpless state lead on to remorse, to a sense of awakening in hell. He remembers "the previous abyss into which he had fallen . . . but it was not so deep as this".[19] Hardy comments: "That had been the breaking in of the outer bulwarks of his hope; this was of his second line".[20] This sentence is important because while indicating Jude's vulnerability, it also emphasises his strength, his "bulwarks". It also suggests that Hardy sees Jude as rather stronger than Freud sees most human beings, since what Hardy calls "bulwarks", Freud calls "palliative remedies". Thus, though Jude is in despair, and tells the curate, "I am melancholy mad", the impression is that his mental state is due to appalling circumstances rather than to any innate psychological weakness. He is certainly not mad, and once he has decided that a meaningful life can be achieved through the "purgatorial course" of becoming a licentiate, he cheers up. This is, of course, unrealistic and shows a lack of self-knowledge, but it also shows his characteristic resilience in adversity.

The subsequent cycles of Jude's development are less fully analysed; as Sue's tantalising, enigmatic nature becomes the dominant one, Jude's emotional changes and basic stability wane in importance and interest. From this point on he is either trying to adjust himself to her needs, or to persuade her to act differently, so that attention is focused away from him. A period of happiness follows Arabella's visit and Sue's capitulation to Jude's "grossness", in spite of society's disapproval. Jude's loss of his religious beliefs has removed one form of conflict, and his resignation to the fact that he cannot go to Christminster another. Even though life with Sue can never be completely satisfying, since she feels "at liberty to yield herself as seldom as she chooses",[21] yet there is enough emotional satisfaction to enable him to "care little about misery". The deaths of the children of course disrupt all this. Sue's neurotic, relentless determination to punish herself leaves Jude with nothing. His mental stability is not undermined, but his will to live is. His death becomes inevitable.

This is not a collapse brought about by psychological weakness, but the disintegration of a man whose strong, healthy impulses and lofty aspirations have been destroyed by a hostile environment.

This aspect of Jude needs emphasising, since many critics have tended to draw attention mainly to his weaknesses (the earlier critics to his supposed inability to control his "animal instincts" and the later ones to his "modern nervousness"), but Hardy's conception is more complex and more challenging than this. Jude's weaknesses and conflicts are closely related to his strengths. Hardy makes much of his "weakness for drink". Yet there are only three occasions in the novel when he gets really drunk: when he recognises the futility of his marriage to Arabella; when he sees simultaneously that Sue will probably marry Phillotson and that he will never get into Christminster; and when Arabella makes him drunk before remarrying him. This hardly suggests a compulsive drinker. He does use drink to numb his pain when it becomes unbearable, but he more often struggles with a period of despair and then finds means of renewed hope. Hardy presents Jude's feelings of guilt about drinking and his perhaps irrational fears of his use of it as part of the conflict which exists between his high aims and his normal humanity. Jude cannot admit that he needs "palliatives" in a harsh world. In this matter he comes into the category of those "who wish to be more noble-minded than their constitution allows",[22] and therefore runs the risk of neurosis; however, in the more important matter of his "weakness for women", he comes to terms with his "constitution", and this is central to the whole conception of Jude, and indeed, of the book as a whole.

In the Preface, Hardy describes one of the subjects of the novel as "the deadly war waged between flesh and spirit". This theme is treated in an extremely complex way and embodied in various facets of the novel: in the contrast between Arabella and Sue; in the conflicts between Sue and Phillotson, and Sue and Jude; in the inner conflicts of Jude, in which he ultimately comes to terms with his own nature; and in Sue's inner conflicts which only intensify as Jude develops in maturity and in certainty about himself and human relationships. But in so far as the Preface seems to suggest that such a war is inevitable, it is misleading. The whole tenor of the book, and in particular of the character of Jude, is towards suggesting it is unnecessary and avoidable. Here lies the originality of Hardy's treatment of Jude. He is illustrating through him that a normal man — a good man — will have strong and varied drives; that the 'flesh' is as much a part of him as the 'spirit'. He is also showing that society and conventional attitudes can be destructive to the whole man, but he does not imply that it is in the nature of existence that this should be so.

Jude's condemnation of his "weakness for women" is, like his guilt about drinking, excessive. But while Jude, at least as a young man, deplores the strength of his 'animal' instincts, Hardy does not endorse this view. In the previous novel, he had suggested that with more of the animal in him, Angel might have been a nobler man. Jude is that nobler man. His adolescent sexual awakening by Arabella was natural and healthy and could have been simply a "liberal education", as could Tess's encounter with Alec. His 'animal' response would not have been harmful if the relationship had remained, what in its nature it was, a temporary experience. It is the demands of society which turn it into a permanently crippling relationship. (Though the social demand — that a man must marry a girl he has made pregnant — on which the marriage is based is a lie, yet it is society's influence on Arabella which makes her think she must marry a man who has aroused her "latent sensuousness"; living with him full-time, she soon finds him boring, yet at the end of the novel she does it again, and finds him boring again). Jude, at this stage, sees this in a rather tentative way, and temporarily loses sight of it later:

> There seemed to him, vaguely and dimly, something wrong in the social ritual which made necessary a cancelling of well-formed schemes involving years of thought and labour, of foregoing a man's one opportunity of showing himself superior to the lower animals, and of contributing his units of work to the general progress of his generation, because of a momentary surprise by a new and transitory instinct which had nothing in it of the nature of vice and could only at the most be called weakness.[23]

Isolated in this way, Hardy's theories about sex seem rather obtrusive; but this impression is modified by the fact that they are embodied in a character who simultaneously illustrates Hardy's awareness of the fluctuating nature of mental and emotional development. At this point, Jude's "vague" and "dim" perceptions coincide with the views that emerge from a reading of the book as a whole. Later, he loses this glimpsed insight, especially that the "instinct had

nothing in it of the nature of vice", under the pressure of Sue's "uncarnate" nature and her wish to "ennoble some man to high aims"
and he attempts to subdue the flesh. Hardy does not regard his efforts to suppress passion by abstinence as either wise or admirable;
"insulted Nature sometimes vindicated her rights".[24] These fluctuations as Jude tries to come to terms with himself and his experience create a sense of the character struggling, and sometimes
failing to understand himself, rather than of an author imposing
preconceived ideas on him.

The night with Arabella at Aldbrickham adds a further level of
complexity. On the surface, it looks like a fairly straightforward battle in "the war between flesh and spirit" with the victory for the flesh
and remorse afterwards. At his first sight of her, Jude is "dazed" and
"indifferent to the fact that Arabella is his wife indeed".[25] Yet he observes minutely her figure, her clothes and her hands, and notices
her animation. There is a similar contradiction implied in his way of
seeing the situation: "the woman between whom and himself there
was no more unity than between east and west, being in the eye of the
Church one person with him".[26] So it is the Church's view which ostensibly and incredibly instigates the night at Aldbrickham and the
disappointment of Sue, waiting for him at Alfredston. The journey
and the arrival at the inn "in time for a late supper" are described
briefly and factually. The gap between supper and half-past nine
the next morning is filled in only retrospectively. This is obviously
due to nineteenth-century fictional convention, yet it contributes to
our sense of the physical affinity between Jude and Arabella. It gives
the impression that they quite naturally converge, without any soul-
searching on Jude's part; that comes later, when he has "an indescribable consciousness of Arabella's midnight contiguity, a sense
of degradation at his revived experiences with her, of her appearance as she lay asleep at dawn, which set upon his motionless
face a look as of one accurst".[27] Even here, the emotions are conflicting, the "indescribable consciousness" is as vivid as the sense of
degradation, and even this seems prompted more by the news of
Arabella's Australian "husband" than by revulsion at the occasion
itself. His, "Why the devil didn't you tell me last night?"[28] is the first
indication of disgust. Before that, he had simply been reminiscing
about his first journey to Christminster. Even after her revelation,
his feelings are mixed: "he pitied while he condemned her".[29]
Though Jude's conscious thoughts after the night with Arabella are
of shame and degradation, he also arrives at a new, clearer aware-

ness that Sue is "so uncarnate as to seem at times impossible as a human wife to any average man . . . how she lived as such passed his comprehension".[30]

Jude's simple shame at this "earthliness" is not unqualified; it is coupled with a realisation that "average" human beings are flesh as well as spirit. But it is an intellectual insight, which does not diminish the attraction of the "ethereal creature . . . whose spirit could be seen trembling through her limbs",[31] nor even prevent him from mortifying the flesh with renewed fervour.

His disillusioning visit to the composer pushes him forward another step; he missed Sue because of it, and felt that this was "another special intervention of Providence to keep him away from temptation" (the meeting with Arabella had ironically been the other), but at the same time, "a growing impatience of faith . . . made him pass off in ridicule the idea that God sent people on fool's errands".[32] After the next meeting with Sue at Shaston, he can acknowledge that "the human was more powerful in him than the Divine".[33] From this point, Jude's internal "war between flesh and spirit" gains momentum. Sue's confession of her unhappiness with Phillotson, their spontaneous, passionate kiss at parting, his admission to himself that whatever his theories and ambitions, "to persist with headlong force in impassioned attentions to her was all he thought of"[34] lead him to question "the artificial system of things, under which the normal sex impulses are turned into devilish domestic gins and springes to hold back those who want to progress",[35] and to the burning of his theological books.

Jude's coming to accept his own nature and the nature of man has not been presented in a doctrinaire way, but as a deeply felt inner struggle. Hardy shows how a sensitive, ambitious and rather conventional man can experience tormenting conflicts and come to terms with them instead of taking the alternative course into neurosis. Freud describes how "in our therapy we often find ourselves obliged to do battle with the superego and work to moderate its demands".[36] Jude has managed to achieve this for himself. From now on, his point of view coincides, most of the time, with Hardy's. Now he talks about "normal sexual impulses" (which Sue calls "grossness"). The epigraph to part V is significant here: "Thy aerial part, and all the fiery parts which are mingled in thee, though by nature they have an upward tendency, still in obedience to the disposition of the universe they are overpowered here in the compound mass of the body". Jude has learnt "obedience to the disposition of the Universe" and is no longer trying to be "all air and fire".

This resolution of his conflicts at this point in the novel might well have caused Hardy some difficulties in the treatment of Jude. He avoids the danger of the character becoming merely the mouthpiece of the author by sustaining the conflicts in other ways and by never allowing Jude's certainty and confidence to be too strongly established. The shift of emphasis from Jude to Sue is also helpful in reducing the impact of the character who might seem to be too emphatically expressing the author's views. But, above all, the actuality of Hardy's method, the feeling he creates, most of the time, of a lived experience, full of conflicting emotions and multiple ways of responding to experience save the novel from becoming what Sue calls "too sermony".

An occasion when the theory is fully embodied in the action is the visit of Arabella to the cottage at Aldbrickham. It occurs after Jude and Sue have been living together sexlessly for a year, and in his exasperation, Jude has had moments of wondering whether Sue is capable of love. His responsiveness to Arabella arises immediately from his state of sexual frustration. Hardy makes this quite explicit: "I've waited with the patience of Job, and I don't see that I've got anything by my self-denial".[37] His feeling that perhaps he has more in common with Arabella after all than with Sue is suggested when he says, "I am coarse too". Also, his pretence to Sue and to himself that he must go out to Arabella because she may need help, is amusingly put into perspective the following morning when he responds "placidly" to Sue's anxiety about her: "You haven't the least idea how Arabella is able to shift for herself".[38] Jude's attitude on this occasion is treated wholly sympathetically and Sue's capitulating through jealousy hardly speaks much for the "ennobling" effects of sexual abstinence. At the same time, Hardy manages to indicate a slightly different angle on the episode through the wry amusement at Jude's pretence of being more high-minded than he is; then he tilts our sympathies towards Sue through her anxiety for Arabella's welfare and her admission that, "I can't help liking her — just a little bit! She's not an ungenerous nature".[39]

These continual shifts in attitude towards the characters and changes in the characters themselves play a very important part in giving a "sense of felt life" to a novel which is concerned with philosophical, sociological and psychological problems. Though Jude's inner "war between flesh and spirit" is resolved, the outer conflict never ceases, and to some extent it undermines his confidence in his own position. His immediate response to Sue's "I give in", was, "And I'll arrange for our marriage tomorrow".[40] At breakfast the next morning he is gaily talking of arranging the banns at once. But, as his repeated efforts to get her to church or registry office fail, he begins to be affected by her attitude, at first feeling, "If you are made uneasy, I am unhappy",[41] and then coming to feel that they were "horribly sensitive" and "queer sort of people" and that her "whims . . . are very much in accord with my own".[42] These shifts and uncertainties about what he really feels serve to keep Jude a living, developing, complicated human being, even though Sue has become the main centre of the interest. Even his response to Sue's mad self-punishment after the children are dead is uncertain and hesitant. Though he insists that it is not God but "man and senseless circumstance"[43] that have brought them to misery, he also starts feeling guilty himself: "I seduced you . . . You were a distinct type — a refined creature intended by Nature to be left intact".[44] This is precisely the line on Sue that Lawrence takes in his "Study", but Jude's opinion cannot be taken as Hardy's, since in his confusion and anguish he repeatedly contradicts himself. His attitude keeps changing as he tries to cope with Sue's frantic guilt. He shifts from accusing himself, to trying to diminish her "monstrous" and "unnatural" remorse, to attacking the Church: "I'm glad I had nothing to do with Divinity — damn glad — if it's going to ruin you in this way".[45] He abandons his theory of her "distinct type" to argue against her view that, "We ought to have lived in mental communion and no more". To this he says, "But people in love couldn't live for ever like that . . . human nature can't help itself". As she continues to argue in favour of "self-mastery", he burst out . . . "You have never loved me as I loved you — never — never! . . . . You are . . . a fay or sprite, not a woman". Her desperate weeping and determination to send him away leads to another violent fluctuation of feeling and he swings back to self-accusation: "My God! How selfish I was! Perhaps — perhaps I spoilt one of the highest and purest loves that ever existed between man and woman".[46]

The violence of the emotions, the changeableness and uncertainty of Jude's state of mind remove this far from any theoretical discussion about right and wrong attitudes to sexual relationships; though both the characters theorise a good deal as they argue, Hardy makes their anguish dominate the scene. "He went to the bed, removed one of the pair of pillows thereon, and flung it to the floor".[47] Rage, helplessness and despairing finality are concentrated in that action. It suggests that he does not believe the accusation which he has just made against himself; it sums up his sheer helpless rage and despair which comes from the realisation that she had never really wanted to be in bed with him. When she comes to say goodbye, he has changed again, and, "with anguish that was well-nigh fierce" insists, "I loved you and you loved me".[48] He sees that "the blow of her bereavement seemed to have destroyed her reasoning faculty", and asks, "Do you love him? You know you don't". His emphatic certainty, so different from his earlier shifts and changes as he adapted himself to Sue springs from the desperation caused by her behaviour; her violent repudiation of their love leads to Jude's equally violent assertion of it. He repeats this at the final meeting at Marygreen when he suggests that they run away together while simultaneously telling her, "You are not worth a man's love".[49] Jude's changing, uncertain and violent responses to Sue are the outcome of her nature as much as of his. This is why Jude, in spite of his complexities and convincingness seems subordinate to Sue in the second half of the novel; he is continually trying to adjust himself to her needs.

In all this passion and anguish, the remarriage to Arabella may seem incongruous, perhaps simply included to complete the tight-knit pattern. But it is more significant than this. Although in his stupefied state, Jude seems utterly indifferent to her, he surprises himself one day by asking her to be home by the seven o'clock train. Yet, he thinks, "She is nothing to me".[50] Hardy is obviously suggesting an unconscious interest here. Similarly, "he yielded in his half-somnolent state",[51] to Arabella, when she had made him drunk. Her "animal magnetism" still evokes a response from him, but Hardy handles this kind of reaction with great caution, especially when his good characters are involved. Both Jude and Tess (in the Chase) have to be seduced when half asleep. It is a way of letting the characters (and perhaps by implication Hardy himself) escape from responsibility for their "animal" natures, and thus avoid the condemnation (he might have hoped) of contemporary readers.

In spite of these instances of evasiveness, one of Hardy's aims in both *Tess* and *Jude* was to assert the harmlessness of "normal sexual impulses" even when unaccompanied by emotional and intellectual sympathies. He was trying to shift "the inert mass of crystallised opinion" which finds expression in, for instance, a review of *Jude*: "the physical part of the question . . . has hitherto been banished from the lips of decent people and as much as possible from their thoughts".[52] That he is battling against such views as these is clear throughout *Tess* and underlies the decision to subtitle it *A Pure Woman*. *Jude* explores the same idea, among many others and in a more complicated context, but with characters which clearly develop out of those in the previous novel. In Sue, he explores in far greater depth the neuroses already examined in Angel. Arabella is not much more complicated than Alec, but her vitality, "latent sensuousness" and real insight in sexual matters as well as her "coarseness" are presented with immediacy and reality, while Alec never fully recovers from the staginess of his early appearances. The relationship between Tess and Jude is less obvious, but very important in the development of Hardy's ideas and feelings about people's sexual nature. They are both basically stable and resilient, and their problems arise more from the attitude of other individuals and of society as a whole than from within. Perhaps their essentially balanced natures reveal themselves most fully in their ability to put up with the unreasonableness of their neurotic partners. Both respect the other person's individuality. Tess will not use emotional blackmail to prevent Angel from leaving her. Jude refrains for a considerable time from putting pressure on Sue to go to bed with him. Just as one can see in Angel's character traits that are developed in Sue, so Tess's sensuousness, imaginativeness, intelligence and stability are developed into a more complicated personality in Jude. The relationships in the two books follow a similar pattern, the stable character in each book having a merely physical relationship with a sensual character and an impassioned yet almost bodiless relationship with a neurotic character. In this way, in both books, Hardy shows the need for human beings to satisfy both "flesh and spirit". It is rather surprising that Lawrence in his interesting but idiosyncratic comparison of Tess and Jude, claims that Jude "had the strong, purist idea that a man's body should follow and be subordinate to and subsequent to his mind".[53] While this is true of Jude during the time when he is attempting to be religious and ascetic, it fails to take into account that he changes and develops. Hardy is even closer to Lawrence than Lawrence realised. Through the two books, Hardy is moving towards an idea of "the whole man alive". *Tess* is a plea for tolerance of, *Jude* for acceptance of human sexuality.

    In these two books especially, Hardy is examining some of the same problems as those Freud dealt with in his more general writings, such as *"Civilised" Sexual Morality and the Neuroses* and *Civilisation and its Discontents*. Their views of the difficulties which civilisation or society imposes on the individual are very similar. In 1908, Freud wrote: "It is one of the obvious social injustices that the standard of civilisation should demand from everyone the same conduct of sexual life — conduct which can be followed without any difficulty by some people, thanks to their organisation, but which imposes the heaviest psychical sacrifices on others".[54] This is not only central to Hardy's treatment of the sexual theme in *Jude the Obscure*, but it is also exactly parallelled in Sue's words: "Domestic laws should be made according to temperaments, which should be classified. If people are at all peculiar in character they have to suffer from the very rules that produce comfort in others".[55] Indeed, it would not be an exaggeration to say that *"Civilised" Sexual Morality and the Neuroses* puts in theoretical terms a very large part of what Hardy has stated in imaginative terms. The following passage reads almost like a summary of Hardy's views:

> civilisation demands of individuals of both sexes that they shall practise abstinence until they are married and that those who do not contract legal marriage shall remain abstinent throughout their lives. The position, agreeable to all the authorities, that sexual abstinence is not harmful and not difficult to maintain, has also been widely supported by the medical profession. It may be asserted, however, that the task of mastering such a powerful impulse as that of the sexual instinct by any other means than by satisfying it is one which can call for the whole of a man's forces. Mastering it by sublimation, by deflecting the sexual instinctual aim to higher cultural aims, can be achieved by a minority and then only intermittently, and least easily during the period of ardent and vigorous youth. Most of the rest become neurotic or are harmed in one way or another.[56]

Of course, the novel being an imaginative creation is far more complex and contradictory and less clearcut than this. Jude's enforced sexual abstinence is only partly due to the demands of society; Sue's hatred of "grossness" plays a major part. Hardy's picture of the effects of this on his whole life corresponds to Freud's analysis. He shows Jude accepting his rejection by Christminster without much struggle; he also abandons his proposed theological training, and after that makes no real effort to improve his education, but simply remains obsessed with the idea of Christminster (nicely highlighted by the Christminster cakes). Hardy does not specifically relate his educational failure to this sexual problems (apart from showing the temporary interruption of his work caused by the fascination of Arabella), but he does emphasise the point that Jude was especially suited to learning and to teaching: "I was never really stout enough for the stone trade . . . . But . . . I could accumulate ideas and impart them to others".[57] His glimpse of the value of manual work[58] is not a criticism of his own ambition to do otherwise. But in spite of this, after his very strenuous youthful struggles, Jude gives up fairly easily the idea of acquiring learning. One reason lies in Hardy's developing interest in Sue. But perhaps, since there were other sources of education besides Christminster and Jude makes no attempt to tap them, nor to fight for education for working men, we should look for psychological reasons for his loss of zest for learning. Freud says, "In general I have not gained the impression that sexual abstinence helps to bring about energetic, self-reliant men of action or original thinkers or bold emancipators and reformers".[59] Freud takes the line that Hardy takes, that the whole man needs to be developed; to thwart one facet of him is to thwart the whole man.

In his conclusion to *Civilisation and its Discontents*, Freud refuses to offer a theory, or the consolation people want; he is prepared to question whether our civilisation "is the most precious thing we possess or could acquire" and is willing to listen, without committing himself, to those who think "that the whole thing is not worth the effort and that in the end it can only produce a state of things which no individual will be able to bear".[60] Hardy is even further from formulating an all-inclusive theory than Freud, but *Jude the Obscure* certainly shows that society and the individual whose "noisy", "reproachful" superego "coincides with the demands of the prevailing cultural superego",[61] work together to make life unbearable. Hardy's picture of the "discontents" associated with civilisation anticipates Freud by 35 years.

In spite of the disclaimers in the Preface, Hardy has no hesitation in using the novel as a vehicle for various theories about the nature of man. For instance, he formulates the theory which became central in Freud's *The Ego and the Id*. When Jude first meets Arabella, Hardy shows how his conscious intentions disintegrate in the face of the powerful, instinctive force of sex; he describes "the commonplace obedience to conjunctive orders from headquarters, unconsciously received by unfortunate men when the last intention of their lives is to be occupied with the feminine".[62] This ponderous generalisation is rather awkward in the context of backchat about Arabella's "missile". Hardy returns to the theory a few pages later and phrases it this time more strongly and vividly:

> as if materially, a compelling arm of extraordinary muscular power seized hold of him — something which had nothing in common with the spirits and influences that had moved him hitherto. This seemed to care little for his reason and his will, nothing for his so-called elevated intentions, and moved him along, as a violent schoolmaster a schoolboy he has seized by the collar, in a direction which tended towards the embrace of a woman for whom he had no respect . . . .[63]

In a parallel passage in *The Ego and the Id* Freud quotes Groddeck, "who is never tired of insisting that what we call our ego behaves essentially passively in life, and that, as he expresses it, we are lived by unknown, uncontrollable forces".[64]

Thus, we see Hardy not only giving expression in narrative form to intuitive insights into human nature, but also formulating psychological theories which were to receive clinical backing in the following century. This particular theory is especially startling, at a time when "self-mastery" was assumed by most people to be the ideal, and, indeed, still was when Freud wrote in 1930 that the cultural superego "enjoins a command and never asks whether or not it is possible for men to obey".[65]

In making the existence of these "unknown, uncontrollable forces" a prominent theme in *Jude the Obscure* and in suggesting the importance of them as an integral part of the personality, Hardy is giving expression to a theme which is to be more fully explored both in the fiction and in the writing of the next century. Psychologists such as Freud, and educationists such as A. S. Neill, saw the dangers of valuing only one aspect of the personality. Forster's "only connect, and the beast and the monk, robbed of the isolation that is life to either, will die",[66] and Lawrence's, "Life is only bearable when the mind and the body are in harmony, and there is a natural balance between them, and each has a natural respect for the other"[67] are instances of later novelists reiterating and developing points made in *Jude the Obscure*. The quotation from Lawrence could almost serve as a negative epigraph to *Jude*: Sue's mind and body are never in harmony, and so her life and Jude's become unbearable. Much of Lawrence's work is concerned with examining the difficulties of achieving this harmony and only *Lady Chatterley's Lover* really suggests that it is something which human beings can perhaps achieve fully.

The recognition of the importance of the instincts is perhaps the most important link between Hardy and Lawrence. Lawrence's varied and powerful ways of suggesting the existence of the unconscious, especially in *The Rainbow* and *Women in Love* go far beyond Hardy's relatively tentative findings, but Hardy had already pointed the way, as the "Study of Thomas Hardy" shows Lawrence realised, however much he distorted Hardy in the process of defining his own intentions. Even in his methods of embodying these themes in character, Hardy makes some tentative steps which Lawrence will follow through. The idea that character in the novel cannot be defined with clarity and definiteness, which Lawrence emphasises in *Women in Love*, when Ursula is revolted by the idea that a person can be treated like an account that is settled, "draw two lines under him and cross him out"[68] is seen already in *Jude.* Sue is "puzzling and unstatable", with "untranslatable" eyes; her quicksilver changes of attitude and mood leave Jude plodding in her wake. Yet he not only develops an understanding and acceptance of his own nature, but is a "changer" too. In this and in other ways he has affinities with Birkin in *Women in Love*. Birkin is a "changer";[69] his views on society and the relationships between the sexes are largely those of his author, yet he is throughout struggling to clarify his thought, contradicting himself (in "Mino" for instance), being attacked by the other characters and accused of being a "preacher". Jude similarly sometimes voices the views of his author, arrives at his author's view on sexual relationships, yet is changing and contradicting himself right to the end of the novel and is criticised as "too sermony".[70] Though Jude is less educated than Birkin, he is not much less articulate. They are both concerned with the same basic problems — how to make "life bearable" in a society which is largely destructive, and how to develop a sexual relationship which will satisfy one's deepest needs. Lawrence is able to explore this more successfully than Hardy, since he has created in Ursula somebody who has both sensitivity and intelligence and also sensuality. The split between the "flesh and spirit" was a necessary stage in Hardy's exploration of sexual themes, but just as Jude comes to see them as equally valuable elements in his personality, by the end of the novel it seems as if Hardy is ready to explore a similar completeness in a woman. The "whole man alive" — and woman too — seems the natural next stage. He could not do this in *Jude* itself, in spite of Lawrence's tendency to rehabilitate Arabella and make her a possible vehicle for this (he maintains that Hardy exaggerated her coarseness "to make the moralist's case against her"[71]), for Arabella remains "a complete female animal"[72] in spite of her "flashes of intelligence".[73] Alvarez argues that she is more intelligent than Sue, but her intelligence — and she does show real insight in Sue's nature — is restricted to the one subject which interests her, sex. She is the antithesis of a whole person.

But Hardy was not ready, nor would the times permit him, to write with candour about two people who could conceivably offer one another the fulfilment of the "whole man" and "whole woman". This, perhaps, is the novel which would have followed *Jude* if he had written another; this, perhaps, is why it was never written. He said, "If you mean to make the world listen to you, you must say now what they will all be thinking and saying five and twenty years hence".[74] *Jude* was rather more ahead of its time than that. It is not surprising that he hesitated to push the novel still further in the direction he had been going, and decided to try another mode of expression: "Perhaps I can express more fully in verse ideas and emotions which run counter to the inert crystallised opinion — hard as a rock — which the vast body of men have vested interests in supporting".[75]

Nevertheless, Hardy's creation of Sue is one of his most remarkable achievements. This character is, as J. I. M. Stewart has said. "virtually a point of major innovation in prose fiction".[76] With her, Hardy is exploring further aspects of personality already developed in Knight and Angel, but in comparison with Sue, these earlier attempts look like merely tentative trial runs. With Sue, he made tremendous advances on all fronts: he explored psychological problems in greater depth than ever before; he dealt with taboo subjects with clarity and honesty; he raised questions about mental health and psychological balance which were to become central in psychological and educational writing and in novels during the following 30 years and beyond; he began to touch on possible new ways of conceiving character in the novel which were to be developed by his successors; and he rendered Sue's personality with concreteness, vividness and immediacy. In the combination of these elements Hardy achieved the peak of his art as a novelist because he here fuses most completely the analytical and creative aspects of characterisation. As we read about Sue, we are fully conscious of her psychological problems, but she is never merely a clinical case; Hardy makes us experience her mode of being. We cannot fully appreciate what Hardy is doing without grasping intellectually the problematic nature of her personality and simultaneously entering into it imaginatively.

The many qualities she has in common with Knight and Angel — their abstemiousness, especially in sexual matters, and their consequent claims to virtue, their rationality — make clear that these particular psychological characteristics have interested Hardy for a long time; with Sue, he reaches a fuller and more profound understanding and realisation of them. The structure of *Jude the Obscure* allows this further treatment. In *Tess of the d'Urbervilles* Angel is subordinate. His major psychological upheaval in Brazil is given cursory treatment so as to avoid shifting the balance of the book away from Tess. In *Jude the Obscure* Sue carries equal weight to Jude in the structure of the novel, and this seems to have been the intention from the start. In the manuscript there is, in the early part, a lot of detail about Sue's life as the niece of the head of a Christminster College, and early ideas for a title included "The Simpletons", "The Malcontents" and "Hearts Insurgent". It seems reasonable to assume that Hardy expected to give more or less equal prominence to Sue and Jude, thus allowing himself the scope to carry out that exploration in depth of her psychological problems which he could not allow himself with Angel. With this fuller treatment, Hardy has space to present Sue dramatically instead of, as often with Angel, through analytical summary. Most of the analysis of Sue is done by herself, or by Jude and Phillotson as they grope towards an understanding of her, or by Arabella, in her limited but shrewd assessments. Thus the whole treatment of Sue is more complete and more extreme than that of Angel. By dealing with a woman rather than a man, Hardy was challenging contemporary opinion more sharply, since women's sexual feelings (if they were admitted to exist) were regarded as an even more indelicate subject than men's. Sue's problems are more extreme than Angel's and eventually develop into mental illness, so that in this respect Hardy is going much further than he has gone before. Also, since he manages to make Sue more interesting, more attractive and more neurotic than Knight and Angel, he achieves a sense of greater intensity, of a more extreme personality with her than with the earlier characters. The originality of the portrait lies in the detailed examination of Sue's particular kind of psychological complexity; the strength lies in the way these insights are used to create a vivid and living character whose emotions we can experience vicariously.

A close reading of the book reveals that as well as being intuitively sympathetic to Sue's feelings, Hardy is consciously aware that he is exploring regions of great psychological complexity; but there is also external evidence which substantiates this point. One of the most valuable contributions to our understanding of *Jude the Obscure* and especially of the character of Sue is Edmund Gosse's review which Hardy said was "the most discriminating that has yet appeared".[77] Gosse stressed the importance of Sue in the book:

The "vita sexualis" of Sue is the central interest of the book, and enough is told about it to fill the specimen tables of a German specialist. Fewer testimonies will be given to her reality than Arabella's because hers is a much rarer case. But her picture is not less admirably drawn; Mr Hardy has, perhaps, never devoted so much care to the portrait of a woman. She is a poor, maimed "degenerate", ignorant of herself and of the perversion of her instincts, full of febrile, amiable illusions, ready to dramatise her empty life, and play at loving though she cannot love. Her adventure with the undergraduate has not taught her what she is: she quits Phillotson still ignorant of the source of her repulsion; she lives with Jude, after a long, agonising struggle, in a relationship that she accepts with distaste, and when the tragedy comes, her children are killed, her poor, extravagant brain slips one grade further down and she sees in this calamity the chastisement of God. What has she done to be chastised? She does not know but supposes it must be her abandonment of Phillotson, to whom, in a spasm of self-abasement and shuddering with repulsion, she returns without a thought for the misery of Jude. It is a terrible study in pathology, but of the splendid success of it, of the sustained intellectual force implied in the evolution of it, there cannot, I think, be two opinions.[78]

In a further letter, ten days after his first appreciative response to the review, Hardy wrote again to Gosse saying "you are quite right" but, nevertheless, modifying Gosse's comments to some extent. He referred to Sue's "abnormalism" and spoke of her sexual instinct as "unusually weak and fastidious", yet said that it was "healthy, as far as it goes". Later in the same letter, he said, "Sue is a type of woman which has always had an attraction for me, but the difficulty of drawing the type has kept me from attempting it until now".[79] It seems that while Hardy felt that Gosse had fully understood his intentions with Sue, he hesitated to endorse phrases like "a terrible study in pathology"; this would indeed equate it with "the specimen tables of a German specialist". Sue's attractiveness for Hardy, stated in this letter, is evident in the whole conception of the character. His great achievement with Sue is that she is simultaneously a suitable case for analysis, and a living, changing, "unstatable" woman, evoking vivid and changing responses from those who know her.

It is interesting to consider here Havelock Ellis's review of *Jude the Obscure*, since he too played down the neurotic element: "Sue is neurotic, some critics say; it is fashionable to play cheerfully with terrible words you know nothing about. 'Neurotic' these good people say by way of dismissing her, innocently unaware that many a charming 'urban miss' of their own acquaintance would deserve the name at least as well".[80] I think these comments can be attributed primarily to Hardy's achievement in conveying Sue's attractiveness and charm, also to the fact that many of her attitudes are (in spite of her revolutionary claims) those of the ideal Victorian maiden, wishing to "ennoble some man to high aims" and to elevate him out of his masculine "grossness", so that she did appear perhaps as one among many "charming urban misses". Ellis is also claiming superior and specialised knowledge of neuroses, but his later psychological writings classify people very similar to Sue as distinctly neurotic:

> We have to recognise that while in its more moderate demands an ideal of sexual abstinence remains within the sphere of sanity, it tends to pass beyond that sphere in its more extravagant demands. The conception of sexual abstinence . . . fails even to evoke any genuine moral motives, for it is exclusively self-regarding and self-centred . . . moreover in this special matter of sex, it is inevitable that the needs of others, and not merely the needs of the individual himself, should determine action.[81]

This might well be a summary of Sue's behaviour. Ellis's description of "exclusively self-regarding and self-centred behaviour" exactly fits her treatment of the undergraduate, of Phillotson, of Jude. It would not be an exaggeration to say that she practises sexual abstinence "passing beyond the sphere of sanity" with the undergraduate

and Phillotson, and even with Jude, it is the self-centred need to keep
him from Arabella which makes her consent to go to bed with him
eventually, although in eloping with him she told him she had "resolved to trust you to set my wishes above your gratification".[82] The
neurotic nature of Sue's attitude to marriage is emphasised by a comparison with Sally in "Interlopers at the Knap" (*Wessex Tales*),
who decides quite calmly and rationally after one disappointment
that she does not wish to marry. Hardy shows her decision to be a sensible one; he appreciates her unconventionality and independence,
and enjoys the discomfiture and incredulity of the somewhat
despised suitor. This mature, well-balanced woman's refusal to
conform to the expected pattern of behaviour contrasts with Sue's
neurotic advances and retreats. This rather slight story shows that
Hardy made a clear distinction between a sane rational rejection of
marriage and the neurotic, hovering on the brink, shifting between
rejection and acceptance of Sue.

Surprisingly, Lawrence is among those who failed to recognise the
real nature of Sue's conflicts. This is probably because he is far more
concerned in his "Study of Thomas Hardy" to work out his own philosophy and development as a novelist than to assess Hardy's. The
study is interesting and illuminating because it shows the affinity between the two novelists and the powerful impact Hardy made on
Lawrence, but, as he said, "it is the story of my heart" and thus illuminates Lawrence more than Hardy. He has some interesting comments on Sue, but simplifies Hardy's treatment of her sexuality. He
says she is completely sexless, "scarcely a woman at all",[83] and argues
that she should have been left intact. "She had a being special and
beautiful . . . . She was not a woman . . . . Why was there no place for
her? . . . . If we had reverence for what we are, our life would take
real form, and Sue would have a place, as Cassandra had a place."[84]
This part of his argument suggests that Sue's sexual problems come
almost exclusively from the outside, from the men who love her and
from a society which cannot accept the existence of sexless beings.
This argument cannot be sustained in the light of Sue's repeated attempts to attract men. Nor can Hardy possibly be construed as saying that society forces a sex life on its unwilling members. Much of
the novel is an indictment of a society which restricts, condemns and
denies sexuality. Possibly Lawrence is here really expressing second
thoughts on Miriam (the essay was written in 1914, the year after the
publication of *Sons and Lovers*). The character he creates out of Sue
has some resemblances to Miriam, in her high evaluation of learning

and knowing (though Sue is far more intellectual and widely read than Miriam) and also in the way he imagines she treats her children. He says Sue "would not be satisfied till she had them crushed on her breast".[85] In fact, Sue only shows an interest in her children when they are dead. She attends to their physical needs, but otherwise seems to have little contact with them. She talks to Little Father Time who is old enough to take part in an intellectual discussion, but the total impression, created largely by omission, is of a cool, detached mother. It is only when they are dead and buried that she becomes passionate about them, struggling hysterically to get to them in their coffins. This is characteristic of all her human relationships. When there is a barrier (Jude is outside the window, or she is communicating with him by letter, or he is departing for the last time), she can feel affectionate, even passionate. Lawrence is using Hardy as a springboard to stimulate his own imagination rather than analysing his art as a novelist.

A close reading of *Jude the Obscure* makes it clear that Hardy with great insight and sympathy, is carefully building up a picture of a personality precariously balanced on the edge of sanity. As Havelock Ellis says, she is not "a monstrosity", but Hardy has created convincingly the weaknesses in her personality, "the channels of least resistance along which the forces of life most impetuously rush",[86] and which in the end undermine her precarious balance. Sue is the culmination of several attempts of this kind — Boldwood, Knight, Angel, possibly Clym — but she is the most complex and the most vital and, as he said to Gosse, exceptionally difficult to depict. One of the difficulties was the ban on saying anything honestly about sexual relationships in contemporary fiction. "Candour in English Fiction" makes it clear that Hardy regarded this as one of the major obstacles to the writing of serious fiction. His final novel is a determined attempt to break down these taboos on "those issues which are not to be mentioned in respectable magazines and select libraries".[87] He is far more explicit in his treatment of Sue's sexual difficulties than his letter to Gosse suggests. There he says,

One point illustrating this I could not dwell upon: that, though she had children, her intimacies with Jude have never been more than occasional, even when they were living together (I mention that they occupy separate rooms, except towards the end) and one of her reasons for fearing the marriage ceremony is that she fears it would be breaking faith with Jude to withhold herself at pleasure, or altogether, after it; though while uncontracted she feels at liberty to yield herself as seldom as she chooses.[88]

But in fact all this is very clear in the book itself. Hardy stresses her intellectual fascination with sex in her "daring" views on "The Song of Songs": "I hate such humbug as could attempt to plaster over with ecclesiastical abstractions such ecstatic, natural human love as lies in that great and passionate song".[89] The implications of this come out quite clearly in her account of her relations with the undergraduate: "he wanted me to be his mistress, but I wasn't in love with him — and on my saying I should go away if he didn't agree to *my* plan, he did so. We shared a sitting-room for fifteen months."[90] Already here she is showing her delight in arousing love and her inability to reciprocate it and her mixture of guilt and self-righteousness because of this. While weeping and accusing herself of cruelty, she says, "People say I must be cold-natured — sexless — on account of it. But I won't have it! Some of the most passionately erotic poets have been the most self-contained in their daily lives," and a little later she speaks of wanting "to ennoble some man to high aims".[91] This attempt to justify herself for alternately attracting and repulsing her lovers is of course a rationalisation of something Hardy suggests is not wholly involuntary. The marriage "rehearsal" with Jude on her wedding morning is deliberately contrived by this "epicure of the emotions".[92] Her sadism is directed towards both lovers. She wilfully tortures Jude by taking his arm for the first time that morning and forcing him through what is almost a mock marriage; then she taunts Phillotson with the fact that they have done this. Between the two episodes, she masochistically expresses remorse for what she had done. Jude thinks, "Possibly she would go on inflicting such pains again and again, and grieving for the sufferers again and again, in all her colossal inconsistency".[93]

The immediate cause of her marrying Phillotson is jealousy at the news of Jude's marriage, but Hardy hints at other reasons too. He stresses Phillotson's age, his restrained, subdued manner. He also shows how Sue retreats whenever Jude becomes demonstrative. He seems to be implying that Sue feels she can marry Phillotson because she hopes that he will not make any sexual demands on her (and Jude thinks that she does not know what marriage means). Hardy makes it clear to the reader that any such expectations are false. He says of Phillotson's celibacy, "It was a renunciation forced upon him by his academic purpose, rather than a distaste for women which had

hitherto kept him from closing with one of the sex in matrimony".[94]
If she had any such hope, it is fading by the evening of the wedding,
when "she has the manner of a scared child". After the wedding,
Hardy unambiguously underlines the physical repulsion Sue feels.
Shortly after the marriage, she defends a hypothetical woman "who
didn't like to live with her husband . . . merely because she had a feeling against it — a physical objection — a fastidiousness".[95] A little
later, she is admitting, "It is a torture to me to live with him as a husband".[96] This feeling on Sue's part is explicable enough. Hardy has
made it quite clear that she is not in love with Phillotson. She has
committed herself to the marriage for a number of largely negative
reasons — annoyance at Jude's marriage, fear of public opinion after
her expulsion from college, and a failure to imagine what marriage
is likely to entail. The fact that she has not foreseen that the sexual
relationship may be a problem is perhaps more revealing than her
dismay when actually confronted by Phillotson as a lover. She is educated, emancipated, independent, and presumably is not simply ignorant of the facts of marriage. Yet she repressed all thoughts about
this aspect of it until it was too late. This suggests a tendency to repression which is often a feature of neurosis and throws some light
on her return to Phillotson's bed at the end of the novel.

There seems to me absolutely no grounds for assuming that
Phillotson has "some unexplained sexual peculiarities". Lerner and
Holmstrom argue that the book is ambiguous on this point, that "a
novelist who has begun to be outspoken must not stop halfway".[97]
Admittedly, there are two hints that Phillotson might be abnormal
sexually, one coming from Aunt Drusilla: "There be certain men
here and there no woman can stomach. I should have said he was
one".[98] But Aunt Drusilla is hardly an unbiased judge since she is a
spinster with a lifelong hatred of marriage. The other suggestion
comes from Widow Edlin:

" 'What is it you don't like about him?' asked Mrs Edlin curiously.
'I cannot tell. It is something . . . I cannot say' ".[99]

But this only shows that the 'normal' Mrs Edlin could not sense anything she "couldn't stomach" in Phillotson. All the other evidence
points to Phillotson being tolerant, long-suffering, generous, but an-
noyed, disappointed and hurt by Sue's horror of a sexual relationship
with him. There is, perhaps, a hint that the marriage was not consummated; when Jude and Sue meet for the first time after it, "she

seemed unaltered — he could not say why".[100] Hardy's intention is not clear here, but there is otherwise no ambiguity about Sue's relations with Phillotson; physically, she cannot stand him, she would rather sleep in a cupboard among spiders than with him, she jumps out of a window to escape him. Lerner and Holmstrom ask, "Is Hardy portraying the sufferings of a woman who has found herself with a physically incompatible mate, or a frigid woman? The difference is surely important, and it implies a further question, what were her sexual relations with Jude like?".[101] They do not answer the question, but Hardy does. He not only shows both relationships in considerable detail, but he makes explicit comments: "the ethereal, fine-nerved, sensitive girl, quite unfitted by temperament and instinct to fulfil the conditions of the matrimonial relationship with Phillotson, possibly with scarce any man".[102] (It is, incidentally, noteworthy that when Sue is weeping and saying that Aunt Drusilla is right about Phillotson, she says "perhaps I ought not to have married", not "perhaps I ought not to have married him".[103])

Of course, there is a difference in her relationship with Jude, for, as Arabella says, "She cares for him — as much as she is able to".[104] But Hardy, nevertheless, builds up a clear picture of her feeling of dislike for any sexual relationship. She wishes that Eve had not fallen "so that some harmless form of vegetation might have peopled Paradise".[105] She asks Jude to elope with her, then demands separate rooms. Hardy gives an outspoken conversation between them with no "stopping short". Sue, obviously, is evasive. The dialogue would be very unconvincing if she were not. But Hardy manages to convey the important point quite clearly in spite of this. At first she says that she is timid, then that Phillotson has been so generous that, "I would rather not be other than a little rigid"(the tortuous negative effectively conveys her nervous tension). Then she admits, "My nature is not so passionate as yours". She tells Jude that Phillotson "was too resigned almost" at letting her go. Here Hardy brings in something he emphasises at every opportunity — Sue's incessant hunger to be loved, even though she knows she can give almost nothing in return. The conversation continues:

'If I loved him ever so little as a wife, I'd go back to him even now'. 'But you don't, do you?' 'It is true — O so terribly true — I don't.' 'Nor me neither, I half fear', he said pettishly, 'Nor anybody perhaps! Sue, sometimes when I am vexed with you, I think you are incapable of real love . . . . '

' . . . . My liking for you is not as some women's perhaps. But it is a delight in being with you, of a supremely delicate kind, and I don't want to go further and risk it by — an attempt to intensify it! . . . . I resolved to trust you to set my wishes above your gratification.'[106]

Here Hardy makes Sue express very clearly her distaste for and fear of sexual intercourse. Her attitude is conveyed with delicacy and subtlety, but the reader cannot misunderstand what she is saying. Had he made her any more explicit, he would have falsified her character. This stilted, rational piece of self-analysis is characteristic and credible. She has what Lawrence calls "sex in the head" rather than the sexlessness he attributes to her, enjoys talking about love and sex, but gets frightened as soon as a physical relationship seems to be a possibility. Lerner and Holmstrom's suggestion that Hardy ought to have answered the question, "Is she frigid? Yes or No?" has something of the crudity of a sex manual or a lawcourt beside Hardy's complex rendering of Sue's conflicting emotions.

Far from "stopping short", Hardy continues to show Sue's fears of sex. When Jude and Sue are both divorced and free to marry one another, Sue says, "I would much rather go on . . . only meeting by day. It is so much sweeter — for the woman at least, and when she is sure of the man".[107] Eventually, of course, she does go to bed with Jude, but this is solely in order to keep him for herself when Arabella threatens her security. She does it saying, "I am not a cold-blooded sexless creature, am I, for keeping you at such a distance?"[108]

But they do not get married. They do not even share a bedroom. Hardy unobtrusively indicates this on the night of Father Time's arrival: "Jude had just retired to bed and Sue was about to enter her chamber adjoining when she heard the knock and came down".[109] This is the point that Hardy said he "could not dwell on" in the letter to Gosse. But he succeeds in making it clear enough that Sue had not wholeheartedly accepted Jude as a lover. "A fortnight or three weeks" after Arabella's influential visit, he shows Sue's jealousy of her aroused again by the sight of Little Father Time. Jude comments, "Jealous little Sue! I withdraw all my remarks about your sexlessness".[110] Hardy certainly intends us to notice the timing of this remark, and later implies that the situation of those first two or three weeks is not much improved after years of living together, when Jude says she is "not quite so impassioned perhaps as I could wish".[111] Hardy further increases the impression that their sexual relationship has not had much positive impact on Sue by showing her, after she has accepted Little Father Time and told him to call her mother, saying, "I feel myself getting intertwined with my kind".[112] Yet making love with Jude has not made her feel this.

So far then Hardy has given a sympathetic portrait of an extremely complex personality for whom some calamitous experience is likely to be traumatic. While enabling us to experience what it is like to be Sue, what it is like to know and love her and be exasperated by her, he has simultaneously outlined the symptoms of psychological weakness which will make any disastrous event traumatic for her. Her particular kind of psychological problem was perhaps particularly prevalent among women at that time, possibly partly as a result of the growing opportunities for education and partial emancipation — a situation which tended to arouse new hopes and frustrate them at the same time. Freud devised what he called a "parable" about two girls which gives in outline the kind of contrast Hardy embodied in Sue and Arabella. Freud's story describes how as little girls the daughters of a landlord and his caretaker play with one another and have sex play together. As they get older the landlord's daughter is kept busy being educated and cannot play with her friend. The caretaker's child continues the same kind of play with other children, sees sexual activity going on at home, has a boyfriend at puberty, soon a lover, marries young, has children and takes it all for granted. For the other girl, life is more difficult:

> The well-brought-up, intelligent and high-minded girl has completely repressed her sexual impulses . . . [she] came under the influence of education and accepted its demands. From the suggestions offered to it, her ego constructed ideals of feminine purity and abstinence which are incompatible with sexual activity; her intellectual education reduced her interest in the feminine part which she was destined to play. Owing to this higher moral and intellectual development of her ego, she came into conflict with the demands of her sexuality.[113]

It is interesting that Hardy and Freud in their portraits of contrasting women are pinpointing precisely the same point of contrast. The kind of woman they are both describing — educated and inhibited — is the modern woman of the late nineteenth and early twentieth century (Freud's account was written in 1917). It is an indication of Hardy's awareness and sensitivity that he was able to observe and understand such psychological problems and then create a character which embodies them more than twenty years before Freud diagnosed them through psychoanalysis. This is a further example of Hardy giving imaginative life to the kind of knowledge about human nature which was explored in a different way with the development of psychoanalysis.

Hardy said that Sue was a type of woman who had always interested him,[114] and this seems to be true of Freud also. Many of the qualities which Hardy portrays so vividly in Sue as she experiences and inflicts joy and anguish were found also by Freud in the neurotic women he analysed. She is similar to those "narcissistic" women whose needs do not "lie in the direction of loving but of being loved".[115] "Strictly speaking, it is only themselves that such women love with an intensity comparable to that of a man's love for them".[116] Such a woman's attitude towards men is cool and she causes her lovers "doubts of her love and complaints of her enigmatic nature".[117] Hardy gives a beautiful illustration of Sue's narcissism when she tries to get Jude to quote from "Epipsychidion", and eventually recites the lines herself, applying them to herself and saying that they are "too flattering".[118] Freud's, "They are plainly seeking themselves as love objects",[119] parallels this. Sue reveals that she regards this as an admirable emotional state when she claims that "some of the most passionately erotic poets have been the most self-contained in their daily lives".[120] Freud uses the words "self-containment" and "inaccessibility" to describe this aspect of narcissism.

Freud maintained that masochism is an element in narcissism since "masochism is actually sadism turned round upon the subject's own ego".[121] As we have seen, Sue continually tortures first her lovers, then herself for having caused them pain. Freud analyses this behaviour:

> We have every reason to believe that sensations of pain, like other unpleasurable sensations, trench upon sexual excitation and produce a pleasurable condition, for the sake of which the subject will even willingly experience the unpleasure of pain. When once feeling pains has become a masochistic aim, the sadistic aim of *causing* pain can arise retrogressively; for while these pains are being inflicted on other people, they are enjoyed masochistically by the subject through his identification of himself with his suffering object. In both, of course, it is not the pain itself that is enjoyed, but the accompanying sexual excitation — so that this can be done especially conveniently from the sadistic position.[122]

Much of this applies to Sue, that "epicure of the emotions" who tantalises and tortures Jude and Phillotson on her wedding day, and before and after. Some of the characteristics, however, do not manifest themselves clearly until after the traumatic experience of the children's deaths, when her whole life is directed towards trying to maintain her precarious mental balance.

The deaths of the children is one of those melodramatic episodes for which Hardy is often criticised. There are obviously some weaknesses in the treatment of it, but the sense of violence and shock is essential to his design. If Sue's psychological vulnerability is to be fully exposed, he must show her precariously built up defences being broken down. He shows the breakdown into hysteria, the frantic struggle at the graveside, then the gradual building of fresh defences, the creation of the neurotic personality as a defence against insanity. All her former qualities are still there; her feelings remain basically the same, though grotesquely exaggerated; it is only the ideas, the theories that change fundamentally. Her sexual fears, her guilt, her masochism persist, increasing wildly: "We should mortify the flesh, — the terrible flesh — the curse of Adam!";[123] "I should like to prick myself all over with pins and bleed out the badness that is in me";[124] she attempts to cope with fear and guilt by a complete reversal of her intellectual position, saying, "It is no use fighting against God".[125] Hardy shows her adopting a harsh, rigid form of Christianity as a way of achieving some kind of self-control; it has to be harsh, because for her nothing milder would be effective.

It is wholly convincing that she should attempt to deal with her emotional problems by self-punishment and rationality. It is reminiscent of Angel's attempt at his time of crisis to solve the problem by thinking, till he was "ill with thinking; eaten out with thinking; withered by thinking". Sue, similarly, applies her intellect to the problem, and comes up with some self-analysis which is strikingly accurate as far as it goes. She tells Jude:

"Your wickedness was only the natural man's desire to possess the woman. Mine was not the reciprocal wish till envy stimulated me to oust Arabella. I had thought I ought in charity to let you approach me — that it was damnably selfish of me to torture you as I did my other friend. But I shouldn't have given way if you hadn't broken me down by making me fear you would go back to her . . . . At first, I did not love you Jude; that I own. When I first knew you I merely wanted you to love me. I did not exactly flirt with you,

Power?.

but that inborn craving that undermines some women's morals almost more than unbridled passion — the craving to attract and captivate, regardless of the injury it may do to the man — was in me; and when I found I had caught you I was frightened. And then — I don't know how it was — I couldn't bear to let you go — possibly to Arabella again — and so I got to love you Jude. But you see, however fondly it ended, it began in the selfish and cruel wish to make your heart ache for me without letting mine ache for you.[126]

That she understand herself as far as this, including her sadistic impulses (she uses the word 'torture') may at first sight seem incompatible with her psychological state. But it is, I think, another example of Hardy's insight into psychological complexities. Such perception on Sue's part is in keeping with her former "sparkling intellect", such close self-obervation is part of her "self-containment"; it is also this which enables her to survive the traumatic experience of the children's deaths combined with her own neuroses without collapsing totally and permanently — which the scene at the graveside shows to have been a possibility. She uses her intellectual recognition of her own guilt to justify her self-punishment (while hardly noticing that Jude will be punished too). Her behaviour is a continuation, in an even more obsessive form, of what it was in the past. When she turns Jude out of the house, she kisses him, and rejects him simultaneously:

> " 'Goodnight', he said, and turned to go. 'Oh but you shall kiss me!' said she, starting up, 'I can't — bear — '."[127]

Thus she builds up her self-protective barriers by forcing Jude to agree to living elsewhere, and then from behind these barriers, demands demonstrations of love.

In their arguments, Sue has always switched from discussion to emotion as soon as they verged on any criticism of herself. Jude feels she is utterly changed, but in fact she has only increased her former tendency to use emotional blackmail when things seemed to be going badly for her. In argument, she has always put her points ruthlessly, sometimes almost contemptuously, adopting a stance of moral superiority. She quotes some words of J. S. Mill to Phillotson and demands to know, "Why can't you act upon them? I wish to always". (The poor man moans, "What do I care about J. S. Mill! I only want to lead a quiet life".)[128] From the heights of her knowledge and understanding she analyses the intellectual phases Jude is going through: "You are in the Tractarian stage now . . . let me see — when was I there? In the year eighteen hundred and —".[129] Yet though she can be so sarcastic and never pulls her punches, she becomes hyper-sensitive when the argument is going against her, and hastily with-draws from it, usually making her opponent seem guilty at the same time. During one of the long discussions on marriage, Sue has made her points as vigorously as Jude has, but when he begins to say that he really fears she cannot love and that women who "play the game of elusiveness" too often "go unlamented to their graves", she "acquired a guilty look; and she suddenly replied in a tragic voice, 'I don't like you so well today as I did Jude! . . . you are not nice — too sermony' ".[130] She then switches round to extreme self-accusation. The same pattern is repeated in the later arguments after the deaths of the children, the main differences being that she starts using emotion as a weapon earlier and her expressions of guilt are far more intense.

During her last meeting with Jude, she performs almost a carica-ture of her earlier actions by repelling him as long as he begs her to come back to him, but as soon as he starts telling her he will never come to see her again and that "she is not worth a man's love", " 'I can't endure you to say that' she burst out . . . 'Don't, don't scorn me! Kiss me, O kiss me lots of times' ". When he does so, her response is, " 'Now I'll hate myself for ever for my sin' ",[131] and she sends him away, coughing into the rain.

Her attitude to physical sexual relationships also remains basically unchanged even though the outcome in behaviour seems completely contradictory. It is characteristic that, when she has sent the dying Jude away and decided, "I am going to make my conscience right on my duty to Richard — by doing a penance, the ultimate thing", it is then, for the first time, when she will never see Jude again that she says, "I love him — O, grossly". This is the first time that she has ever admitted to any "grossness" in herself. She immediately follows this with her decision to go to bed with Phillotson, "shuddering" and "with a look of aversion . . . and clenched teeth";[132] this epitomises her conscious attitude towards sexual intercourse as something terri-fying and "gross". She sees her decision as a way of enabling herself to cope with her otherwise overwhelming sense of guilt, ostensibly guilt because she left Phillotson in the first place, then guilt because she has kissed Jude, and probably above all, guilt because of the "grossness" of her feelings for him.

Phillotson is very hesitant about admitting her to his bedroom, asks if she realises what she is letting herself in for, and leaves her waiting on the threshold while he fetches a testament on which he makes her swear that she will not see Jude again. Her persistence in the face of all this is characteristic; it is when she is being rebuffed that she demands love.

We do not necessarily have to accept Sue's interpretation of her behaviour as simply a way of expiating her guilt. As we have seen, her self-analysis has been extremely accurate in many respects, but Jude repeatedly feels that since the deaths of the children her intellect has been destroyed: "Her once clear vision was dimmed"; "bereavement seemed to have destroyed her reasoning faculty".[133] Her desire to punish herself is understandable, however unreasonable; she does it by wearing herself out scrubbing the stairs "since eight" and simultaneously washing away her guilt. Hardy often shows neuroses emerging in minor typical modes of behaviour which are very effective in giving substance and actuality to the psychological states he is describing (Boldwood's clothes fetishism is a comparable example of his use of a clinical symptom). However, scrubbing the stairs all evening is a different matter from forcing herself on a hesitant man, while shrinking, clenching her teeth, but managing to utter no cry.

If at this point, we return to Freud, we find a possible interpretation of this episode which differs from Sue's explanation of her motives but corresponds more closely with Hardy's total treatment of her. Freud says:

> Of the many symptomatic pictures in which obsessional neurosis appears, the most important turn out to be those provoked by the pressure of excessively strong sadistic sexual impulses (perverse therefore in their aim). The symptoms, indeed in accordance with the structure of an obsessional neurosis, serve predominantly as a *defence* against these wishes or give expression to the struggle between satisfaction and defence. But satisfaction does not come off too badly either; it succeeds in roundabout ways in putting itself into effect in the patient's behaviour and is preferably directed against themselves and makes them into self-tormenters.[134]

Freud is here talking about people who find a substitute for the sexual act, but Sue's "prostituting" herself to Phillotson is just as much an "abnormal method of sexual excitation"[135] as any other perverse inclination. Freud's suggestion that such people are creating a defence against strong sexual impulses does not fit in with Sue's own view of her refinement and elevating "freedom from grossness" but it does give a more plausible explanation of her repeated attracting and repulsing than any she offers herself.

I have up to this point been arguing that Hardy's psychological insight is fully conscious, that he is interested in and aware of psychological theory as well as being particularly able to enter imaginatively into the mode of being of psychologically disturbed characters. With Sue, I think, we have an example of an intuitive glimpse of an idea which has not been fully formulated though it has been embodied in the novel. Hardy does not at any point in the novel state explicitly that Sue's aversion to sexual relationships derives from exceptionally strong drives which have been suppressed. All the characters, including Sue herself, assume the opposite. Yet the story shows her continually creating cliff-hanging situations (by living with the undergraduate, by marrying Phillotson, by eloping with Jude) in which the possibility of a sexual relationship is always present but kept at bay. In the description of the return to Phillotson, her aversion is shown to be so violent that it seems almost incredible that she would go through with it; if, however, Hardy has intuitively sensed that people like Sue have violent but repressed sex drives which they are terrified of, then the shuddering and clenched teeth fit the total picture. As Freud said, "satisfaction does not come off too badly either". Later in the same work, he accounts for this by saying, "It seems that an accumulation of narcissistic libido beyond a certain amount is not to be tolerated".[136] The step from Sue's admission of her feelings about Jude — "I love him — O grossly!"[137] to Phillotson's bed is explicable in this way.

Whether we accept Freud's theory as psychologically accurate or not, there is much in the novel to suggest that Hardy was thinking on similar lines. Sue cannot allow her sexual feelings into her consciousness, but Hardy shows them emerging in other ways. When she says, "I should like to prick myself all over with pins and bleed out the badness that is in me",[138] the image is a sexual, as well as a masochistic one. This advanced, modern young woman is totally incapable of telling Little Father Time about childbirth; she will never express feelings of love except when their fulfilment has become impossible. (Even on the happy day at the Agriculture Show, when Jude tries to get her to say that she is happy "because *we* have come" to the show, she replies, "You are always trying to make me confess to all sorts of absurdities. Because I am improving my mind, of course".)[139] At the time, these responses seem to support her own view that she is too re- fined for sex, but her later developments cast doubt on this. That she should choose sex as punishment, and actually force herself upon Phillotson at a time when she has managed to set up the kind of situation which she has always apparently sought — living with a man who loves and admires her but makes no sexual demands on her — makes her explanation suspect. It is worth remembering also that it is at the point when she has established precisely the same Platonic relationship in her first marriage to Phillotson that she de- cides to leave him for Jude. Freud says that we must not "judge every- thing as it appears to the ego of the neurotic subject";[140] certainly by the last chapters of the book we accept that Sue's "once clear vision is dimmed". Hardy's treatment of the story suggests "the repressed and repudiated demands of sexuality", and also that this repudiation is not prompted by the straightforward distaste which she claims, since she follows each successful repudiation by seeking a new set-up where a sexual relationship will become a possibility again.

I am not claiming that it is necessary to have read Freud in order to understand Hardy's Sue; all the points I have made can be grasped from the text. But I must admit that Freud did clarify many points for me, which now seem self-evident and I am surprised that I had not noticed them before. Nor am I suggesting that Hardy for- mulated Freud's theory about the repression of libido in the novel. This seems to be one of the few occasions when Hardy intuitively glimpsed an explanation of an aspect of human behaviour without being completely conscious of what he was doing. It is perhaps sig- nificant that it is in the Preface to *Jude* that Hardy says, "no doubt there can be more in a novel than the author consciously puts there".

I think this element was subconscious rather than unconscious and this affects not only the content of Sue's character but also the method of presenting her in the novel. The detailed exploration of sexual neuroses was the most striking innovation at the time, but the whole conception and treatment of Sue as a character in a novel is also a major innovation. From his earliest writings Hardy had been conscious that human beings are ultimately unknowable. Eustacia's enigmatic character is viewed speculatively from the outside; Hen- chard's behaviour is not wholly explicable; Grace is seen as "a con- jectural creature". With Sue, the uncertainty is emphasised more strongly. She cannot be pinned down, defined or explained. She has "indefinable charm"[141] and "liquid untranslateable eyes".[142] There is "the elusiveness of her curious double nature",[143] which makes her impossible to understand completely. The other characters continually puzzle over her. Phillotson calls her "puzzling" and "unstateable" and says, "her exact feeling for him [Jude] is a riddle to me — and to him, too, I think — possibly to herself".[144] Jude confirms this: "she was a riddle to him"; "her conduct was one lovely conundrum to him".[145] He can never make up his mind about her. At first he is attracted by her apparent unconventionality, by her calling across the road to him at the Martyrs' Memorial and by her "advanced" ideas. But before long he is saying, "You seem to me to have nothing unconventional at all about you,"[146] and yet the next day, "I believe you are as innocent as you are unconventional".[147] Later, he tells her, "You are as enslaved to the social code as any woman I know".[148]

Much of Jude's thinking about her is expressed interrogatively. Meditating on the broken heart of her undergraduate friend, he wonders whether he is to be the next one.[149] He wonders whether her reference to himself as her "married relation" has its source in "satire or suffering".[150] During the wedding he tries to analyse her personality, and finds no answer to his question — "How could Sue have had the temerity to ask him to do it? [to give her away] . . . was she simply perverse? . . . possibly she would go on inflicting such pains again and again".[151] When he meets her again, "She seemed unaltered . . . he could not say why".[152]

In these ways, Hardy creates a living, changing, incompletely comprehensible being. He avoids the effect of a too precise clinical analysis so that there is no suggestion of a case history in spite of the mass of clinical psychological material embedded in the novel. In these ways he moves further away than ever from the comparative certitude about characterisation of his nineteenth-century predecessors. Though he explores her psychological complexities in great depth, he deliberately avoids giving the impression that she is a finite being whose personality can be wholly explained or encapsulated in words. The alteration of "unpredictable" in the first edition to "unstateable" in later editions confirms that Hardy wanted to emphasise that however minutely he analyses the character, there always remains an area of her being which is unknowable. Puzzling, unstateable Sue with her violent contradictions and inconsistency ("You mustn't love me" on one page; "If you want to love me you may"[153] on the next), leads straight to those fluctuations of feeling, to that awareness of the ebb and flow of emotion which Lawrence showed so powerfully in his characters. Hardy's insistence on her elu-

siveness parallels Ursula's rejection of the idea that you can add someone up and draw a line underneath.[154] Lawrence went very much
further in finding ways of suggesting, without defining, the unconscious processes of his characters. In Hardy we do not get that positive sense of the existence of "darkest avenues of the soul",[155] which
Lawrence creates. But by establishing so vividly Sue's elusiveness
and contradictoriness he points towards the region which Lawrence
was to make a central area of his novels.

Lawrence's language is more sensuous, rhythmical, powerful,
adventurous than Hardy's. Nevertheless, Hardy has succeeded in
finding ways of conveying the indefinable and unconscious aspects
of Sue's personality, both in the ways I have mentioned and in his use
of dialogue. This is an aspect of Hardy's novels that has come in for
an excessive amount of adverse criticism. I have defended some instances of the use of stilted language by his inhibited characters, and
would go further here and claim that the language he gives Sue
expresses her nature fully and accurately. Alvarez complains that
"Jude and Sue speak to one another as though they had just been
introduced at a vicarage tea-party".[156] But this is just as it should be.
In theory so daring, in practice so inhibited, Sue naturally talks,
especially about emotional matters, in this stiff, intellectual way.
When Jude first meets her shouting across the road to him, and attacking conventional attitudes, she seems to be free and adventurous
in outlook and speech. But as Hardy develops her inconsistencies
and shows her fears and inhibitions, he also conveys an ambiguity in
her language. As Heilman has pointed out, her attack on marriage
as "a sordid contract" seems original at first, but in her continued descriptions of it as "vulgar", "low" and "sordid" she is using just the
words which were applied at the time (and often in reviews of Hardy's
novels) to anything to do with sex. Sue uses them as part of her cam-
paign against marriage, but they are also an expression of her conventional anti-sex attitude.[157] The conversation with Little Father
Time the night before the murders is an example of how Hardy
can convey in a few lines of dialogue a whole range of shifting
thoughts and feeling and unconscious fears and hesitations. Sensitive Sue is so wrapped up in her own troubles that she is totally insensitive to the effect she may be having on the child. She decides to be
"honest and candid" with him, then when the matter of childbirth
comes up she speaks "hesitantly", "murmurs", "can't explain", cannot finish her sentences, will explain when he is older, and lets the
boy go away thinking that she has simply "sent for another" baby.[158]

Even the involvement of Jude in this evasive language seems to me justified. He is attracted by "sprite-like" qualities and perpetually afraid of frightening her away altogether, and is always anxious to avoid anything she might feel was "gross" and ready to apologise ("Forgive me for being 'gross' "). This is highlighted effectively on the night of Arabella's visit when, fed up with Sue's insistence on celibacy, he decides to go out after Arabella, and his language becomes blunt and forthright. The sense of awkwardness sometimes conveyed by the dialogue is never a blemish when Sue is speaking, but an element in the successful presentation of her character.

In "Candour in English Fiction", Hardy argued that most contemporary fiction was weak and insincere because of the taboos against "the explicit novel"; the remedy lay, he suggested, in "intellectual adventurers" attempting "original treatment" of the passions. He admitted that originality was dangerous, risked failure or at least "crude results".[159] Hardy attempted this adventure in his creation of Sue. There are some crudities in the novel (the over-insistent symbolism of Little Father Time, for instance) but in the characterisation of Sue Hardy combines originality with subtlety. Hardy in 1895 is writing the first twentieth-century novel. He has rejected Victorian taboos and written explicitly about sexual relationships, emotional disturbances, unconscious fears and motives. It cannot be denied that, chronologically at least, this was an advance; where Hardy led, many twentieth-century novelists followed. It is arguable that, aesthetically, it was not a forward step and that since Hardy the novel has become obsessed with sex and neuroses to its detriment. But, whatever the long-term effect of this development of subject-matter and approach, Hardy was justified in feeling that it had to be made if the novel was to be meaningful "to men and women of full age". He would have agreed with Lawrence that, "If a novel reveals true and vivid relationships it is a moral work, no matter what the relationship consists in";[160] it is, after all, the core of the argument of "Candour in English Fiction". Hardy's claim that *Jude* ... makes for morality more than any other book I have written"[161] expresses much the same thought.

I think it is important to stress that Hardy's originality does not lie in his treatment of "a special case" but that he is concerned, in depicting Sue, with questions of wide relevance which became matters of more general concern in the earlier years of the twentieth century. Sue's unbalanced state is shown as partly due to the fact that she has educated her intellect without developing emotionally at the same time. Her reading is of an abstract, rational kind. The only poets she mentions are Shelley and Swinburne and they seem to appeal to her primarily because of their atheism. Hardy shows in her a lack of balance between intellect and emotions which develops into a suppression of instinctual drives. The dangers of this kind of development were to become apparent to many kinds of writers after Hardy. Among novelists, Forster with his theory of "the undeveloped heart" and Lawrence with his stress on the need for a harmonious balance between mind and body are clearly developing themes that were central in Hardy's work. Educationists such as A. S. Neill suggested the development of *Hearts not Heads in School*. All of them would have agreed with Freud that society overvalued man's rational powers, that

> the cultural super-ego . . . does not trouble enough about the mental constitution of human beings; it enjoins a command and never asks whether or not it is possible for them to obey it. It presumes, on the contrary, that a man's ego is psychologically capable of anything that is required of it — that his ego has unlimited power over his id. This is an error; even in so-called normal people the power of controlling the id cannot be increased beyond certain limits. If one asks more of them, one produces revolt or neurosis in individuals or makes them unhappy.[162]

In this, one of his latest works, Freud sums up in psychological terms the dangers of the kind of imbalance that Hardy showed in Sue. In 1893, Hardy wrote to Mrs Henniker, "If you want to make the world listen to you, you must say now what they will all be thinking and saying five and twenty years hence".[163] On this topic he seems to have got the timing just about right.

Hardy's main innovations lie in his subject matter. By opening up the novel to new areas of thought and feeling, by making conscious matters which in the nineteenth century tended to be repressed, he was enlarging its scope immensely and increasing its relevance to the "men and women of full age" to whom he was addressing it. This inevitably had an effect on his mode of characterisation. He has that capacity, which Forster thought was characteristic of the modern novelist, to put down a bucket into the unconscious and accept whatever came up. The change in the concept of characterisation, with the emphasis on the existence of unknowable areas of the personality, is not quite so striking as the change in subject matter, but it is a natural consequence of it. Lawrence wrote, "The novel has a future. It's got to have the courage to tackle new propositions without using abstractions; it's got to present us with new, really new feelings, a whole new line of emotions, which will get us out of the emotional rut".[164] A little hesitantly and cautiously, Hardy is doing this. These developments are embodied in a character that has so much vitality and is depicted with such sympathy that it is indeed "a point of major innovation in prose fiction".

10 Conclusion

Hardy's psychological insight is the basis of the kind of novels he wrote. Their diversity, the multiplicity of interests expressed in them, spring from his sensitivity to, and humane sympathy for a wide variety of human beings, a compassion which includes all living things. It is this variousness which has given rise to the many divergent notions of what is the central quality of his art. Some of his contemporaries thought his intention was to shock and disgust, some later readers felt that primarily he evoked nostalgia for a lost, rural past, others saw him as a fatalist and pessimist. Recent criticism has been concerned to define his philosophical position more precisely and to show its relevance to the modern world. Ian Gregor has pointed out that while there are "a number of quite definable interests running through" the novels, "nevertheless, separate and distinctive as these interests are, they do not seem to compromise, much less to threaten the unity and coherence of the novels".[1] Gregor's central theme is that we must not look in Hardy for the kind of enclosed Jamesian structure, but see a Hardy novel rather as "a gradually unfolding process".[2] I find his argument wholly convincing; indeed, by a quite different route, I have come to conclusions very similar to Gregor's. Both the diversity and the coherence of Hardy's novels arise from the great breadth of his sympathies. His ability to enter into a wide variety of modes of being underlies the basic structure of his novels.

"The book is all contrasts", Hardy said of *Jude the Obscure*.[3] The variety of contrasts, some of which Hardy lists in the letter, is perhaps greater in this novel than in the others, but they are all based on a structure which emphasises the possibility of choice, of the different ways of reacting to a given situation which are open to human beings. The different responses to the storm in *Far from the Madding Crowd*, to the Heath in *The Return of the Native*, to the bad weather in *The Mayor of Casterbridge* are clearcut examples of the structure in all the novels. The choices the characters make arise from the nature of the personality ("Character is Fate")[4] which Hardy is in the process of creating and analysing. The structure and the action of the novels derive from the personalities of the characters.

Any reader who enters imaginatively into Hardy's world will experience the emotions of the more immediately apprehensible and sympathetic characters, will weep with Tess, share Jude's anguish. The psychological depth of the treatment of the neurotic characters may be overlooked because of the intensity of the involvement with the others. But it is vital to a full understanding of Hardy's art to recognise that we are being asked to respond to a variety of modes of experiencing. One of the things Hardy particularly admires in Tess is her willingness to let other people be themselves, her refusal to impose her wishes on others. He reveals something of his own quality as a novelist in this. He creates and explores complex and difficult personalities, and in doing so extends to them tolerant acceptance and understanding.

These difficult and disturbed characters on which I have mainly focused are particularly important for understanding the impression of the world Hardy is showing us, and the kind of fiction he is creating to embody it. I have taken the risk of perhaps distorting Hardy's total picture by putting so much emphasis on this aspect of it. I have done this partly because, though his psychological insight is now recognised, it does not seem to have been fully explored, partly because it becomes increasingly important as Hardy develops as a novelist, and partly because it is the basis of all the varied elements in the novels. His concern for the individual, his conception of society which arises from that concern, and his aspirations for the novel form as a vehicle for that concern, all spring from his awareness of human complexity and vulnerability.

The range of Hardy's psychological insight leads to his sense of society's unaccommodating attitude to individuals. Sue's idea that laws ought to be adjusted according to individual needs is his own theory; he wrote to the Parisian paper, *L'Ermitage*, in 1893: "I consider a social system based on individual spontaneity to promise better for happiness than a curbed and uniform one under which all temperaments are bound to shape themselves to a single pattern of living. To this end I would have society divided into *groups of temperaments*, with a different code of observances for each group".[5] While he recognised that there were plenty of "irremediable ills" in life, he maintained that "it is certain that men make it much worse than it need be".[6] He knew the difficulty of adjusting to both remediable and irremediable ills, and understood those who failed to make such an adjustment. There is certainly no doubt that one of the things he wanted to do through his novels was to make life more bearable both by changing people's attitudes ("the inert crystallised opinion — hard as a rock — which the vast body of men had vested interests in supporting",[7]) and through this, the social structure. In an unpublished letter to the Fawcett Society, written in reply to a request for his support of the suffragette movement, he wrote,

> "I have for a long time been in favour of women-suffrage. I fear I shall spoil the effect of this statement (if it has any) in my next sentence, by giving you my reason. I am in favour of it because I think the tendency of the women's vote will be to break up the present pernicious conventions in respect of women, customs, religion, illegitimacy, the sterotyped household (that it must be the unit of society), the father of a woman's child (that it is anybody's business but the woman's own) . . . and other matters which I got into hot water for touching on many years ago . . . ."

The letter is dated 30 November 1906. It shows how far-reaching Hardy's criticism of social structures was, as well as underlining, once more, his concern for the individual, his understanding of the variety of human needs and possibilities. In the novels we see an increasing stress on the difficulties of adjusting to the changes which were occurring in his day, such as "the decline in belief in a beneficent Power",[8] and the development of scientific attitudes and techniques, which were combined with the retention of a rigid moral code; this combination, he felt, was making it more and more difficult for people to come to terms not only with society, but with themselves. Tess, pregnant, thinking herself "an anomaly" but really at one with nature,[9] is just one illustration of the impact of society's codes on the individual's concept of himself.

The development of the treatment of psychological difficulties through the major novels indicates a growing sense of the loss of instinctive harmony between mind and body. As the characters develop their intellects, they lose touch with their intuitive faculties, begin to despise the body and senses as "animal" and "gross". Clym's educational plans would totally disregard, even disparage, this aspect of human beings; Angel and Sue cannot admit that it exists within themselves; they inevitably become neurotic. By *Jude the Obscure*, Hardy seems to feel there is no way out. One must either crush oneself, like Sue ("we must conform") or be crushed by the external world's refusal to allow fulfilment. "The war between flesh and spirit" is the central conflict in Hardy's novels, impinging, as he sees it on all aspects of man's life — on his relationships to other people, to himself, to society and to nature. It culminates in *Jude*, where Hardy reaches his impasse, because, while concluding that such a war is unnecessary, he can see no way of persuading mankind of the truth of this, nor of embodying the concept in a positive rather than negative way in a novel.

One of the difficulties lies in the nature of the warring elements. Primitive, instinctive drives are obviously by their nature more difficult to bring into consciousness and express in words than intellectual ones. Hardy wants to convey both the nature of the unconscious and its importance. Ian Gregor quotes approvingly Virginia Woolf's comments on that

> little blur of unconsciousness, that halo of freshness and margin of the unexpressed which often produce the most profound sense of satisfaction. It is as if Hardy was not quite aware of what he did, as if his consciousness held more than he could produce, and he left it for his readers to make out his full meaning and to supplement it from their own experience.[10]

In so far as this corresponds to Hardy's, "no doubt there can be more in a book than the author consciously puts there",[11] it is a valid comment. But in her picture of Hardy "not quite aware of what he did" we are moving dangerously close to the "poor innocent" Hardy found in some of the criticism of Virginia Woolf's contemporaries. That "little blur of unconsciousness" is there because Hardy *is* aware of its existence in *all of us* and far from leaving it to his readers to make it out, he is searching for ways of expressing it in the novels without analysing it precisely and thus defeating his purpose. Hence his experiments with modes of characterisation which will suggest the "conjectural", "puzzling", "unstateable" aspects of personality and hint at the existence of those "darkest avenues of the soul"[12] which Lawrence with his more experimental use of language was able to suggest so vividly. Hardy's movement towards a new conception of character in the novel arises directly from his psychological knowledge and perceptions.

The affinities between Hardy and Lawrence are striking and profound. It is conceivable that if Hardy had gone on writing novels after 1895 he would have written something very similar to those of Lawrence: he might have found ways of expressing the unconscious more fully; he might even have imagined a harmonious relationship with no warring between flesh and spirit. Yet there is a fundamental difference between the two writers. Lawrence was completely ruthless; he shocked people and was banned, whereas Hardy managed to shock people without being banned; Lawrence's technical experiments are bold and far-reaching, Hardy's restrained and tentative. These differences are characteristic of their attitudes to human life. For Lawrence, deadly or destructive people deserve no compassion; the Mater in *The Virgin and the Gipsy* can be left to drown, Banford in "The Fox" can be killed without compunction, Clifford Chatterley can be conceived without any sympathy, because they are "dead men in life".[13] For Hardy, such a conception is inconceivable. The only things he is intolerant of are intolerance and cruelty. There are some minor figures who are treated without sympathy — the farmer at Flintcomb Ash, Angel's brothers, the gossips who object to an unmarried pregnant woman engraving the ten commandments, and the occasional character in the short stories, like Uplandtowers in "Barbara and the House of Grebe"; but these are used primarily as a means of conveying society's communal intolerance. As soon as the characters start to be developed and to be individualised, Hardy's sympathies come into play. Alec d'Uberville is a good example of a character who refuses to remain purely a figure for the author's disapprobation. If Hardy had started to imagine an inner life for the farmer at Flintcomb Ash, he too would have received his compassion. It is this wide-ranging compassion which gives the novels their particular quality, their insight into different modes of being, their sense of the supreme value of the human being, however bewildered, tormented, or even cruel he or she may be.

The openness to all kinds of human experience is of a piece with his frequently stated theory of the novels, that they are "*seemings*, provisional impressions only".[14] This is an echo of his description of *Jude* as "an endeavour to give shape and coherence to a series of seemings or personal impressions".[15] In the Preface to *Poems of the Past and the Present* he said, "unadjusted impressions have their value, and the road to a true philosophy of life seems to lie in humbly recording diverse readings of its phenomena as they are forced upon us by chance and change". Here he was writing about a collection of poems on a variety of subjects written at widely different times, but what he says is relevant to the fiction. The novels give a sense of continuing exploration, of probing deeper and deeper into personality and watching it develop and change in the process, so that we observe not only diverse modes of being among different characters but even within a single character. Even the endings of the novels avoid a sense of completion. In *The Return of the Native* Hardy actually offers alternative endings. In *The Mayor of Casterbridge* we contemplate death, indeed total extinction, but are made aware too of the unforeseen happiness of Elizabeth-Jane's continuing life. In *The Woodlanders* we are invited to speculate about Grace's future while recognising Marty's unchanging devotion. Tess is dead but Angel and Liza-Lou "arose . . . and went on". Even in *Jude* there is the suggestion that later generations may benefit from the "pioneering" of Jude and Sue; there is also a chilling look at the more immediate future, at Sue's life "till she's as he is now". Hardy leaves us with an impression simultaneously of finality and of continuity. At the end, his "seemings" are still divergent and he makes no attempt to reconcile the opposing elements, just as, all through the novels, but especially in the later ones, we have been made aware of the impossibility of defining an individual. The endings take this feeling further. Jude is dead, but the Christminster crowds are cheering the boatraces; Tess's walking across Wessex is finished, but the others are going on. Hardy has lit up for a moment a brief span of time, a few lives, has peered as far as he can into the depths of a few personalities. He ends by insisting that this is only a glimpse, fleeting and uncertain. In this, as in so much else, he has much in common with Freud:

> It is clearly his conception of truth as something hidden, repressed, driven underground, but to which he had come closer than others, that made Freud, despite his belligerent positivism, go so far beyond the materialism of his generation in science in saluting the great novelists and poets. Surely it was this sense of truth as a "mystery" . . . that made Freud venerate those who like Joseph could uncover dreams, or like Moses, see God in fire.[16]

Hardy would perhaps have emphasised the "mystery" even more strongly. The "doctrine of the unknowable" which underlies his philosophy and his psychology is embodied in the form of his novels: "I am utterly bewildered to understand how the doctrine that, beyond the knowable, there must always be the unknown, can be displaced".[17]

Notes

CHAPTER 1

1. *One Rare Fair Woman*: *Thomas Hardy's Letters to Florence Henniker, 1893 — 1922*, edited by E. Hardy and F. B. Pinion (Macmillan, 1972), p. 26.
2. Roy Morrell, *Thomas Hardy, the Will and the Way* (University of Malaya Press, 1965).
3. Jean Brooks, *Thomas Hardy: the Poetic Structure* (Elek, 1971).
4. *Hardy's Personal Writings*, edited by Harold Orel, University of Kansas, 1966 (Macmillan, 1967), p. 137.
5. Ibid., p. 137.
6. Ian Gregor, *The Great Web* (Faber, 1974), p. 321.
7. *Hardy's Personal Writings*, op. cit., pp. 127 — 8.
8. *Tess of the d'Urbervilles* (Collins, 1958), Chapter 35.
9. D. H. Lawrence, 'A Propos of *Lady Chatterley's Lover*' (Penguin, 1961), p. 92.
10. *Tess of the d'Urbervilles*, Chapter 18.
11. *The Return of the Native* (Macmillan, 1960), Book First, Chapter 1.
12. Letter to Harper and Brothers, 7 April 1894, R. L. Purdy, *Thomas Hardy: A Bibliographical Study* (Oxford University Press, 1954), p. 90.
13. Florence Emily Hardy, *The Life of Thomas Hardy* (Macmillan, 1933).
14. *The Literary Notes of Thomas Hardy*, edited by Lennart A. Björk (Göteborg, 1974).
15. I am indebted to Lennart Björk for this information, which is partly derived from his edition of the *Notebooks* and also from his lecture on the influence of Fourier on Hardy's social and psychological thinking given at the 1975 Hardy Society Summer School.
16. Björk, op. cit., p. 76.
17. Ibid., p. 117.
18. Ibid., p. 119.
19. Preface to *Poems of the Past and the Present*, *Complete Poems* (Macmillan, 1976), p. 84.
20. *The Yorkshire Post*, 8 June 1896.
21. *Blackwood's Magazine*, January 1896.
22. Edmund Gosse, Review of *Jude the Obscure* in *St. James's Gazette*, November 1895.
23. *The Savoy*, October 1896.
24. Donald Davidson, "The Traditional Basis of Hardy's Fiction", *The Southern Review*, Hardy Centenary Number, 1940.

25. F. R. Leavis, *The Great Tradition* (Chatto and Windus, 1948), Chapter 1.
26. Lord David Cecil, *Hardy the Novelist* (Constable, 1943), Chapter 5.
27. Davidson, op. cit.
28. A. J. Guerard, *Thomas Hardy* (New Directions, 1964), p. 87.
29. Cecil, op. cit., Chapter 4.
30. Pierre d'Exideuil, *The Human Pair in the Works of Thomas Hardy*, translated by F. W. Gosse (Humphrey Toulmin, 1930).
31. "The Integrity of Hardy", *Essays and Studies of the English Association*, 1948.
32. Roy Morrell, *Thomas Hardy, the Will and the Way*.
33. F. E. Hardy, op. cit., p. 177.
34. *The Return of the Native*, Book Third, Chapter 2.
35. Letter quoted by Theodor Reik in *From Thirty Years with Freud* (New York and Toronto, 1940), p. 175.
36. F. E. Hardy, op. cit., p. 284.

CHAPTER 2

1. *Desperate Remedies* (Macmillan, 1960), Chapter 3.
2. Chapter 8.
3. Chapter 4.
4. Chapter 5.
5. Chapter 5.
6. Chapter 6.
7. Chapter 6.
8. Chapter 6.
9. Charles Morgan, *The House of Macmillan* (Macmillan, 1943), pp. 93–4.
10. *The Spectator*, 22 April 1871.
11. Chapter 8.
12. *A Laodicean* (Macmillan, 1960), Chapter 3.
13. Chapter 6.
14. Chapter 6.
15. Chapter 18.
16. Chapter 6.
17. Chapter 12.
18. Chapter 9.
19. Chapter 11.
20. M. Millgate, *Thomas Hardy* (Bodley Head, 1971), pp. 172–3.
21. "The Distracted Preacher", V (*Wessex Tales*, Macmillan, 1960).
22. Ibid., IV.
23. Note on *Wessex Tales*, 1912.
24. *Desperate Remedies*, Chapter 8.
25. F. E. Hardy, op. cit., p. 370.
26. H. R. Beech, *Changing Man's Behaviour* (Penguin, 1969) p. 27.
27. B. F. Skinner, *Science and Human Behaviour* (Macmillan, 1953), p. 59.
28. In the final chapter of *Introduction to Comparative Psychology* (Walter Scott, 1894).
29. Skinner, op. cit., p. 59.
30. D. Blackman, *Operant Conditioning* (Methuen, 1974), p. 215.

31. Beech, op. cit., p. 153.
32. Ibid., p. 155.
33. Ibid., p. 169.
34. Ibid., p. 178.
35. *After Strange Gods* (Faber, 1934).
36. *The Woodlanders* (Macmillan, 1960), Chapter 14.
37. Ibid., Chapter 14.
38. F. E. Hardy, op. cit., p. 204.

CHAPTER 3

1. Ibid., p. 284.
2. Ibid., p. 287.
3. Ibid., p. 286.
4. *The Well-Beloved* (Macmillan, 1960), Part I: 1.
5. Part I: 2.
6. Part I: 2.
7. Part II: 5.
8. Part II: 13.
9. Part II: 11.
10. Part II: 9.
11. Part I: 9.
12. Part I: 8.
13. Part I: 2.
14. Part I: 2.
15. Part II: 6.
16. Part III: 8.
17. *Illustrated London News*, 3 December 1892.
18. Jung, *Integration of the Personality* (Routledge & Kegan Paul, 1940), Chapter 1.
19. Ibid., Chapter 1.
20. Ibid., Chapter 1.
21. Jung, *Archetypes of the Collective Unconscious, Collected Works*, translated by Hall (Routledge & Kegan Paul, 1954), Vol. 9 (i).
22. Jung, *Integration of the Personality*, Chapter 1.
23. Jung, *Archetypes of the Collective Unconscious, Collected Works*, Vol. 9 (i), p. 27.
24. Jung, *Aion, Collected Works*, Vol. 9 (ii), p. 268.
25. *The Well-Beloved*, Part I: 2.
26. Jung, *Archetypes of the Collective Unconscious, Collected Works*, Vol. 9 (i), p. 25.
27. *The Well-Beloved*, Part II: 3.
28. Part II: 3.
29. Part II: 12.
30. Jung, *Archetypes of the Collective Unconscious, Collected Works*, Vol. 9 (i), p. 286.
31. *The Well-Beloved*, Part II: 6.
32. Jung, *The Integration of the Personality*, p. 82.
33. Jung, *Aion, Collected Works*, Vol. 9 (ii), p. 268.

34. *The Well-Beloved*, Part II: 1.
35. Part II: 1.
36. Jung, *Archetypes of the Collective Unconscious, Collected Works*, Vol. 9 (i), p. 26.
37. *The Well-Beloved*, Part II: 6.
38. Part II: 6.
39. Part II: 1.
40. Part I: 7.
41. Part II: 9.
42. Part I: 9.
43. Part II: 5.
44. Part II: 6.
45. Jung, *Archetypes of the Collective Unconscious, Collected Works*, Vol. 9 (i), p. 26.
46. Ibid., p. 30.
47. Ibid.
48. *The Well-Beloved*, Part I: 7.
49. Jung, *The Integration of the Personality*, p. 19.
50. *The Well-Beloved*, Part III: 2.
51. Jung, *Collected Works*, Vol. 9 (i), p. 270.
52. F. E. Hardy, op. cit., p. 286.
53. Ibid.
54. Ibid., p. 287.
55. Proust, *Letters*, edited by Curtis (Chatto & Windus, 1950).
56. F. E. Hardy, op. cit., p. 217.
57. Proust, *La Prisonnière*, II, translated by C. K. Scott-Moncrieff, (Chatto & Windus, 1922), p. 236.
58. Proust, *Le Temps Retrouvé*, p. 255.
59. F. E. Hardy, op. cit., p. 286.
60. Proust, *Le Côté de Guermantes*, p. 112.
61. *The Well-Beloved*, Part II: 2.
62. F. E. Hardy, *Life of Thomas Hardy*, p. 217.
63. Proust, *A l'Ombre des Jeunes Filles en Fleur*, I, p. 670.
64. Proust, *A l'Ombre*, p. 627.
65. *The Well-Beloved*, Part I: 2.
66. Proust, *A l'Ombre*, I, p. 670.
67. *The Well-Beloved*, Part II: 6.
68. Proust, *A l'Ombre*, I, p. 627.
69. Proust, *Le Temps Retrouvé*, p. 261.
70. F. E. Hardy, op. cit., p. 432.
71. Ibid., p. 177.

CHAPTER 4

1. *Far from the Madding Crowd* (Macmillan, 1960), Chapter 35.
2. Chapter 31.
3. Chapter 49.
4. Chapter 51.
5. Chapter 51.

6. Chapter 52.
7. Chapter 31.
8. Chapter 12.
9. Chapter 14.
10. Chapter 17.
11. Chapter 18.
12. Freud, *Repression, Standard Edition*, translated by James Strachey (Routledge, 1915) Vol. XIV, p. 146.
13. Freud, *Repression*, p. 150.
14. Freud: *Autobiographical Study, Standard Edition* (Routledge & Kegan Paul, 1924), Vol. XX, p. 23.
15. *Far from the Madding Crowd*, Chapter 12.
16. Chapter 14.
17. Chapter 17.
18. Chapter 17.
19. Chapter 18.
20. Chapter 19.
21. Chapter 32.
22. Chapter 18.
23. Freud, *Autobiographical Study*, p. 29.
24. Chapter 31.
25. Freud, *Inhibitions, Symptoms and Anxiety*, Vol. XX, p. 109.
26. Chapter 18.
27. Preface to *Jude the Obscure* (Macmillan, 1960).
28. Preface to *Poems of the Past and the Present, Complete Poems* (Macmillan, 1976).
29. Freud, *Repression*, p. 146.
30. Schopenhauer, *The World as Will and Idea*, (1844) Vol. 3, p. 169, translated by Haldane and Kemp (Trubner, 1883).
31. Freud, *Autobiographical Study*, p. 23.
32. Freud, *On the History of the Psychoanalytical Movement* (1914), Vol. XIV, p. 16.
33. *Far from the Madding Crowd*, Chapter 14.
34. Freud, *Autobiographical Study*, p. 23.
35. *Far from the Madding Crowd*, Chapter 35.
36. Chapter 35.
37. Chapter 12.
38. Chapters 19 and 53.
39. Chapter 19.
40. Chapter 19.
41. Chapter 49.
42. Chapter 55.
43. Chapter 55.
44. Chapter 55.
45. Chapter 15.
46. Chapter 38.
47. Chapter 18.
48. Chapter 53.
49. Chapter 18.

50. Chapter 18.
51. Chapter 18.
52. Freud, *Inhibitions, Symptoms and Anxiety, Standard Edition* (1926), Vol. XX, p. 109.
53. Chapter 14.
54. Chapter 14.
55. "The Mirror and the Sword", *Nineteenth Century Fiction* (March 1964).
56. 24 May 1909. From *One Rare Fair Woman*.

CHAPTER 5

1. Preface to *The Mayor of Casterbridge* (Macmillan, 1960).
2. *The Mayor of Casterbridge*, Chapter 2.
3. Chapter 17.
4. Chapter 5.
5. Chapter 5.
6. Chapter 5.
7. Chapter 9.
8. Chapter 10.
9. Chapter 12.
10. Chapter 31.
11. Chapter 13.
12. Chapter 15.
13. Chapter 27.
14. Chapter 19.
15. Chapter 19.
16. Chapter 19.
17. Chapter 27.
18. Chapter 22.
19. Chapter 25.
20. Chapter 25.
21. Chapter 26.
22. Chapter 27.
23. Chapter 27.
24. Chapter 29.
25. Chapter 31.
26. Chapter 33.
27. Chapter 37.
28. Chapter 35.
29. Chapter 38.
30. Chapter 38.
31. Chapter 40.
32. Chapter 41.
33. Chapter 41.
34. Chapter 41.
35. Chapter 42.
36. Chapter 43.
37. Chapter 44.

38. Chapter 44.
39. Chapter 44.
40. Freud, *Civilisation and its Discontents* (Hogarth Press, 1930), p. 54.
41. *The Mayor of Casterbridge*, Chapter 17.
42. Adler, *Aggressiontrieb*, (1908), *The Individual Psychology of Alfred Adler*, translated by H. L. and R. R. Ansbacher (Allen and Unwin, 1958), p. 35.
43. Ibid., p. 7.
44. Ibid.
45. Lorenz, *On Aggression* (Methuen, 1966), p. 239.
46. Storr, *Human Aggression* (Penguin, 1968), p. 148.
47. *The Mayor of Casterbridge*, Chapter 16.
48. Freud, *Civilisation and its Discontents*, p. 60.
49. Adler, op. cit., p. 271.
50. Ibid., p. 273.
51. Storr, *Human Aggression*, p. 99.
52. Ibid.
53. *The Mayor of Casterbridge*, Chapter 34.
54. Chapter 35.
55. Storr, op. cit., p. 105.
56. *The Mayor of Casterbridge*, Chapter 2.
57. Chapter 19.
58. Chapter 40.
59. Chapter 45.
60. Storr, op. cit., p. 114.
61. *The Mayor of Casterbridge*, Chapter 43.
62. Adler, op. cit., p. 270.
63. *The Mayor of Casterbridge*, Chapter 19.
64. Chapter 27.
65. Chapter 27.
66. *Hardy's Personal Writings.*
67. Freud, *Civilisation and its Discontents*, p. 60.
68. Storr, op. cit., p. 130.
69. D. J. West, *Murder Followed by Suicide* (Heinemann, 1965), p. 150.
70. *The Mayor of Casterbridge*, Chapter 17.
71. Chapter 17.
72. Guerard: *A Study of Thomas Hardy* (New Directions, 1964), p. 87.
73. R. D. Laing, *The Self and Others* (Tavistock Publications, 1961), Chapter 9.
74. *The Mayor of Casterbridge*, Chapter 41.
75. Chapter 27.
76. Chapter 42.
77. Storr, op. cit., p. 115.
78. Ibid., p. 116.
79. *The Mayor of Casterbridge*, Chapter 15.
80. Chapter 19.
81. Chapter 12.
82. Chapter 44.
83. F. E. Hardy, op. cit., p. 177.
84. *The Mayor of Casterbridge*, Chapter 1.
85. Chapter 5.

86. Chapter 5.
87. Chapter 12.
88. Chapter 34.
89. Chapter 31.
90. Chapter 17.
91. Chapter 19.
92. Chapter 24.
93. Chapter 19.
94. Chapter 31.
95. Chapter 25.
96. Chapter 26.
97. Chapter 28.
98. Chapter 31.
99. Chapter 17.
100. Chapter 33.
101. Chapter 17.
102. Chapter 26.
103. Chapter 42.
104. Chapter 43.
105. Chapter 44.
106. Chapter 17.
107. Chapter 44.
108. Chapter 43.
109. F. E. Hardy, op. cit., p. 177.
110. *The Mayor of Casterbridge*, Chapter 45.
111. Chapter 43.
112. *Winter Words, Complete Poems* (Macmillan, 1976), p. 886.
113. *The Mayor of Casterbridge*, Chapter 14.

CHAPTER 6

1. F. E. Hardy, op. cit., p. 102.
2. *The Woodlanders*, Chapter 27.
3. Chapter 30.
4. F. E. Hardy, op. cit., p. 177.
5. Ibid., p. 358.
6. *The Woodlanders*, Chapter 14.
7. Chapter 40.
8. Chapter 3.
9. Chapter 4.
10. Chapter 11.
11. Chapter 12.
12. Chapter 22.
13. Chapter 5.
14. Chapter 5.
15. Chapter 5.
16. D. H. Lawrence, *Women in Love* (Secker, 1921), Chapter 23.
17. E. M. Forster, *Aspects of the Novel* (Arnold, 1927), Chapter 4.
18. *The Woodlanders*, Chapter 6.

19. Chapter 9.
20. Chapter 9.
21. Chapter 9.
22. Chapter 11.
23. Chapter 12.
24. Chapter 12.
25. Chapter 13.
26. Chapter 15.
27. Chapter 22.
28. Chapter 22.
29. Chapter 23.
30. Chapter 24.
31. Chapter 24.
32. Chapter 24.
33. Chapter 28.
34. Chapter 28.
35. Chapter 29.
36. Chapter 30.
37. Chapter 30.
38. Chapter 33.
39. Chapter 35.
40. Chapter 35.
41. Chapter 39.
42. Chapter 40.
43. Chapter 40.
44. Chapter 41.
45. R. D. Laing, *The Divided Self* (Tavistock Publications, 1960), Chapter 4.
46. R. D. Laing, *The Self and Others*, Chapter 3.
47. *The Woodlanders*, Chapter 40.
48. R. D. Laing, *The Self and Others*, Chapter 3.
49. R. D. Laing, *The Divided Self*, Chapter 4.
50. Ibid., Chapter 11.
51. *The Woodlanders*, Chapter 38.
52. Chapter 40.
53. R. D. Laing, *The Self and Others*, Chapter 7.
54. *The Woodlanders*, Chapter 24.
55. Chapter 47.
56. F. E. Hardy, op. cit., p. 220.
57. Ian Gregor, op. cit., p. 156.
58. Letter to Edmund Gosse, 20 November 1895, quoted in F. E. Hardy, op. cit., p. 272.
59. Quoted by C. J. Weber in *Hardy and the Lady from Madison Square* (Colby College Press, 1952), p. 89.
60. Letter to Mrs Henniker, 29 September 1907, in *One Rare Fair Woman*, op. cit., p. 134.
61. F. E. Hardy, op. cit., p. 252.
62. *The Woodlanders*, Chapter 7.
63. Chapter 28.
64. Chapter 3.

65. Chapter 48.

CHAPTER 7

1. F. E. Hardy, op. cit., p. 284.
2. Irving Howe, *Thomas Hardy* (Masters of Literature Series, Weidenfeld and Nicolson, 1968), p. 58.
3. Ibid.
4. *The Return of the Native*, Book First, Chapter 1.
5. D. H. Lawrence, "The Novel and the Feelings", *Phoenix* (Heinemann, 1936), p. 756.
6. *The Return of the Native*, Book First, Chapter 6.
7. D. H. Lawrence, "The Novel and the Feelings", op. cit., p. 756.
8. *The Return of the Native*, Book First, Chapter 3.
9. Book First, Chapter 6.
10. Book First, Chapter 6.
11. Book First, Chapter 7.
12. Book First, Chapter 7.
13. Book First, Chapter 7.
14. Book First, Chapter 6.
15. Book First, Chapter 7.
16. Book First, Chapter 7.
17. Book Second, Chapter 3.
18. Book Fourth, Chapter 3.
19. Book Fourth, Chapter 3.
20. Book Fifth, Chapter 14.
21. *One Rare Fair Woman*, p. 139 (See Chapter 4, page 55).
22. *The Return of the Native*, Book Fifth, Chapter 8.
23. Book Fifth, Chapter 8.
24. Book Fifth, Chapter 8.
25. Book Fifth, Chapter 8.
26. Book First, Chapter 2.
27. Book Fifth, Chapter 8.
28. Book First, Chapter 7.
29. Book First, Chapter 1.
30. Book Third, Chapter 2.
31. Book Second, Chapter 6.
32. Book Third, Chapter 1.
33. Book Third, Chapter 1.
34. Book Third, Chapter 2.
35. Book Third, Chapter 2.
36. Book Third, Chapter 1.
37. Book Third, Chapter 1.
38. Book Third, Chapter 1.
39. Book Fourth, Chapter 2.
40. Book Third, Chapter 2.
41. Book Third, Chapter 4.
42. Book Third, Chapter 4.
43. Book Third, Chapter 4.

44. *Jude the Obscure* (Macmillan, 1960), IV, 3.
45. *The Return of the Native*, Book Third, Chapter 4.
46. Book Third, Chapter 5.
47. Book Third, Chapter 3.
48. Book Third, Chapter 2.
49. Book Third, Chapter 4.
50. Book Third, Chapter 5.
51. Book Fourth, Chapter 1.
52. Book Fifth, Chapter 1.
53. Book Fifth, Chapter 2.
54. Book Fifth, Chapter 1.
55. Book Fifth, Chapter 2
56. Book Fifth, Chapter 2.
57. Book Fifth, end of Chapter 2, beginning of Chapter 3.
58. Book Fifth, Chapter 6.
59. Book Fifth, Chapter 9.
60. Book Sixth, Chapter 4.
61. Book Fifth, Chapter 3.
62. Book Third, Chapter 5.
63. Book Fourth, Chapter 2.
64. Freud, *Civilisation and its Discontents*, p. 77.
65. Ibid.
66. *The Return of the Native*, Book Third, Chapter 2.
67. Book Sixth, Chapter 6.
68. Book Sixth, Chapter 6.
69. Book Third, Chapter 3.
70. Book Third, Chapter 3.
71. Book Third, Chapter 4.
72. Book Fourth, Chapter 2.
73. Book Fifth, Chapter 3.
74. Jung, A Commentary on "*The Secret of the Golden Flower*", *Collected Works*, Vols. 13, 15, p. 11.
75. *The Return of the Native*, Book First, Chapter 1.
76. Jung, *Archetypes of the Collective Unconscious*, p. 288.
77. *The Return of the Native*, Book First, Chapter 1.
78. Jung, *Archetypes of the Collective Unconscious*, p. 287.
79. Ibid., pp. 4–5.
80. *The Return of the Native*, Book First, Chapter 1.
81. Book First, Chapter 1.
82. Jung, *Archetypes of the Collective Unconscious*, p. 288.
83. Ibid., p. 5.
84. *The Return of the Native*, Book First, Chapter 1.

CHAPTER 8

1. *A Pair of Blue Eyes* (Macmillan, 1960), Chapter 13.
2. Freud, *"Civilised" Sexual Morality and the Neuroses*, *Standard Edition*, 1908, Vol. IX, p. 186.

3. Ibid., p. 197.
4. Ibid.
5. Ibid., p. 193.
6. *A Pair of Blue Eyes*, Chapter 35.
7. Chapter 13.
8. Chapter 19.
9. Chapter 30.
10. Chapter 20.
11. Chapter 32.
12. Jung, *Memories, Dreams and Reflections* (Routledge, 1963), p. 185.
13. *A Pair of Blue Eyes*, Chapter 20.
14. Chapter 22.
15. Chapter 28.
16. Freud, *Totem and Taboo, Standard Edition* (1913), Vol. XIV.
17. *A Pair of Blue Eyes*, Chapter 19.
18. Chapter 18.
19. Chapter 30.
20. Chapter 33.
21. Chapter 35.
22. Chapter 34.
23. Chapter 38.
24. Chapter 22.
25. Chapter 20.
26. Chapter 34.
27. Chapter 35.
28. Chapter 30.
29. In *The Academy*, 6 February 1892, quoted in Lerner and Holmstrom, *Thomas Hardy and His Readers* (Bodley Head, 1968), p. 77.
30. Conversation with Raymond Blathwayt, printed in *Black and White*, 27 August 1892, Lerner and Holmstrom, ibid., p. 96.
31. *Tess of the d'Urbervilles*, Chapter 2.
32. Chapter 18.
33. Chapter 23.
34. Chapter 25.
35. Chapter 26.
36. Chapter 27.
37. Chapter 23.
38. Chapter 24.
39. Chapter 24.
40. Chapter 24.
41. Chapter 24.
42. Chapter 24.
43. Chapter 24.
44. Chapter 24.
45. Chapter 24.
46. Chapter 24.
47. Chapter 24.
48. Chapter 26.
49. Chapter 31.

50. Arnold Kettle, Introduction to *Tess of the d'Urbervilles, Standard Edition*, (Harper & Row, 1966), p. xiv.
51. *Tess of the d'Urbervilles*, Chapter 32.
52. Chapter 21.
53. Jung, *Two Essays in Analytical Psychology, Collected Works*, Vol. 7, p. 188.
54. Jung, *Aion*, p. 13.
55. Jung, *The Development of the Personality, Collected Works*, Vol. 17, p. 198.
56. *Tess of the d'Urbervilles*, Chapter 35.
57. Chapter 35.
58. Chapter 36.
59. Chapter 36.
60. Freud, *Delusions and Dreams in Jensens's "Gradiva", Standard Edition*, Vol. IX, p. 25.
61. Ibid., p. 68.
62. Ibid., p. 83.
63. Ibid., p. 89.
64. *Tess of the d'Urbervilles*, Chapter 37.
65. Chapter 35.
66. Chapter 37.
67. Chapter 35.
68. Chapter 19.
69. Chapter 30.
70. Chapter 65.
71. Chapter 36.
72. Freud, *The Taboo of Virginity, Standard Edition*, 1917, Vol. XVI, p. 199.
73. Freud, *On Narcissism, Standard Edition*, 1914, Vol. XIV, p. 80.
74. *Group Psychology, VIII, Being in Love and Hypnosis, Standard Edition*, 1921, Vol. XVIII, p. 112.
75. Schopenhauer, "The Metaphysics of Love", *Essays of Schopenhauer*, translated by Dircks (Walter Scott, 1897), p. 182.
76. *Tess of the d'Urbervilles*, Chapter 39.
77. Chapter 40.
78. Chapter 40.
79. Chapter 36.
80. Chapter 36.
81. Chapter 37.
82. Freud, *Civilisation and its Discontents*, Chapter 5, p. 112.
83. *Tess of the d'Urbervilles*, Chapter 37.
84. Chapter 40.
85. Chapter 39.
86. Irving Howe, *Thomas Hardy*, p. 123.
87. *Tess of the d'Urbervilles*, Chapter 35.
88. *Complete Poems*, op. cit., p. 314.
89. *Tess of the d'Urbervilles*, Chapter 35.
90. Preface to *Jude the Obscure*.
91. Preface to *Poems of the Past and the Present*. (*Complete Poems*, op. cit., p. 84.)
92. *Tess of the d'Urbervilles*, Chapter 36.

93. Freud, *"Civilised" Sexual Morality and the Neuroses*, p. 191.
94. *Tess of the d'Urbervilles*, Chapter 25.
95. Chapter 18.
96. Freud, *The Taboo of Virginity* op. cit., p. 193.
97. *Tess of the d'Urbervilles*, Chapter 39.
98. Chapter 39.
99. Chapter 14.
100. Chapter 15.
101. Chapter 19.
102. Chapter 19.
103. Chapter 15.
104. Chapter 35.
105. Ian Gregor, op. cit., p. 187.
106. *Tess of the d'Urbervilles*, Chapter 42.
107. Gregor, op. cit., p. 188.
108. Ibid., p. 183.
109. *Tess of the d'Urbervilles*, Chapter 30.
110. Chapter 45.
111. Chapter 55.
112. Chapter 47.
113. D. H. Lawrence, *A Propos of Lady Chatterley's Lover* (Penguin, p. 92).

CHAPTER 9

1. Hardy, Letter to Gosse, 20 November 1895, quoted in F. E. Hardy, op. cit., p. 272.
2. F. E. Hardy, op. cit., p. 208.
3. Preface to *Jude the Obscure*.
4. F. E. Hardy, op. cit., p. 249.
5. Hardy in William Archer, *Real Conversations* (Heinemann, 1904).
6. *Jude the Obscure*, Part First, II.
7. Part First, I.
8. Part First, II.
9. Part First, II.
10. Part First, III.
11. Part First, IV.
12. Part First, V.
13. Part First, V
14. Freud, *"Civilised" Sexual Morality and the Neuroses*, p. 197.
15. *The New Review*, June 1894.
16. *Jude the Obscure*, Part First, XI.
17. Part First, XI.
18. Freud, *Civilisation and its Discontents*, p. 28.
19. *Jude the Obscure*, Part Second, VII.
20. Part Second, VII.
21. Hardy, Letter to Gosse, 20 November 1895, quoted in F. E. Hardy, op. cit., p. 272.
22. Freud, *"Civilised" Sexual Morality and the Neuroses*, p. 191.

23. *Jude the Obscure*, Part First, IX.
24. Part Third, IX.
25. Part Third, VIII.
26. Part Third, VIII.
27. Part Third, IX.
28. Part Third, IX.
29. Part Third, IX.
30. Part Third, IX.
31. Part Third, IX.
32. Part Third, X.
33. Part Fourth, I.
34. Part Fourth, III
35. Part Fourth, III.
36. Freud, *Civilisation and its Discontents*, pp. 142−3.
37. *Jude the Obscure*, Part Fifth, II.
38. Part Fifth, II.
39. Part Fifth, III.
40. Part Fifth, II.
41. Part Fifth, IV.
42. Part Fifth, IV.
43. Part Sixth, III.
44. Part Sixth, III.
45. Part Sixth, III.
46. Part Sixth, III.
47. Part Sixth, III.
48. Part Sixth, IV.
49. Part Sixth, VIII.
50. Part Sixth, VI.
51. Part Sixth, VII.
52. Mrs Oliphant, "The Anti-Marriage League", *Blackwood's Magazine*, January 1896, quoted in Lerner and Holmstrom, *Thomas Hardy and His Readers*, p. 127.
53. D. H. Lawrence, "Study of Thomas Hardy" *Phoenix*, op. cit., p. 505.
54. Freud, *"Civilised" Sexual Morality and the Neuroses*, p. 192.
55. *Jude the Obscure*, Part Fourth, III.
56. Freud, *"Civilised" Sexual Morality and the Neuroses*, p. 193.
57. *Jude the Obscure*, Part Sixth, X.
58. Part Second, VI.
59. Freud, *"Civilised" Sexual Morality and the Neuroses*, p. 197.
60. Freud, *Civilisation and its Discontents*, p. 80.
61. Ibid., p. 76.
62. *Jude the Obscure*, Part First, VI.
63. Part First, VII.
64. Freud, *The Ego and the Id, Standard Edition*, 1923, Vol. XIX, p. 23.
65. Freud, *Civilisation and its Discontents*, pp. 144−5.
66. E. M. Forster, *Howards End*, (Arnold, 1910), Chapter 22.
67. D. H. Lawrence, A Propos of *"Lady Chatterley's Lover"*, op. cit., p. 92.
68. D. H. Lawrence, *Women in Love*, Chapter 19.
69. Ibid., Chapter 8.

70. *Jude the Obscure*, Part Fifth, I.
71. D. H. Lawrence, "Study of Thomas Hardy", *Phoenix*, op. cit., p. 494.
72. *Jude the Obscure*, Part First, VI.
73. A. Alvarez, "Essay on *Jude the Obscure*", *Beyond All This Fiddle* (Allen Lane, 1968), p. 182.
74. Letter to Mrs Henniker, 16 September 1893, *One Rare Fair Woman*, p. 26.
75. F. E. Hardy, op. cit., p. 284.
76. J. I. M. Stewart, "The Integrity of Hardy" (*Essays and Studies of the English Association*, 1948).
77. Letter to Gosse, 16 November 1895, quoted in F. E. Hardy, op. cit., p. 271.
78. Edmund Gosse, review of *Jude the Obscure* in *St James's Gazette* (November 1895).
79. Letter to Gosse, 20 November 1895, quoted in F. E. Hardy, op. cit., p. 272.
80. Havelock Ellis, review of *Jude the Obscure*, *The Savoy*, October 1896.
81. *Studies in the Psychology of Sex* (London University, 1900–10), Vol. VI, Chapter 6.
82. *Jude the Obscure*, Part Fourth, V.
83. D. H. Lawrence, "Study of Thomas Hardy", *Phoenix*, op. cit., p. 496.
84. Ibid., p. 510.
85. Ibid., p. 508.
86. Review of *Jude the Obscure* in *The Savoy*.
87. *Hardy's Personal Writings*, p. 130.
88. Letter to Gosse, 20 November 1895, quoted in F. E. Hardy, op. cit., p. 272.
89. *Jude the Obscure*, Part Third, IV.
90. Part Third, IV.
91. Part Third, IV.
92. Part Third, VII.
93. Part Third, VII.
94. Part Third, VI.
95. Part Fourth, II.
96. Part Fourth, II.
97. Lerner and Holmstrom, op. cit., p. 150.
98. *Jude the Obscure*, Part Third, IX.
99. Part Sixth, IX.
100. Part Second, III.
101. Lerner and Holmstrom, op. cit., p. 151.
102. *Jude the Obscure*, Part Fourth, III.
103. Part Third, IX.
104. Part Fifth, V.
105. Part Fourth, III.
106. Part Fourth, V.
107. Part Fifth, I.
108. Part Fifth, II.
109. Part Fifth, III.
110. Part Fifth, III.
111. Part Sixth, III.

112. Part Fifth, III.
113. Freud, *General Theory of the Neuroses, Standard Edition*, 1917, Vol. XVI, p. 353.
114. Letter to Gosse, 20 November 1895, quoted in F. E. Hardy, op. cit., p. 272.
115. Freud, *On Narcissism, Standard Edition*, 1914, Vol. XIV, p. 89.
116. Ibid., p. 89.
117. Ibid.
118. *Jude the Obscure*, Part Fourth, V.
119. Freud, *On Narcissism*, p. 88.
120. *Jude the Obscure*, Part Third, IV.
121. Freud, *The Instincts and their Vicissitudes, Standard Edition*, 1915, Vol. XIV, p. 127.
122. Ibid., p. 128.
123. *Jude the Obscure*, Part Sixth, III.
124. Part Sixth, III.
125. Part Sixth, III.
126. Part Sixth, III.
127. Part Sixth, III.
128. Part Fourth, III.
129. Part Third, IV.
130. Part Fifth, I.
131. Part Sixth, VIII.
132. Part Sixth, XI.
133. Part Sixth, IV.
134. Freud, *General Theory of the Neuroses*, p. 309.
135. Ibid.
136. Ibid., p. 421.
137. *Jude the Obscure*, Part Sixth, IX.
138. Part Sixth, III.
139. Part Fifth, V.
140. Freud, *General Theory of the Neuroses*, p. 142.
141. *Jude the Obscure*, Part Sixth, V.
142. Part Second, II.
143. Part Fourth, II.
144. Part Fourth, IV.
145. Part Third, I.
146. Part Third, II.
147. Part Third, IV.
148. Part Fourth, V.
149. Part Third, IV.
150. Part Third, VII.
151. Part Third VII.
152. Part Third, IV.
153. Part Third, V.
154. D. H. Lawrence, *Women in Love*, Chapter 19.
155. D. H. Lawrence, "The Novel and the Feelings", *Phoenix* II, (Heinemann, 1968), p. 759.
156. A. Alvarez, op. cit., p. 185.

157. R. Heilman, "Hardy's Sue Bridehead", *Nineteenth Century Fiction*, 1965—66, Vol. 20.
158. *Jude the Obscure*, Part Sixth, II.
159. *Hardy's Personal Writings*, pp. 126—7.
160. D. H. Lawrence, "Morality and the Novel", *Phoenix*, op. cit., p. 530 .
161. F. E. Hardy, op. cit., p. 280.
162. Freud, *Civilisation and its Discontents*, p. 77.
163. *One Rare Fair Woman*, p. 26.
164. D. H. Lawrence, "Surgery for the Novel — or a Bomb", *Phoenix*, op. cit., p. 520.

CHAPTER 10

1. Gregor, op. cit., p. 25.
2. Ibid., p. 51.
3. Letter to Gosse, 20 November 1895, quoted in F. E. Hardy, op. cit., p. 272).
4. *The Mayor of Casterbridge*, Chapter 17.
5. F. E. Hardy, op. cit., p. 258.
6. Archer, *Real Conversations*.
7. F. E. Hardy, op. cit., p. 284.
8. *Tess of the d'Urbervilles*, Chapter 18.
9. Ibid., Chapter 13.
10. Virginia Woolf, *Collected Essays*, (Hogarth Press, 1966), Vol. I, p. 258, quoted by Gregor, op. cit., p. 33.
11. 1912 Preface to *Jude the Obscure*.
12. D. H. Lawrence, "The Novel and the Feelings", *Phoenix*, op. cit., p. 535.
13. D. H. Lawrence, "Why the Novel Matters", *Phoenix*, op. cit., p. 535.
14. F. E. Hardy, op. cit., p. 375.
15. Preface to *Jude the Obscure*.
16. Alfred Kazin, *Contemporaries*, (Secker and Warburg, 1963), p. 378.
17. F. E. Hardy, op. cit., p. 370.

Bibliography

WORKS BY HARDY

FICTION

Desperate Remedies, Macmillan, 1960.
A Pair of Blue Eyes, Macmillan, 1960.
Far from the Madding Crowd, Macmillan, 1960.
The Return of the Native, Macmillan, 1960.
A Laodicean, Macmillan, 1960.
The Mayor of Casterbridge, Macmillan, 1960.
The Woodlanders, Macmillan, 1960.
Wessex Tales, Macmillan, 1960.
Tess of the d'Urbervilles, Collins, 1958.
A Group of Noble Dames, Macmillan, 1960.
Life's Little Ironies, Macmillan, 1960.
Jude the Obscure, Macmillan, 1960.
The Well-Beloved, Macmillan, 1960.
(first published in *The Illustrated London News,* 1892)
A Changed Man, Macmillan, 1960.

NON-FICTION

The Complete Poems edited by James Gibson, Macmillan, 1976.
The Life of Thomas Hardy by Florence Emily Hardy, Macmillan, 1933.
Hardy's Personal Writings, edited by Harold Orel, Macmillan, 1963.
One Rare Fair Woman: Thomas Hardy's Letters to Florence Henniker, 1893 — 1922, edited by E. Hardy and F. B. Pinion, Macmillan, 1972.
The Literary Notes of Thomas Hardy, edited by Lennart A. Björk, Göteborg, 1974.

212

WORKS BY OTHER AUTHORS

Adler, A. *The Individual Psychology of Alfred Adler*, translated by H. L. and R. R. Ansbacher, Allen & Unwin, 1958.

Allen, Grant. *The Woman Who Did*, John Lane, 1895.

Alvarez, A. *Beyond All This Fiddle*, Allen Lane, 1968.

Archer, W. *Real Conversations*, Heinemann, 1904.

Beech, H. R. *Changing Man's Behaviour*, Penguin, 1969.

Blackman, D. *Operant Conditioning*, Methuen, 1974.

Blathwayt, R. *Conversation with Hardy, Black and White*, 27 August 1892.

Brooks, Jean. *Thomas Hardy: The Poetic Structure*, Elek, 1971.

Carpenter, R. C. "The Mirror and the Sword", *Nineteenth Century Fiction*, March 1964.

Cecil, Lord David. *Hardy the Novelist*, Constable, 1943.

Davidson, Donald. "The Traditional Basis of Hardy's Fiction", *Southern Review*, Hardy Centenary Number, 1940.

Eliot, T. S. *After Strange Gods*, Faber & Faber, 1934.

Ellis, Havelock. Review of *Jude the Obscure*, *The Savoy*, October 1896.

Ellis, Havelock. *Studies in the Psychology of Sex*, London University 1900—10.

d'Exideuil, P. *The Human Pair in the Works of Thomas Hardy* translated by F. W. Gosse, Humphrey Toulmin, 1930.

Forster, E. M. *Howards End*, Arnold, 1910.

Forster, E. M. *Aspects of the Novel*, Arnold, 1927.

Fourier, C. *Passions of the Human Soul*, translated by J. R. Morell, Hyppolyte Balliere, London, 1951.

Freud, Sigmund. *Standard Edition of the Complete Psychological Works of Sigmund Freud*, translated and edited by James Strachey, Hogarth Press, 1953—74:

Freud, Sigmund. *Delusions and Dreams in Jensen's "Gradiva"* Vol. IX, 1907.

Freud, Sigmund. *"Civilised" Sexual Morality and the Neuroses* Vol. IX, 1908.

Freud, Sigmund. *Totem and Taboo*, Vol. XIV, 1913.

Freud, Sigmund. *On the History of the Psychoanalytical Movement*, Vol. XIV, 1914.

Freud, Sigmund. *On Narcissism*, Vol. XIV, 1914.

Freud, Sigmund. *Repression*, Vol. XIV, 1915.

Freud, Sigmund. *The Instincts and their Vicissitudes*, Vol. XIV, 1915.

Freud, Sigmund. *General Theory of the Neuroses*, Vol. XVI, 1917.

Freud, Sigmund. *The Taboo of Virginity*, Vol. XVI, 1917.

Freud, Sigmund. *Group Psychology VIII: Being in Love and Hypnosis*, Vol. XVIII, 1921.

Freud, Sigmund. *The Ego and the Id*, Vol. XIX, 1923.

Freud, Sigmund. *Autobiographical Study*, Vol. XX, 1924.

Freud, Sigmund. *Inhibitions, Symptoms and Anxiety*, Vol. XX, 1926.

Freud, Sigmund. *Civilisation and its Discontents*, Vol. XXI, Hogarth Press, 1930.

Gosse, E. Review of *Jude the Obscure*, St. *James's Gazette*, November 1895, and *Cosmopolis* January 1896.

Gregor, Ian. *The Great Web*, Faber & Faber, 1974.

Guerard, A. J. *Thomas Hardy*, New Directions, 1964.

Heilmann, R. "Hardy's Sue Bridehead", *Nineteenth Century Fiction*, 1965—66, Vol. 20.

Howe, Irving. *Thomas Hardy*, Masters of World Literature Series, Weidenfeld and Nicolson, 1968.

Jung, C. G. *Aion, Collected Works*, Routledge & Kegan Paul, 1953—71, Vol. 9 (ii).

Jung, C. G. *Archetypes of the Collective Unconscious, Collected Works*, Vol. 9 (i).

Jung, C. G. *A Commentary on "The Secret of the Golden Flower"*, *Collected Works*, Vol. 13.

Jung, C. G. *The Development of the Personality, Collected Works*, Vol. 17.

Jung, C. G. *The Integration of the Personality*, Routledge & Kegan Paul, 1940.

Jung, C. G. *Memories, Dreams and Reflections*, Routledge & Kegan Paul, 1963.

Jung, C. G. *Two Essays in Analytical Psychology, Collected Works*, Vol. 7.

Joyce, James. *Ulysses*, Bodley Head, 1937.

Kazin, A. *Contemporaries*, Secker and Warburg, 1963.

Kettle, Arnold. Introduction to *Tess of the d'Urbervilles, Standard Edition*, New York, Harper & Row, 1966.

Laing, R. D. *The Divided Self*, Tavistock Publications, 1960.

Laing, R. D. *The Self and Others*, Tavistock Publications, 1961.

Lawrence, D. H. "A Propos of *Lady Chatterley's Lover*", Penguin, 1961.

Lawrence, D. H. "The Novel and the Feelings", *Phoenix*, Heinemann, 1936.

Lawrence, D. H. "Morality and the Novel", *Phoenix*, Heinemann, 1936.

Lawrence, D. H. "Study of Thomas Hardy", *Phoenix*, Heinemann, 1936.

Lawrence, D. H. "Surgery for the Novel — *or a Bomb*", *Phoenix*, Heinemann, 1936.

Lawrence, D. H. "Why the Novel Matters", *Phoenix*, Heinemann, 1936.

Lawrence, D. H. "The State of Funk", *Phoenix II*, Heinemann, 1968.

Lawrence, D. H. *Sons and Lovers*, Duckworth, 1913.

Lawrence, D. H. *The Rainbow*, Methuen, 1915.

Lawrence, D. H. *Women in Love*, Secker, 1921.

Lawrence, D. H. "The Fox", in *The Ladybird*, Secker, 1923.

Leavis, F. R. *The Great Tradition*, Chatto & Windus, 1948.

Lerner L. and Holmstrom, T. *Thomas Hardy and his Readers*, Bodley Head, 1968.

Lorenz, Konrad. *On Aggression*, Methuen, 1966.

Millgate, M. *Thomas Hardy*, Bodley Head, 1971.

Morrell, Roy. *Thomas Hardy, The Will and the Way*, University of Malaya Press, 1965.

Morgan, Charles. *The House of Macmillan*, Macmillan, 1943.

Morgan, C. Lloyd. *Introduction to Comparative Psychology*, Walter Scott, 1894.

Neill, A. S. *Hearts not Heads in School*, Herbert Jenkins, 1945.

Oliphant, Mrs. "The Anti-Marriage League", *Blackwood's Magazine*, January 1896.

Pavlov, I. P. *Lectures on Conditioned Reflexes*, Oxford University Press, 1927.

Proust, Marcel. *A la Recherche du Temps Perdu*, translated by C. K. Scott-Moncrieff, 1929.

Proust, Marcel. *Letters* (edited by Curtis), Chatto, 1950.

Purdy, R. L. *Thomas Hardy: A Bibliographical Study*, Oxford University Press, 1954.

Reik, T. *From Thirty Years with Freud*, International Universities Press, 1940.

Schopenhauer, A. *The World as Will and Idea*, 1844, translated by Haldane and Kemp, Trubner, 1883.

Schopenhauer, A. *Essays of Schopenhauer*, translated by Dircks,

Walter Scott, 1897.

Skinner, B. F. *Science and Human Behaviour*, Macmillan, 1953.

Stewart, J. I. M. "The Integrity of Hardy", *Essays and Studies of the English Association*, 1948.

Stewart, J. I. M. *Thomas Hardy: A Critical Biography*, Longmans, 1971.

Storr, Anthony. *Human Aggression*, Penguin, 1968.

Thorndike, E. L. *The Psychology of Learning*, Kegan Paul, 1913.

Von Hartmann, E. *The Philosophy of the Unconscious*, Trubner, 1884.

Watson, J. B. *Behaviourism*, Kegan Paul, 1931.

Watson, William. Review of *Tess of the d'Urbervilles*, *The Academy*, 6 February 1892.

Weber, C. J. *Hardy and the Lady from Madison Square*, Colby College Press, 1952.

West, D. J. *Murder followed by Suicide*, Heinemann, 1965.

Woolf, Virginia. *Collected Essays*, Hogarth, 1966, Vol. 1.

Index